REPAIRING HOUSES

A Step-by-Step Guide

Trevor James is an architect working with the Solon Cooperative Design Group,
and has written and illustrated *Repairing Houses*
while involved with a number of short-life housing groups at Solon.

REPAIRING HOUSES

A Step-by-Step Guide

TREVOR JAMES

SPHERE BOOKS LIMITED
30-32 Gray's Inn Road, London WC1X 8JL

First published in Great Britain by
Sphere Books Ltd 1981

Whilst great care has been taken in the preparation of this volume,
many of the techniques described are dangerous
and the correct safety precautions should be observed before undertaking work.
The Author and Publishers cannot accept liability for damage or injury suffered
as a result of failure to take such care.

Set in VIP Century Schoolbook

Printed and bound in Great Britain by
©ollins, Glasgow

CONTENTS

INTRODUCTION

Building repairs can be simple as long as you understand what you are doing and tackle them with calm and common sense. Do not pretend knowledge if you do not understand an instruction or a technique in this book, but read it through again until you feel confident. Used wisely this book should save you money and provide the satisfaction of a job well done.

Many people think of building work as an exclusively male pastime. But this is not true and I hope that the illustrations make this clear. My assumption is that anyone, woman or man, can use this book to carry out house repairs having had no previous knowledge or experience. Repairs are described in full and there are very few occasions where it is suggested that a professional be called in to solve a problem.

I have tried to describe and illustrate the majority of techniques and repairs which will be necessary when undertaking the repair or extension of an old house. Inevitably some problems will arise which are not covered but most will be easily solved if you adapt the solutions described for similar repairs. The methods illustrated are based on personal experience, discussion with building tradespeople and research. Every effort has been made to ensure that simple and safe practices are described throughout. Much of the experience has been gained in the repair of old houses which have a 'short life' using limited finance. Most of the inexpensive techniques devised for that work can be used for 'permanent' houses but the text notes techniques which have only a limited life.

When using the book please observe the safety comments and take adequate precautions. Do not try to avoid having gas or electrical appliances checked for safety. Care has been taken to describe good practice but no liability can be accepted for any loss, damage or injury resulting from instructions or recommendations contained in this book.

Now, how about starting work on that house?

Acknowledgements

My thanks to my fellow workers and the
management committee of Solon Cooperative
Housing Services Ltd, who allowed me leave of
absence to produce this book as well as giving
me encouragement and support. Particular
thanks to Suzy Nelson who covered for me
whilst I was away writing.

A special mention is also due to Marie-Louise
who provided not only the incentive to stop
talking and start writing, but also a refuge
where I could begin.

Trevor James   August 1980

REGULATIONS

We all know the saying 'An Englishman's Home is his Castle' but the old cliche is not true in Britain, whatever your sex or nationality. Rules, regulations and laws affecting the process of living in, repairing or extending your home are abundant. They can be considered under four broad headings; Planning, Building, Services and Health. It would take a very long, complex book to cover all the regulations and to act as a guide through the maze. I have neither the inclination nor the detailed knowledge to write such a book and even if I had, much of it would have little relevance to the average house repair. Instead, I will try to explain the areas which are affected by legislation and the role of the public employees who implement the rules.

Planning

Planning Legislation is administered by the Local Authorities Planning Department whose officers have the task of enforcing as well as advising on the requirements of the Town and County Planning Acts. The average house repair will only come under the scrutiny of the local planning department if it includes a change of appearance to the front of the house, the building of an extension to the front or sides. An extension to the rear will only require planning permission if the volume exceeds one tenth of the total volume of the house. If there is to be a change of use, for example from a house to flats or bedsitters, from a home to a workshop, this will also require planning permission.

If the house is in a conservation area or has been listed as a building of architectural or historical interest then any proposed change to the external appearance must be agreed with the planning department. In addition if the house is listed Grade I, permission will also be required to make changes to the interior.

Mature or rare trees may be the subjects of tree preservation orders in which case they cannot be chopped down without prior consent, and failure to acquire consent can result in a heavy fine. Damaging or badly pruning the tree can also render the occupant liable to a fine.

It is common practice for people using houses on a short life basis to ignore planning consents since the repairs rarely affect the external appearance of the property and change of use does not often occur. However the home owner is advised to consult the local planning department since if they are unhappy with work

done they could issue an enforcement notice which carries a fine for non compliance and the cost of redoing the offending work for compliance.

When planning permission is required then an application must be made to the planning department. To make an application you will need four copies of an application form obtainable from the department and four copies of a drawing or drawings showing the proposed changes. These drawings need to be accurate, therefore unless you are able to draw scale plans and elevations, it will be necessary to enlist the services of an architect, surveyor or architectural technician, many of whom will carry out drawings for an hourly rate.

Before having drawings done or making a submission, discuss your proposals with the planning officer dealing with the area. There is little point in making an application which does not have the prior agreement of the planning officers since they have to make a recommendation to the committee. Once the application has been made it will be considered by the planning officer who makes a report that is then presented with the application to a planning committee made up of local councillors. It can take several months between application and approval and it is therefore advisable to make an early submission.

Building

The quality of building work is controlled by 'The Building Regulations 1976' and subsequent amendments in most parts of the country. However in the Inner London Boroughs and Bristol building standards are contained in local Building Bye-laws. All are concerned to ensure that buildings are erected or repaired in such a way as to be safe, both for the users and the public at large, are not dangerous to health and provide a comfortable environment by modern standards.

The Building Regulations are administered by the local authority, the relevant department often being simply called Building Control. The London Building Bye-Laws are administered by District Surveyors of the Greater London Council who work in a number of local offices.

There are a wide range of topics covered by the Building Regulations relating to structural stability, fire safety, thermal insulation, sound insulation, ventilation, refuse disposal, the construction of staircases, drainage, heating and sanitation. These are covered in detail and include tables or schedules of construction techniques or materials which are 'deemed to satisfy'; they run to more than 300 pages. Before carrying out major building work it is necessary to submit copies of the proposals to the Building Control Department for approval. When simply repairing a house it is in practice usually only advisable to contact the Building Inspector when carrying out structural work or making alterations. Most of the provisions of the Regulations do not apply to old houses although some such as the adequate sizing of a new beam to replace an old timber beam which is rotten should have the Building Inspector's approval.

The London Building Bye-Laws are much less detailed than the Regulations and leave the District Surveyor more scope for discretion. In the repair of houses the District Surveyor's main concern will be with any work which is structural, such as replacing a beam, cutting a new opening, digging foundations. He will also want details of any alterations that are to be carried out. On minor works it will often not be necessary to make a formal submission to the District Surveyor who may agree to meet at the house and discuss any proposed work and indeed will frequently give advice on the appropriate size of beam or suitable remedy for a repair. The District Surveyors operate on a fee basis, the fee being charged in relation to the cost of the elements of the job in which the surveyor is involved.

In addition to the Bye-Laws and the Regulations, buildings which contain separate flats or are more than 2 storeys (3 storeys in London) will require measures to be incorporated to provide precautions against and means of escape in case of, fire. Although there is reference to these matters in the Regulations, they also refer back to Codes of Practice. The requirements relating to fire precautions are administered both by the Building Control Department and by the Fire Department. The exact method will vary depending on the local authority and the Building Inspector or District Surveyor will normally involve the appropriate department when necessary.

Services

Services in this context means the supply of Electricity, Gas and Water. These supplies are governed by regulations which require that household installations are made to an adequate standard before a supply is connected. The representatives of the various boards are entitled to enter into a home to inspect an installation or to read a supply meter.

The affect of these Regulations are noted in sections 9.00, 13.00 and 14.00 where they are relevant to the repair of houses.

Health

There are a number of laws on the Statute Book which deal with standards related to health and are collectively referred to as the Health Acts. These are administered by the Public Health Inspector now more commonly referred to as the Environmental Health Department of the local authority. The Environmental Health Officers (EHO's) are empowered to inspect houses which they have reason to believe are sub-standard and to serve notices on the occupants or the owners requiring that modifications or repairs are made to bring the house up to the standards defined in the Acts.

If the house, flat or room is, in the opinion of the EHO, unfit for human habitation under the terms of the Act then he may issue a 'closing order' which means that the property which is the subject of the order must not be used until the necessary work has been carried out to bring it up to standard. Common grounds for issuing an order are excessive damp, inadequate daylighting, poor ventilation and a faulty electrical installation. Many other defects may be included under the terms of an EHO's inspection.

The EHO's will normally concentrate on rented accommodation and property in the ownership of the local authority, although they can also visit owner occupiers. People using short-life houses in the ownership of the local authority will usually be able to continue to use property which would normally be the subject of an order, provided that they do sufficient work to make them 'adequate for the time being . . .' This will include minimising dampness, providing safe services and making sure the house is weather proof and hygienic.

Conclusion

The Regulations which govern housing, whilst over prolific, are in the main sensible. Many can be ignored in the repair of houses and only those relating to safety, structural stability and the well being of the occupants should always be observed. If in any doubt, consult the relevant officers who are usually reasonable and concerned more with the overall spirit of the Regulations being adhered to than attention to exact detail.

1
DEMOLITION

REMOVING RUBBISH

The removal of rubbish caused by building works can be a problem in urban areas, and the normal practice is to hire a rubbish skip. However, before ordering a skip the following should be considered:–

(a) Skip licences

Before placing a skip on the road outside of a house, a skip licence is required. This may be obtained from the Engineer's Department of the Local Authority. Issuing techniques vary; one Local Authority will issue a licence over the telephone, another may require that a licence is collected from the Town Hall, while a third will require a written application. Some skip hire firms will obtain a licence as part of their service. On busy streets a licence may be restrictive, for example on a commuting route, the licence may only allow skips to be placed on the street from 10.00 a.m. to 4.00 p.m. on weekdays.

(b) Skip lighting

Skips are required to be lighted during the hours of darkness and the hire firm should provide lights, although responsibility rests with the holder of the licence.

(c) Skip loading

A skip should only be ordered when there is sufficient rubbish to fill it in one day, otherwise it will be filled by other people. Skips are expensive, approximately £30.00 for a normal size, so not only should they not be left for others to fill, but care should also be taken to see that bulky objects, badly placed timbers, etc. do not create voids which are not filled. Skips should not be filled above their sides. If they are, the extra rubbish may be dumped in the street for the licence holder to dispose of – even if the extra rubbish was placed there by other people.

(d) Other ways of disposing of rubbish

Where there is not enough rubbish for a skip, it can be bagged in heavy-duty polythene sacks and taken to the local refuse tip, where household waste can be deposited for little or no charge. Timber and paper waste can be burnt, but plastics, rubber, old linoleum, etc. should not be, and anyone burning rubbish is advised to check how the Clean Air Act is applied in their area.

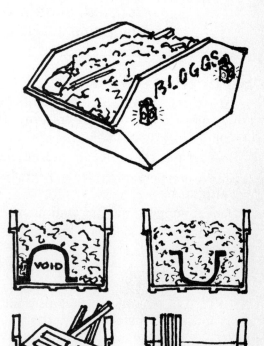

(e) Handling rubbish

A lot of energy can be wasted by double handling of rubbish, and thought should be given to ways of reducing this wastage, for example by the construction of a chute, or rigging up a pulley system to get rubbish down from upper storeys, using a wheelbarrow or polythene sacks to transport rubbish to a skip. Heavy-duty polythene bags or sacks (not refuse sacks) are obtainable from builder's merchants, and are also useful to stockpile rubbish while awaiting the arrival of a skip. These can be emptied and re-used. When clearing dusty debris, such as old plaster, it is advisable to wear a face mask and goggles.

(f) Recycling

Don't throw away materials that can be re-used, and save all metal waste to sell for scrap.

1.02
DEMOLITION

When part of a building is to be demolished, either because it has failed, or because improvements or alterations are being made, extreme care should be taken. The advice of an architect, building surveyor, District Surveyor, Building Inspector, or someone equally qualified, should be sought before starting demolition.

(a) Structural Wall

Check if a wall is structural. If uncertain then ask these questions. If the answer to any of the following is YES, then IT IS:–

 i   Does it support any floor or ceiling joists?
 ii Does it support any rafters, beams, or wallplates?
 iii Does it support another wall above?
 iv Does it provide sideways support to another wall?
 v   Does it give support to ground at a higher level?

If the wall is structural, then alternative support must be provided before the wall is removed. 'Acrow' props, which are adjustable metal supports, are normally used for this purpose, although timber props and wedges may also be used. When providing support for a substantial load, such as a floor, props must be taken down to the ground. Where there is a cavity below the lowest floor this may either be achieved by placing a set of props below the floor or by removing the floor boards, and using one set of extended props between the ground and the underside of the next floor. Temporary supports should only be removed when a replacement structure has been built.

(b) Non-structural Walls

Non-structural walls can be removed without providing props. However, first re-check that the answers to the previous questions are NO. If in doubt ask.

(c) Part of a Building

When part of a building, for example a rear addition, is to be demolished, then work should start at the top and work down, removing loads from walls and beams before they in turn are demolished. Save all re-usable materials.

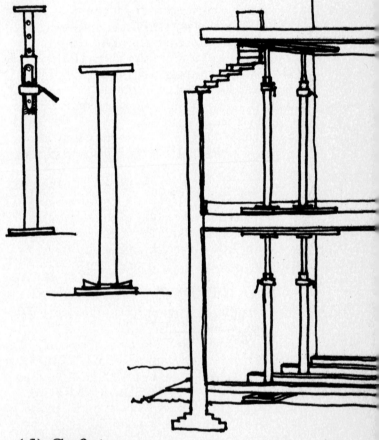

(d) Safety

Demolition is dangerous, and safety rules should be observed:–

– Make sure that the rest of the building is adequately supported!
– Do not allow anyone not working on the demolition into the building!
– Keep the building secure. Do not let children, or the public gain access!
– Cordon off the area where debris will fall and signpost it!
– Do not demolish parts of the building you are standing on!
– Wear a helmet and other protective clothing!

NEW OPENING IN BRICK WALL

Knock 75×100 mm slots through the wall at a maximum of 900 mm centres, the depth of the lintel above the top of the required opening. If opening is for a narrow window or single door, the lintel will normally be 75 mm deep, so that holes occur in the second brick course above the top of the opening.

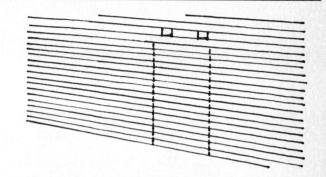

1

Feed 75×100 mm timbers (known as 'needles' when used in this way), through the holes and support each end on an 'Acrow' prop. The load will require supporting down to ground level. If the wall is a structural wall, i.e. is carrying the load of another wall, a floor, or the roof, additional supports may be necessary and professional advice should be sought.

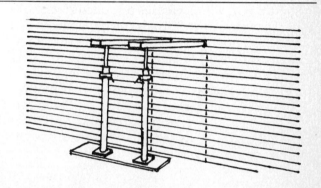

2

Mark the size of the opening and the position of the lintel, which should sit in a brick course and oversail the opening by 150–225 mm on each side. When demolishing brickwork for an opening, a little care will save work later, so cut a hole in the middle of the opening near the top and then, using a bolster and club hammer, lift bricks out by breaking up the mortar courses. Leave bricks which partly project into opening, cut out slot for lintel.

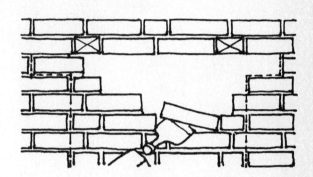

3

Slide in a pre-stressed pre-cast concrete lintel, rough side facing up and point in place with 1:6 cement-sand mortar.

    After a day the 'needles' and props may be removed and the brickwork above the lintel made good, using 1:6 cement-sand mortar and new, or second-hand bricks.

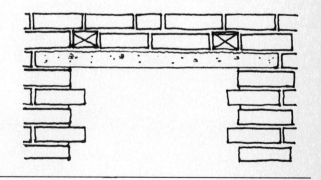

4

Trim off projecting pieces of brick, working from the top down, using a bolster and club hammer. First tap the bolster on the face and then the top of the brick with the hammer to mark a break line, then striking the break line on the face of the brick with the bolster and hammer, chop off protruding piece. Tidy up any small protrusions and fill any recesses on the side of the opening with mortar, or cut bricks and mortar.

5

In many older houses, the external walls consist of a 225 mm (9″) solid inner leaf with a 105 mm (4″) outer leaf which carries no added structural load. To match in with the external appearance it is possible in these cases to support the inner leaf on a precast pre-stressed concrete lintel as described, and to support the outer leaf on a 50×6 mm mild steel bar, galvanised or painted to prevent rust. The bar should be built 225 mm into the mortar course to either side of the opening, and if required the brickwork above can be rebuilt as an 'arch' of headers.

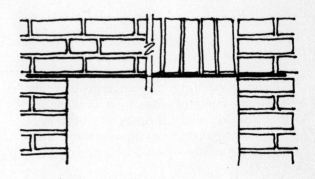

6

1.04
NEW OPENING IN STUD WALL

In older houses, studwork, i.e. timber framed walls, are often structural, the house in fact being a timber frame, with a brick outer skin. Holes should therefore not be indiscriminately cut through studwork. 'Studs' are vertical timbers in a partition.

Remove plaster to one side of the wall to reveal the positions and arrangement of the studwork.

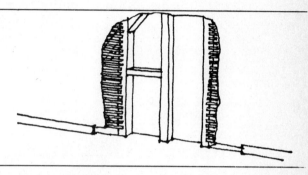

1

Having finalised the position of the opening, take off plaster and lathes or plasterboard to both sides. If stud wall is structural then support floor or ceiling above by placing a scaffold plank or a 100×50 mm timber parallel to the wall at floor and ceiling level, separated by 'Acrow' props at 900 mm centres. If studwork is brick filled, take out bricks in area of opening.

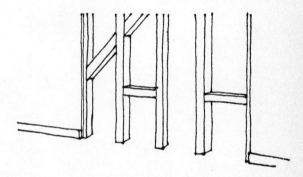

2

For relatively small openings such as a doorway, it is possible to introduce a lintel into existing studwork, and it is then only necessary to cut out the section of studwork, above the height of the opening plus the lintel. For larger openings a more complex arrangement may be required, in order to integrate the new lintel with the studwork. Professional advice should be sought before introducing a large opening in a structural studwork wall.

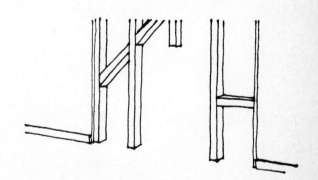

3

To the stud at either side of the opening bolt a piece of timber of the same size as the stud from the bottom of the lintel to the floor, using 4 No. 12 mm diameter coach bolts.

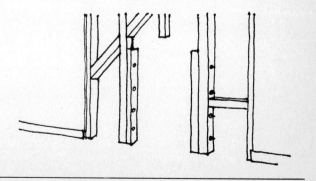

4

Position the timber lintel making sure that it is a tight fit and skew nail the lintel into the studs. Also skew nail the new supports and the cut off studs into the lintel.

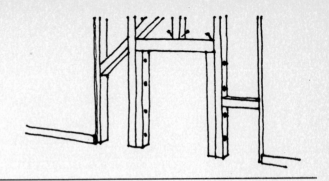

5 _____

Make good wall finishes around opening. (See sections 2.03, 2.04.)

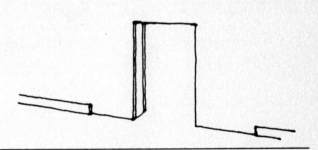

6 _____

2
WALLS

2.01
LEAVE BRICK FINISH

Cleaned brickwork can be a very effective finish to an internal wall.

Hack off perished plaster with a 100 mm (4″) cold chisel, known as a bolster. If the brick is to be left, then take care not to damage the bricks.

1

Clean off remains of plaster with a stripping knife followed by a wire brush.

2

Clean out the mortar from the joints to a depth of 10 mm with a plugging chisel and a club hammer.

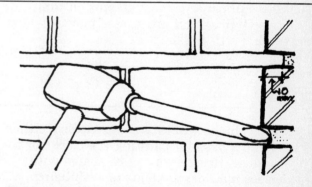

3

Brush the joints and the brickwork down to remove dust and old mortar. Brush water over the wall and the joints, soaking the brickwork so that it will not absorb moisture from the new pointing mortar.

4

Mix enough mortar to do about 1 square metre (a bucket full), using 1 part of Portland cement to 6 parts sand by volume. Use enough water so that mortar is smooth but firm. Don't make mortar too dry; it should be smooth enough to roll across the board when a piece is cut off and pushed across the spotboard with a sawing action of the trowel.

5

Load some of the mortar onto a 'hawk' and, using a small pointing trowel, pick up a strip of mortar on the bottom edge of the face with an upward sweep of the back of the trowel.

Rotate the wrist so that the bottom edge becomes the top edge and force the mortar into the joints, first a vertical joint and then the horizontal joint above and below it. Leave mortar flush with bricks.

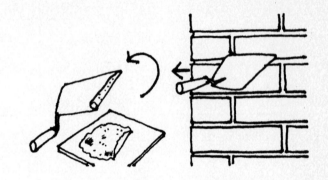

6

Internal brickwork is usually irregular and a flush joint is usually simplest. A flush joint is made by waiting until the mortar has started to go 'off' and then rubbing the joint, in one direction only, with a piece of dry sacking. Damp sacking will cause cement strains on the brickwork. Brush off any excess mortar when dry with a stiff brush.

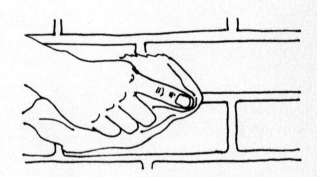

7

It is advisable to seal internal brickwork either to provide a base for painting the bricks or to reduce dust. Brickwork can be sealed with colourless masonry sealants or stabilising solutions. These are simply liberally brushed over brickwork, but make sure the room is well ventilated and read the safety instructions on the can carefully.

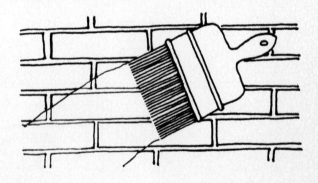

8

PLASTERING BRICK OR BLOCKWORK

This is a description of how to plaster a patch, but the same techniques can be applied to areas of new plaster where the base coat should be 12 mm thick with a 3 mm thick finish coat.

Hack off perished plaster, back to a firm edge, with a 100 mm bolster. Clean off any remaining plaster with a stripping knife or a wire brush.

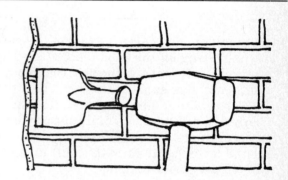

1

Brush the joints and the brickwork down to remove dust and loose mortar. Mix 1 part of Uni-bond adhesive to 10 parts of water and brush this solution over the brickwork, mortar joints and edges of the retained old plaster – this will give the new plaster a better 'key' so that it will stick firmly.

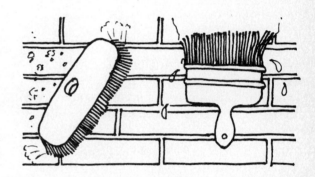

2

Mix the base coat plaster, such as Seraphite or Carlite Browning, in a plastic bucket or a galvanised metal tub, by adding plaster to clean water and working with a plunger made out of a piece of gas pipe and copper wire or a bicycle-pedal cog wheel attached to a stick. Work plaster to an even consistency so that it is stiff enough to stand in peaks when the plunger is removed.

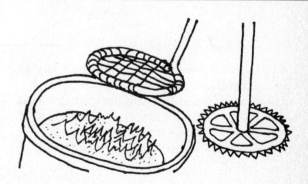

3

Empty the plaster onto a wet 'spot' board which is supported on a stool or trestle. Wet the area to be plastered with clean water, flicked and brushed onto the wall and keep the brush and water near at hand.

4

Load the hawk from the spotboard with the face of the trowel. Take a trowel-load of plaster and apply it firmly to the wall – there is no need to be too forceful, but plaster weakly placed just drops off. Spread the plaster by working strokes away from the body, work from the bottom upwards or from the top down, depending on which seems easiest to your arm action.

5

Run a straight edge down the face of the patch, each end resting on the good plaster to either side, and check the level of the base coat plaster. The base coat plaster should be 3 mm below the surface level of the finished plaster, (the face of the batten,) and should be built out or shaved down accordingly. It is worth taking some time to get the level right, since this will make the finishing coat easier to apply.

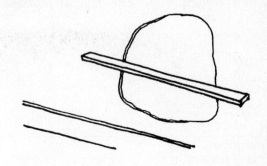

6

When the plaster begins to set, scratch a 'key' into it, with a comb made up of oval nails hammered into a piece of scrap wood at 10 mm centres. Criss cross the scratching.

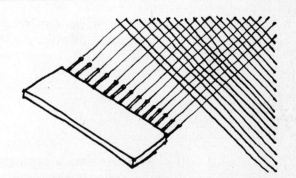

7

The finish coat plaster can be applied any time from an hour after the base coat has been completed. Mix the finish plaster in a clean bucket with a clean plunger until it is as smooth as soft butter. Brush down the base coat to remove any loose plaster and wet with a brush.

8

Using a clean, wet trowel, apply the finish coat and spread it evenly over the base coat. Keep the trowel clean and wet. When the whole of the base coat has been covered then begin to even out the finish coat with sweeping strokes, flicking water at the plaster and wetting the trowel from time to time. This process will show up localised indentations which sould be filled and small humps that should be smoothed out.

9

When the surface is level, the most difficult part of plastering begins. In order to give the plaster a hard smooth finish, it must be polished. This is done using a wet clean trowel and applying pressure whilst working back and forth across, up and down the patch with sweeping strokes. The trowel should be almost flat to the plaster but not quite or else it will stick and pull off some of the plaster. While polishing, water should be flicked at the wall to provide lubrication. Once the patch has an initial polish it can be left for half an hour before completing the polishing.

10

PLASTERBOARD TO STUD PARTITION

Where a large area of plaster has failed on a stud partition, it is simpler and quicker to remove all of the plaster and replace it with gyproc square edged wallboard, hereafter simply called plasterboard, rather than to patch plaster.

Remove remains of old plaster and laths from stud partition. Take off skirting and retain, if re-usable. Run any electrical cables or pipework which are to be concealed in the partition.

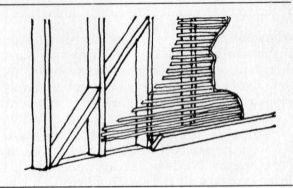

1

Measure distance between centres or left-hand face to left-hand face of timber studs. Plasterboard is easily available in two sizes, 1,830×900 mm and more commonly 2,440×1,200 mm and unless the studs are more than 450 mm apart, 9 mm thick plasterboard is adequate. Plasterboard sheets should meet on a stud vertically and on a horizontal timber nailed between the studs, called a 'noggin'. Order plasterboard sizes to reduce waste.

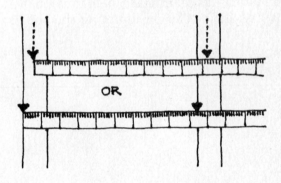

2

Plasterboard doesn't have to go down to the floor, only 10 mm below the top of the skirting; so it will only be necessary to introduce noggins where walls are taller than 2,440 mm plus the height of the skirting. Where a noggin is needed it should be 50 mm deep, as wide as the two vertical studs and long enough to fit tightly between them. They should be made of sawn softwood and skew-nailed into place.

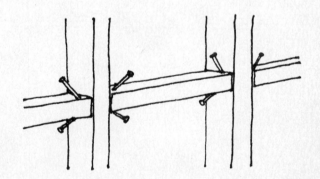

3

To cut plasterboard, use a sharp craft knife and cut through the ivory face and deeply score the plaster core. Lift the board, tap it along the back of the cut, causing the rest of the plaster core to crack and the board to bend along the line. Cut through the grey paper side of the board using the cut plaster as a guideline.

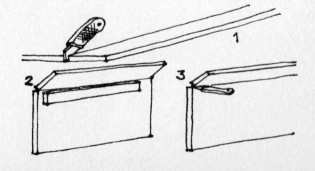

4

Nail plasterboard in place using 32 mm galvanised clout nails. Try not to hit the board or to puncture the ivory paper surface of the board with the nail head. Nails should be at approximately every 150 mm. Sheets should meet on top of a stud or noggin and the gap between boards should be no more than 5 mm.

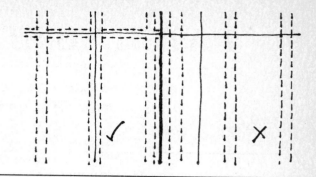

5

Using a hammer and a punch, slightly recess all nail heads, without breaking the paper surface. Using a palette knife, fill nail heads and joints with a filler, such as Polyfilla. Using plasterboard offcuts to pack it out to the level of the plasterboard, nail the skirting back onto the studs.

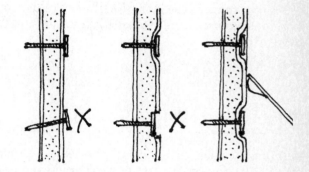

6

PATCH TO STUD PARTITION

Where a small area of plaster has failed on a stud partition it is appropriate to patch in new plaster.

Carefully remove damaged or bulging plaster but do not remove the laths. Pulling out old laths will cause more plaster to lose its key and fall off the wall.

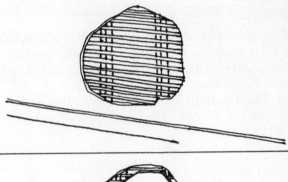

1

Old plasterwork will normally be 19 mm thick or more, so to save plaster and to avoid exerting pressure on the laths, which could disturb more plaster, cut a patch of 9 mm plasterboard to approximately fit the hole. Nail the plasterboard grey face outwards, over the laths, into the studs with 38 or 50 mm galvanised clout nails.

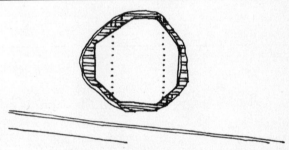

2

Mix up some bonding plaster in a bucket, by adding the plaster to clean water and working with a plunger. Work plaster to an even consistency until it is stiff enough to stand in peaks when the plunger is removed.

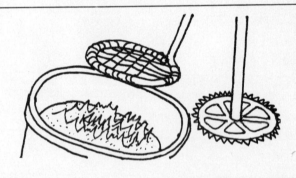

3

Empty the plaster onto a wet 'spot' board which is supported on a stool or trestle. Wet the edges of the old plaster with clean water applied with a brush.

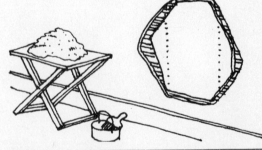

4

Load the hawk from the 'spot' board with the face of the trowel. Fill in between the edge of the old plaster and the plasterboard, pressing the plaster firmly into place so that it squeezes between the laths and forms a key. Build up the plaster over the face of the plasterboard patch.

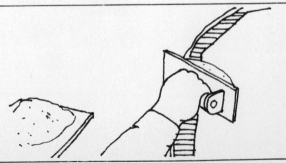

5

Run a straight edge down the face of the patch, each end resting on the good plaster to either side, and check the level of the base coat plaster. The base coat plaster should be 3 mm below the surface level of the finished plaster, (the face of the batten,) and should be built out or shaved down accordingly. It is worth taking some time to get the level right, since this will make the finishing coat easier to apply.

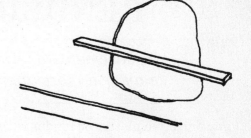

6

When the plaster begins to set, scratch a 'key' into it, with a comb made up of oval nails hammered into a piece of scrap wood at 10 mm centres. Criss cross the scratching.

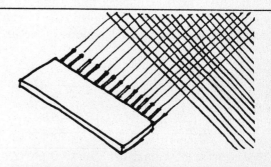

7

The finish coat plaster can be applied any time from an hour after the base coat has been completed. Mix the finish plaster in a clean bucket with a clean plunger until it is as smooth as soft butter. Brush down the base coat to remove any loose plaster and wet with a brush.

8

Using a clean, wet trowel, apply the finish coat and spread it evenly over the base coat. Keep the trowel clean and wet. When the whole of the base coat has been covered then begin to even out the finish coat with sweeping strokes, flicking water at the plaster and wetting the trowel from time to time. This process will show up localised indentations which should be filled and small humps that should be smoothed out.

9

When the surface is level, the most difficult part of plastering begins. In order to give the plaster a hard smooth finish, it must be polished. This is done using a wet clean trowel and applying pressure whilst working back and forth across, up and down the patch with sweeping strokes. The trowel should be almost flat to the plaster but not quite or else it will stick and pull off some of the plaster. While polishing, water should be flicked at the wall to provide lubrication. Once the patch has an initial polish it can be left for half an hour before completing the polishing.

10

*In basements or walls prone to damp, render
may be a more appropriate finish than plaster.*

Hack off any defective plaster or render with a
100 mm bolster and take back to firm edge. Rake
out any loose mortar from brick joints to a depth
of 10 mm. Brush off any dust or loose mortar.

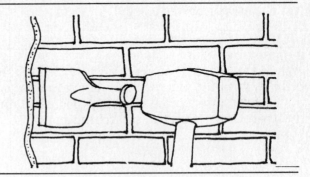

1

Mix up a mortar of 1 part cement to 6 parts of
fine sand and add a waterproofing agent, such as
'Febprufe' or similar. Add water so that mix is
smooth enough to 'roll' with the sawing action of
a brick-laying trowel but is still firm; too much
water will produce a weak mix that will fall off
the hawk and off the wall. The mix should be
even in colour with no dry areas.

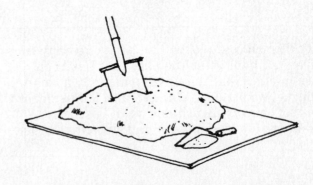

2

If a large area is to be rendered, battens may be
used as a guide to the depth of render. Nail a 12
mm-deep vertical batten in the corner of the
wall to be rendered, using masonry nails. Nail
battens at regular intervals not exceeding 1,800
mm along the wall.

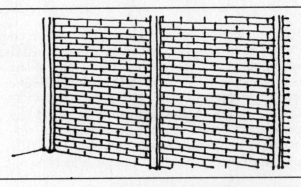

3

Load some of the render mixture onto a wet spot
board supported on a trestle or stool. Wet down
the wall by flicking and brushing clean water
over the surface.

4

Load some mortar onto the hawk by holding it flush with the spot board and using the trowel to scrape onto it several trowel loads of mortar. Holding the hawk near to the bottom of the wall cut off a trowel load of mortar, tip the hawk towards you, load the trowel then push the mortar against the wall and spread upwards. Any dropped mortar that has fallen onto a clean floor, boards or dust sheet can be picked up and re-used.

5
___

Working in this way, fill in between the first pair of battens. Take a straight edged board, place it on the battens and work down the wall, sawing off any excess mortar. Fill in any depressions and again bring the straight edge down the battens, repeat this process until the area of render between the battens is level. Fill in between remaining battens in similar fashion.

6
___

Allow 4 or 5 hours for mortar to set then remove battens and fill in with mortar and level off. Using a comb, made out of oval nails hammered into a batten at 15 mm centres, scratch mortar to provide a random 'key' for the next coat.

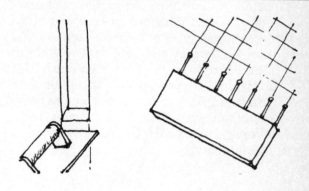

7
___

After 24 hours mix up mortar as before and dampen the wall. Apply a 3 mm thick coat of mortar to the previous coat using wide sweeping strokes to spread mortar evenly over all of the surface. Use a wooden trowel or float for a matt finish and a steel trowel/float for a smooth finish but do not over work as this will cause the cement to separate out of the mortar.

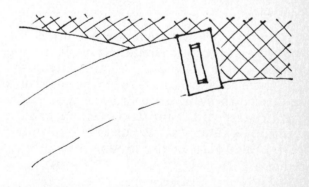

8
___

DRY-LINING: PLASTERBOARD

Dry-lining is useful where a wall in a basement is damp or where extra insulation is required. The plasterboard used is 9 mm thick, foil-backed, gyproc square edged wallboard.

Hack off any plaster and brush off loose particles adhering to the wall surface. If the wall is in a basement or damp then apply 2 coats of Synthaprufe or Aquaseal 5 to seal the surface.

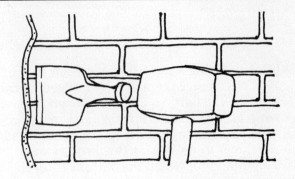

1

Cut 50×25 mm sawn softwood battens to the height of the wall to be dry-lined and paint battens with 2 coats of wood preservative or creosote – don't forget the sawn ends. Fix the first batten vertically in the corner of the wall using either 75 mm masonry nails or 75 mm No. 10 screws and rawlplugs at 450 mm centres. Fix remaining battens to wall, the first at 400 mm from centre line to corner face of corner batten, then at 400 mm centres. If wall is higher than 2,400 mm then fix horizontal battens between vertical battens, but with 2 No. 10 mm holes drilled vertically through the batten to provide ventilation of cavity.

2

Cut plasterboard to height of room minus 10 mm. Offer up plasterboard to battens, ivory side out and nail in place using 25 mm galvanised clout nails, taking care not to hit the board or to break surface of the new board with nail heads. Stop plasterboard 5 mm below ceiling when dry-lining a damp wall, but up to ceiling where dry-lining is only for insulation.

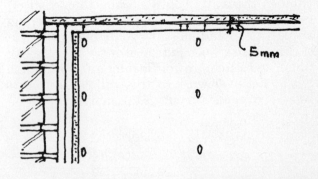

5mm

3

Nail on a 100×19 mm sw chamfered skirting or skirting to match existing and to damp walls drill 2 No. 10 mm diameter holes through skirting and plasterboard between each pair of battens to provide ventilation for the cavity.

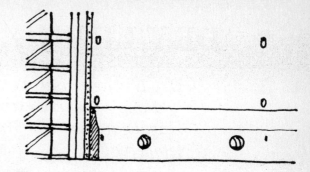

4

Where a board is to abut an irregular wall it may be marked by placing it in front of the next to last board. Then run one end of a 1,220 mm long batten down the irregular wall, keeping the batten horizontal and mark the board to be cut with a pencil held at the other end of the board. This will give the cut line for the last board; cut and nail in place.

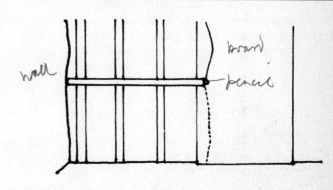

5

Recess nail heads with a punch – taking care not to puncture paper surface of board – and fill nail heads and joints with Polyfilla or similar filler applied with a palette knife.

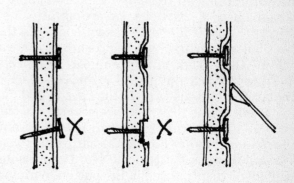

6

2.07
DRY-LINING: HARDBOARD

Dry-Lining is useful where a wall in a basement is damp or where extra insulation is required. Hardboard used is 3 mm thick and old tempered.

Hack off any plaster and brush off loose particles adhering to the wall surface. If the wall is in a basement or damp then apply 2 coats of Synthaprufe or Aquaseal 5 to seal the surface.

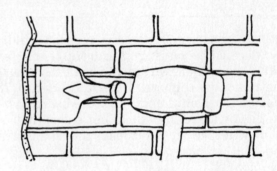

1

Cut 50×25 mm sawn softwood battens to the height of the wall to be dry-lined and paint battens with 2 coats of wood preservative or creosote – don't forget the sawn ends. Fix the first batten vertically in the corner of the wall using either 75 mm masonry nails or 75 mm No. 10 screws and rawlplugs at 450 mm centres. Fix remaining battens to wall, the first at 400 mm from centre line to corner face of corner batten, then at 400 mm centres. If wall is higher than 2,400 mm then fix horizontal battens between vertical battens, butt with 2 No. 10 mm holes drilled vertically through the batten to provide ventilation of cavity.

2

Hardboard should be stored flat and before use for dry-lining it must be 'conditioned' which is done by laying the board flat and scrubbing 1 litre of clean water into the back of each 2,400×1,200 mm sheet. Sheets should then be stored flat in the room to be dry-lined for 72 hours, to allow them to adjust to the moisture content of room. Paint back of board with 2 coats of Synthaprufe or Aquaseal 5.

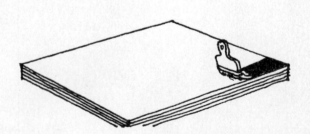

3

Cut hardboard to height of room minus 10 mm using a saw. Offer up hardboard to battens and nail in place with 15 mm hardboard pins. For damp rooms stop hardboard 5 mm below ceiling line to ventilate cavity.

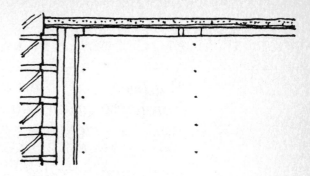

4

Nail on a 100×19 mm sw chamfered skirting or skirting to match existing and to damp wall drill 2 No. 10 mm diameter holes through skirting and hardboard between each pair of battens to provide ventilation for the cavity.

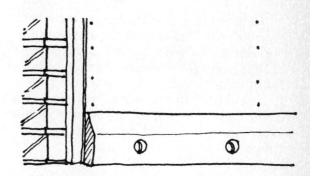

5

Recess pin heads with a punch and tape joints with a 50 mm wide self-adhesive paper tape.

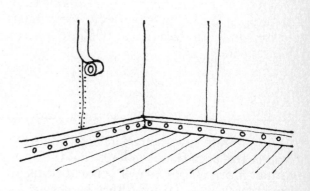

6

2.08
NEW STUDWORK PARTITION

Studwork partitions are usually non-loadbearing and are used to subdivide existing space. The name derives from the vertical timber members, which are traditionally called 'studs'.

Before positioning a new studwork partition check whether it runs across the span of the joists or along the joists. If it runs across floor and ceiling joists there should be no problem, but if it runs with the joists the line of the partition should either be moved so that it sits above and below a joist, or if this is not possible then additional timbers will be required between the floor and ceiling joists.

At ceiling level introduce 50×75 mm sawn softwood 'noggins' at 600 mm centres, skew nailed into joists. At floor level introduce 50 mm×depth of joist minus 50 mm (to avoid disturbing ceiling below) sawn softwood timbers supported on metal hangers at 600 mm centres between joists.

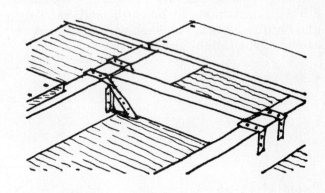

1

Cut a 50×75 mm sawn softwood 'head' plate for the top of the partition, the length of the partition. Mark off position of vertical studs at 400 mm centres (or larger where a door or opening is to be included). Screw head plate in position, since nailing could damage the existing ceiling.

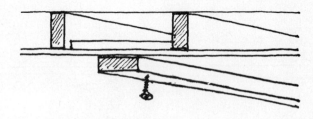

400 mm = 40 cm = 16"

2

Using a level or plumb line drop verticals down from head plate and mark floor. Cut a 50×75 mm sawn softwood 'sole' plate for the base of the partition, remembering that there is no sole plate across the bottom of doorways. Using the plumb line to set the first, mark out the positions of vertical studs. Nail sole plate to floor taking care not to damage any pipes or wires below the floor. Where the sole plate sits on a solid floor then it should be treated with wood preservative, placed on a damp proof course of polythene or bituminous felt and masonry nailed to the floor.

3

Cut vertical studs of 50×75 mm sawn softwood to fit tightly between head and sole plates. Locate studs on marks and skew nail in place.

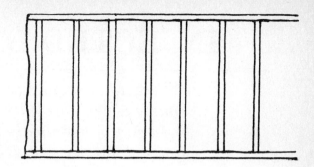

4

If partition exceeds 2,400 mm in height then 'noggins' will be required to support the edges of the boards where they meet horizontally. Noggins of 75×50 mm sawn softwood should be located at 1,200 mm centres vertically even if partition is less than 2,400 mm high and are skew nailed in place. Drill holes for any service runs, such as wiring, in noggins and studs.

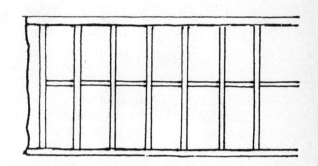

5

Offer up 9 mm gyproc square edged plasterboard to one side of the partition, ivory face out, and nail in place with 32 mm galvanised clout nails, taking care not to damage the board by hitting it with a hammer or breaking the paper surface with the nails. Run any services that are to be hidden within the partition before plasterboarding the second side.

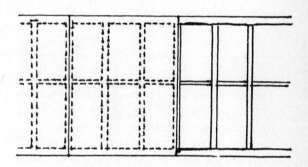

6

Scribe end boards to match any irregularity in the walls and fix into place.
N.B. When setting out stud positions on the sole and head plates, allowance must be made for the first stud to each side of the partition to carry the plasterboard tight up against the adjoining wall.

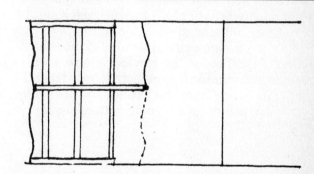

7

Recess nail heads without breaking surface of board and fill nail heads and joints to boards with Polyfilla or similar filler applied with a palette knife. Nail on a skirting to match existing skirtings.
N.B. The forming of doorways and similar openings to studwork partitions is covered on sheet 3.12.

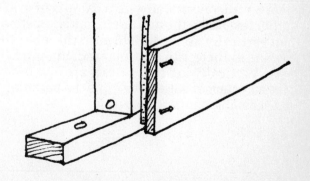

8

2.09
INJECTED DAMP COURSE

Where a house does not have an effective damp course a new one may be provided by the injection of chemicals into the brickwork. For long life property it is more sensible to have this work done by a reputable specialist who will give a 20 year guarantee, but for those in short life accommodation the following method has been found to be effective.

When a specialist carries out this work he will remove the plaster to a height of 1 m and remove the skirting board. This is to both dry out the wall and to reveal the brickwork. In rooms where the plaster is sound and the skirting is 150 mm or more above the outside ground level, it is possible just to take off the skirting.

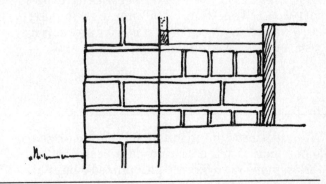

1

If a number of houses or a large extent of damp course injecting is to be done, it is worth hiring an injection machine; if not, the process can be done by hand. If a machine is to be used, the holes drilled must be large enough to take the nozzles of the particular machine; a Number 12 masonry bit will produce a large enough hole for hand injection. Drill holes from the inside at a slight downwards angle, into every brick, but no more than 100 mm apart, at a height of 150 mm above the outside ground level and into the centre of the face of the bricks. Where a wall exceeds 225 mm in thickness drill once from the inside and once from the outside, but be sure that holes are not deep enough to connect.

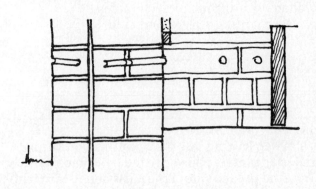

2

Where a wall joins a wall with a damp course at a higher level then the new damp course must be taken vertically up the wall to meet the other to ensure that there is a continuous damp-proof course. Vertically injected courses are also used where an external garden wall hits the building and is causing damp penetration.

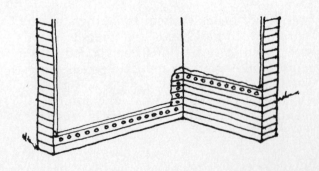

3

When using a machine follow the injection instructions, inserting the nozzles into the holes, injecting and repeating the procedure.

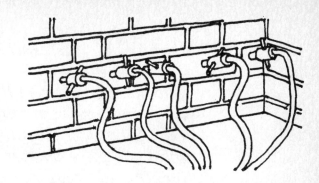

4

The wall may be injected by hand by using a tube attached to an old washing-up-liquid bottle, the tube being placed into the hole and the bottle squeezed. This process is repeated at intervals of 24 hours, 3 times for each hole.

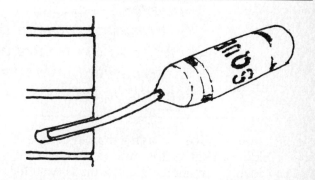

5

Alternatively, a series of funnels attached to tubes may be used. The tubes are placed deep into the holes and sealed in place with putty to prevent leakage around the tube and the funnel is then supported above the hole and filled with fluid and left in position for 24 hours, the fluid being transferred to the bricks by capillary action.

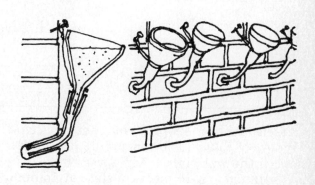

6

When the damp course has been completed, it should be left for at least 1 week before the holes in the brickwork are plugged with mortar. Any replastering or replacement of the skirting should be left for as long as possible to aid the drying out of the wall.

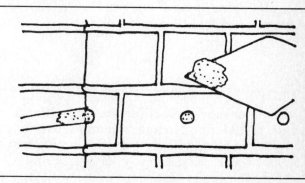

7

Where the damp course is above internal floor level the plasterwork should be hacked off up to the new damp course, the wall so revealed painted with 3 coats of Synthaprufe or Aquaseal 5, the last coat having sand thrown against it while it is still wet. This part of the wall should then be rendered.

Suitable fluid for damp-proof course injection is Grangers Waterproofing fluid.

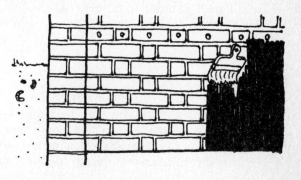

8

2.10
DAMP COURSE, CUT-IN

This method of providing a damp-proof course is normally more expensive when carried out by experts but has the advantage of introducing a solid one-piece barrier which is likely to last longer and prove less problematic than an injected system.

Providing a cut-in damp-proof course relies on the ability to hire a brick cutting saw. Extreme caution and rigorous safety measures should be enforced when using this method.

Using the saw, slice through a mortar course of the brickwork that is 150 mm above external ground level. Saw along the mortar course for 900 mm before stopping.

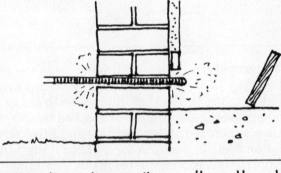

1

Feed a lead core damp-proof course or polythene damp-proof course, wide enough to pass right through the wall, into the slot so formed and hold it in place with pieces of slate at 150 mm intervals. Joins in the damp-proof course should be overlapped by at least 300 mm.

2

Continue around the perimeter, cutting for a length of 900 mm, feeding in damp course and holding it in place with slate until complete. Cut off any overhanging damp-proof course and point up the cut to both sides of the wall in mortar of 1 part cement to 6 parts sand.

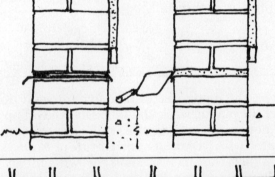

3

This technique is not suited for vertical damp-proof courses but steps may be achieved by overlapping saw cuts on two mortar courses, removing a brick (or bricks) and relaying so that a continuous damp course steps up to the next level.

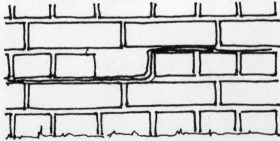

4

STITCHING CRACKS TO INTERNAL WALLS

Where an internal wall has cracked due to settlement or some other form of movement which has now ceased, it is advisable to 'stitch in' the cracked area before renewing the plasterwork.

Cut out cracked bricks and rake out pointing to one brick length on either side of the crack.

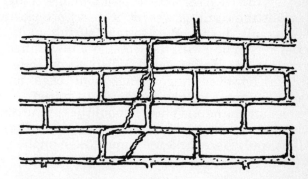

1

Lay in new brick in place of cracked brick (a 'common' brick or second-hand brick is usually adequate for this purpose) bedded in 1:6 cement-sand mortar.

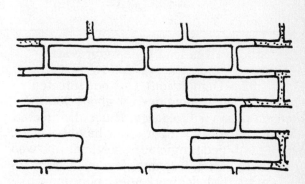

2

Repoint brickwork with mortar of 1 part of cement to 6 of sand. (See sheet 2.20.)

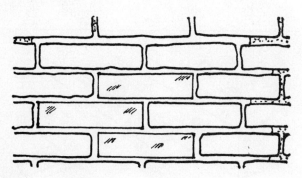
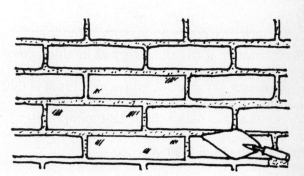

3

REPAIRING A STUD PARTITION

Existing stud partitions have often been affected by wet or dry rot when in contact with damp floors or external walls or by insect attack. Where such attack is localized the partition can be repaired.

Remove partition covering, such as lath and plaster, to reveal the extent of the damage. If the decay is the result of wet rot or insect attack it will usually be adequate to take off the coverings in line with the sections of the timber which are no longer sound. When dry rot is present, however, the coverings should be taken back 900 mm past any contact with rotten timber and laths and plaster should be carefully examined for traces of spores or fine plant-like fibres, and where these are found, taken further back.

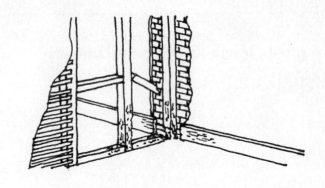

1

If the stud wall is load bearing provide alternative support using 'Acrow' props (see sheet 1.02 – Demolition). Cut out infected timber, in the case of dry rot about 300 mm to 900 mm past visible decay. Burn all infected timber and spray timbers that have been left with a combined fungicide, insecticide and wood preservative (e.g. Cuprinol 5 star). Where studwork joins brickwork play a blow lamp over the brickwork and burn off any visible spores before spraying.

2

Select timber of the same section as the rotten timber and paint with wood preservative. Cut new sections for studs to give a minimum of 600 mm overlap. Bolt new sections onto ends of damaged studs using three 12 mm diameter coach bolts with timber connectors in between the two pieces of timber.

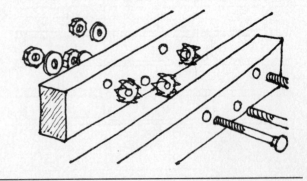

3

When bolting on new sections of timber, the holes for the bolts should be placed central to the top and bottom third of the depth of the timber and no bolt should be nearer than the depth of the timber from any end. Bolts should alternatively be taken through the top and bottom thirds of the timber.

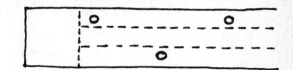

4

When head or sole plate timbers have been affected they should be replaced, before the studs are replaced, with treated timber. Noggins should be added when the studs have been replaced in order to strengthen the construction.

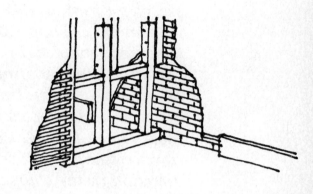

5

The repaired studwork may now be recovered as described in 2.03 Plasterboard to Stud partition or 2.04 Patch to Stud partition.

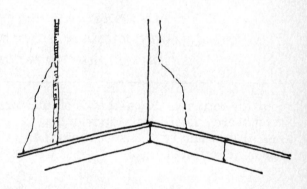

6

Dry rot is a virulent fungus that extracts moisture from timber, breaking it down in the process and leaving the timber dry, brittle and with practically no strength. It is capable of travelling through plaster and brickwork in its search for fresh timber to devour and can carry its own water supply through microscopic tendrils to enable it to do so. It can exhibit itself in a number of ways, including a fungus usually referred to as a fruiting body, a white fluffy down, or it may appear as fibres, not unlike plant roots. Given the right conditions it can spread rapidly, being able to travel up to 4 metres in any direction in the course of one year.

Dry rot commonly occurs when timbers are in contact with or are part of an external wall and it is not enough to replace the rotten timber.

Cut out the rotten timber and take off plaster, skirting boards, floorboards, and window linings in the vicinity to ensure that other timber is not affected.

Cut back plaster until no spores are visible in
either brick or plaster and then cut back plaster
for a further 900 mm.

2

Take a blow lamp and burn the surface of the
brickwork, getting the flame into any openings
or recesses. When cool, spray with fungicide.

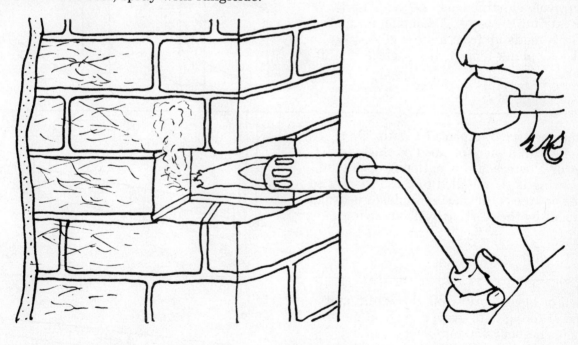

3

Leave wall to thoroughly dry out, then replaster
as 2.02 Plastering.

4

REPLACING EXISTING SKIRTING OR FITTING NEW SKIRTING

Skirtings protect the bottom of the wall from damage, from feet, carpet sweepers, vacuum cleaners, brushes etc.

If the existing skirting is rotten or damaged, prise it off the wall using a crowbar. Sometimes the skirting may be trapped in position by another length of skirting butted against it or by architrave which has been cut out to fit over the skirting. In these cases take care not to cause unnecessary damage.

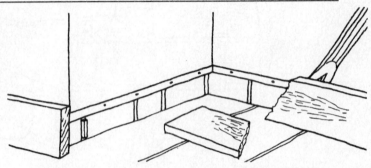

1

The form of the replacement of the skirting will depend on whether the appearance or cost is the most important factor. An inexpensive skirting can be formed using secondhand floorboards or new ex-100×19 mm S.W. chamfered skirting. Alternatively skirtings may be made up to match existing patterns. A common form of skirting is made up from a piece of ex-150×25 mm (6″×1″) plank topped with a piece of staff beading.

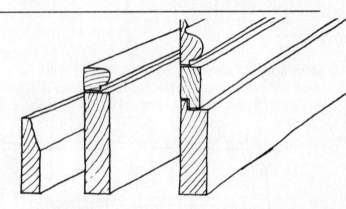

2

Skirtings are fixed in place by nails. On a studwork wall a piece of wood as thick as the plaster or plasterboard is nailed to each stud. The skirting is then nailed to these spacers so that the bottom of the plaster or plasterboard is overlapped by the skirting by about 25 mm (1″).

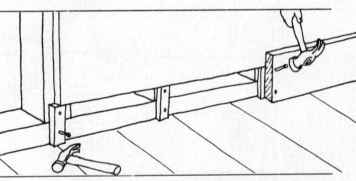

3

In brick or block work walls the traditional method of fixing is to leave a vertical mortar course open about 450 mm apart. Wooden wedges are then hammered into open mortar courses until flush with the face of the brickwork. Pieces of wood as thick as the plaster or the plasterboard are nailed to each wedge and the skirting is nailed to these spacers so that the bottom of the plaster or plasterboard is overlapped by the skirting by about 25 mm (1″). Wedges roughly cut with an axe will twist into place and grip the wall.

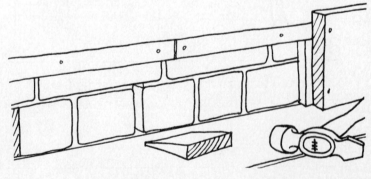

4

2.15
REPOINTING

Defective pointing in a brick wall will allow rain to soak through the wall. Repointing should be done over an area of approximately 1 square metre at a time and should not be done from a ladder but from scaffolding, a scaffold tower, or a stable platform. It is most comfortable to work at chest height.

Clean out the facing mortar from the joints to a depth of 10 mm with a plugging chisel and a club hammer.

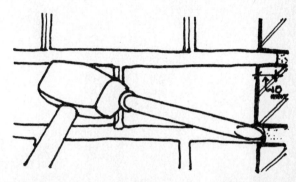

1

Brush the joints and the brickwork down to remove dust and old mortar. Brush water over the wall and the joints, soaking the brickwork so that it will not absorb moisture from the new pointing mortar.

2

Mix enough mortar to repoint about 1 square metre, using 1 part of Portland cement to 6 parts of sand by volume. Use enough mortar so that mortar is smooth, but firm, so that when a piece is cut off and pushed across the spotboard with a sawing action of the trowel it will roll into a 'sausage'.

3

Load some of the mortar onto a 'hawk' and, using a small pointing trowel, pick up a strip of mortar on the bottom edge of the face with an upward sweep of the back of the trowel. Rotate the wrist so that the bottom edge becomes the top edge and force the mortar into the joints, first a vertical joint and then the horizontal joint above and below it. Leave mortar flush with bricks.

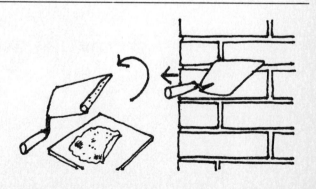

4

Pointing can be completed in a number of different ways such as 'flush', 'rubbed', 'recessed' and 'weather struck'. Of these the simplest is a flush joint. A flush joint is made by waiting until the mortar has started to go 'off' and then rubbing the joint, in one direction only, with a piece of dry sacking. Damp sacking will cause cement strains on the brickwork. Brush off any excess mortar when dry with a stiff brush.

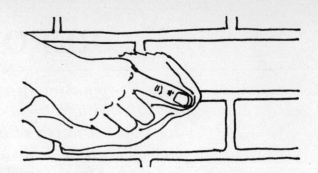

5

REBUILD SECTION OF BRICKWORK

This instruction sheet deals specifically with the rebuilding of small sections of wall; new walls are covered on sheet 2.20.

Clean off old mortar from existing brickwork with a bolster and a club hammer. Brush off dust and particles of mortar and brush clean water into brickwork so that it will not absorb too much water from the new mortar.

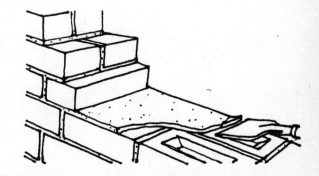

1

Mix up a mortar of 1 part cement to 1 part of hydrated hydraulic lime to 6 parts fine sand and load mortar onto a spotboard. Mortar should be wet enough so that it can be rolled into a firm 'sausage' with a sawing motion of the trowel.

2

If new brickwork is to be built between two existing vertical sections, or corners of brickwork, then run through a line level with the top of the first course of bricks. The line can be run between masonry pins nailed into the existing mortar with a piece of stick at each end to keep the string just clear of the brickwork. Where no vertical sections exist proceed as sheet 2.20 C.

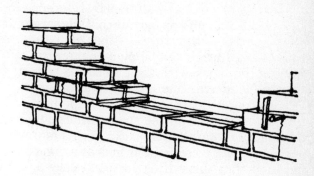

3

Much of the art of good bricklaying lies in the way the trowel is used to pick up the mortar. Do not just scoop up a trowel load of mortar from the spotboard, since this will give an uncohesive, badly distributed load which will drop everywhere and more importantly will not give an even mortar bed when placed. Instead, cut off a piece of mortar, roll it across the spotboard with a sawing action, curving the back of the slice until is has formed a firm sausage shape. Scoop up the sausage in one clean sweep of the trowel, the point of the trowel moving from end to end of the sausage with the blade flat to the spotboard.

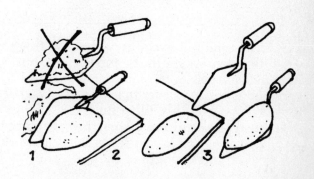

4

Lay the mortar onto the brickwork by holding the trowel above the bricks, tipping the mortar off and at the same time pulling the trowel back down the line of the brick. Spread the mortar using the point of the trowel to make a series of 'V'-shaped depressions. Cut off any mortar which oversails the front edge of the brickwork with an upwards stroke of the trowel and place the extra mortar onto the mortar bed. When spread, the mortar bed should be slightly more than 10 mm thick. With brickwork more than one course thick, lay parallel sections of mortar before spreading with the trowel.

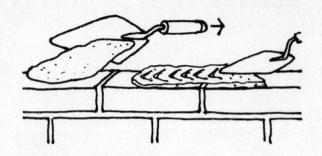

5

Take a brick in the left hand, scoop up ⅓ of a trowel full of mortar, keeping the trowel flat, shake it once with a sudden up/down movement to compact the mortar and to shake off any excess. Now press or strike the mortar onto the end or face of the brick which will abut the existing brickwork and spread the mortar to about 10 mm thick, using the point of the trowel.

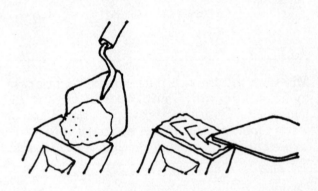

6

Press the brick firmly into place, checking that it is level and vertically aligned by reference to the line, and cut off any mortar that squeezes out with the edge of the trowel. Minor adjustments of a too-high brick can be made by gently tapping the brick with the end of the trowel handle. If a mortar course is too thick or too thin do not attempt to adjust it but scrape it off. Remix the mortar on the spotboard and start again. Lay remainder of bricks in this manner, working along a course of bricks at a time and checking that the wall is vertical every 3 courses.

7

Old bricks tend to have a very shallow 'frog' which is a depression in the top surface, but some modern bricks have deeper 'V' shaped frogs and it will be easier to lay an even bed of mortar if the frogs are filled flush first. Frogs must always face upwards; when they are placed facing down they form cavities in the brickwork and weaken the strength of the wall.

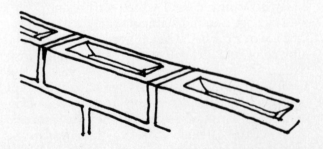

8

When filling a vertical joint between the last new brick and the existing brickwork, throw mortar into the top of the open joint using the end of the trowel and then compact it with a chopping action of the tip of the trowel edge. Repeat this process until the joint is filled, then trim off any excess mortar.

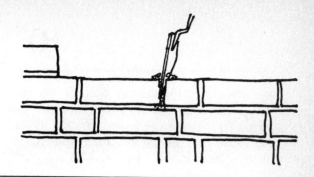

9

When a section of brickwork has been completed it should be pointed before the mortar hardens. One of the simplest forms of pointing is 'rubbed' or 'bucket handle' which traditionally was done with a piece of rounded galvanised metal bucket handle, but a curved piece of pipe can also be used. Rub it up and down the vertical mortar joints to form a smooth, curved slightly hollow joint, repeat the process for the horizontal joints and then brush off any excess mortar.

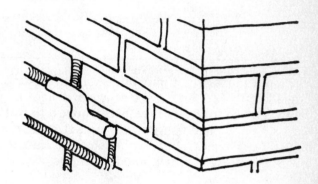

10

2.17
RENDER

Hack off any defective render with a 100 mm bolster and club hammer. Rake out mortar from brick joints to a depth of 10 mm. Brush off any dust and loose mortar. Brush surface with solution of 1 part P.V.A. adhesive to six parts water.

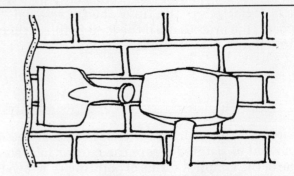

1

Mix up a mortar of 1 part of cement to 4 parts graded soft sand with a waterproofing agent. Add water so that mix is smooth enough to roll across a spotboard using a sawing action of a bricklayer's trowel, but firm enough so that it forms a 'sausage' which holds its shape.

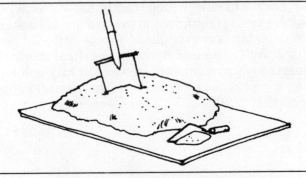

2

If an apron is to be rendered, a 15 mm thick batten, masonry nailed to the wall, will act as both a stop and a guide to the required depth of mortar. For large areas nailing 15 mm deep battens to the wall at 1,200 to 1,800 centres will give both a depth/level guide and workable bays.

3

Load some of the render mixture onto a wet spotboard supported on a trestle or stool. Wet down wall by flicking and brushing clean water over the surface.

4

Load some of the mortar onto the hawk by holding it flush with the spotboard and using the trowel to scrape onto it several trowel loads of mortar. Holding the hawk near to the bottom of the wall, cut a trowel load of mortar, tip the hawk towards you, load the trowel then push the mortar against the wall and spread upwards. Any dropped mortar that has fallen on boards, a polythene sheet, or other clean surface can be re-used.

5

Working in this way fill in up to the batten, in the case of an apron upstand or between the first pair of battens, when rendering a large area. Take a straight-edged board, place it on the battens and move it down the wall, sawing off any excess mortar. Fill in any depressions and again bring the straight edge down the battens, repeating the process until the render is level.

6
_____

Polish the render with sweeping strokes, using a metal trowel (or float) for a smooth finish and a wooden trowel (or float) for a matt finish. Do not over polish as this will cause the cement to separate out of the mortar.

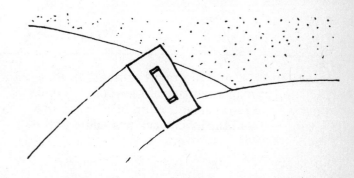

7
_____

After 3 or 4 hours carefully remove the levelling battens and fill in the holes with mortar. Polish surface of mortar to match remainder of render.
   For a rendered apron the top batten should be carefully removed after 3 or 4 hours and a sloping top edge added to the apron with a pointing trowel.
N.B. For buildings with a permanent life a 2 coat render as described in sheet 2.05 is more appropriate using a 15 mm base coat and a 3 mm top coat.

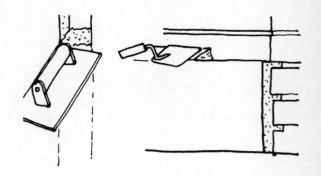

8
_____

Hack out render to either side of a crack to give a 50 mm wide channel or until render is sound, using a cold or plugging chisel and a club hammer.

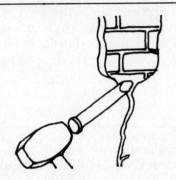

1

Brush out dust and mortar fragments from crack and mix up a solution of 1 part of Unibond adhesive to 6 parts of water and brush this into the crack to seal the brickwork and edges of the render.

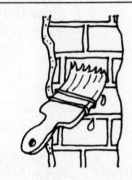

2

Mix up 1 part of cement to 4 parts fine sand and add a waterproofing agent or a P.V.A. liquid to give more adhesion. Add sufficient water so that mortar is firm, but capable of being smoothly rolled across a spotboard with a bricklayer's trowel.

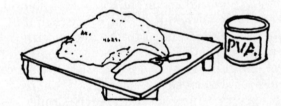

3

Fill crack with mortar and trowel flush and smooth in relation to surrounding render.

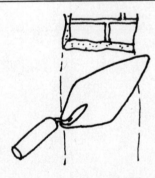

4

If an exterior brick wall has cracked due to settlement or some other form of movement it will no longer be totally weatherproof. If the movement which caused the cracking has ceased it is therefore necessary to restore the external surface.

Cut out cracked bricks and rake out pointing to a depth of 10 mm, to one brick length to either side of crack. Where the crack exceeds 19 mm in width then take out one brick to either side of the cracked brick. Work on 4 courses of brickwork vertically at a time, starting from the base of the wall.

1

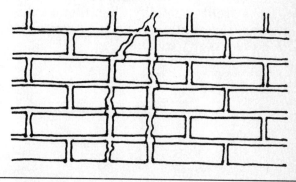

Hack off any old mortar and brush over to remove bits of mortar and dust. Brush surrounding brickwork with clean water.

2

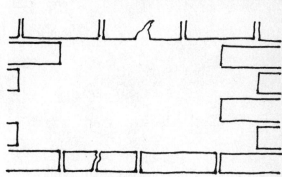

Lay in new or second-hand bricks, preferably to match existing, using a mortar of 1 part cement to 1 part lime to 6 parts fine sand. Where the crack has exceeded 19 mm then introduce expanded metal reinforcing into every fourth mortar course.

3

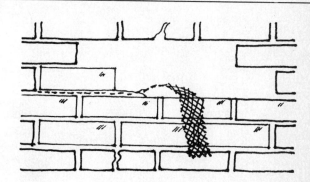

Repoint wall using a mortar of 1 part cement to 1 part hydrated hydraulic lime to 6 parts fine sand, using a joint to match the existing pointing.

4

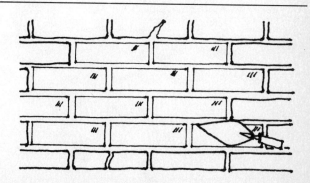

Where cracks in brickwork are hairline cracks it may be simpler to grout them with a wet mortar made up of 1 part cement to 2 parts hydrated hydraulic lime to 9 parts soft sand. The face of the crack should first be covered with potters clay, plasticine or dryish putty to stop the grout leaking out of the face of the crack. Then a small hole is made at the top of the crack with a cold chisel, large enough to take the end of a flexible tube of 10–15 mm diameter. A funnel is attached to the other end of the tube and, with the tube pushed as far into the wall as possible, the liquid grout is poured into the funnel and allowed to trickle down the crack. Leave for 4–5 hours to allow the grout to solidify, then remove the temporary covering and rub off any excess grout with a piece of dry sacking.

5

When constructing a new brick wall it is possible to use a number of different types of brick bonding and the type of foundation will depend on the soil conditions, the load on the wall and other factors. This information sheet therefore describes the most common form of new brick construction which is known as the cavity wall and assumes a foundation design which is appropriate to domestic (i.e. housing) construction in most areas of Inner London.

A Setting out

Before building a new wall, it is necessary to mark out its position and that of the foundations. This is done by setting up two profile boards in line with but about 1.2 m past the end of each stretch of wall. A profile board is made by driving two lengths of 50×50 mm sawn softwood into the ground about 900 mm apart, at right angles to the line of the wall. A piece of straight-edged plank is then nailed to the two pegs so that its top surface is level. It is normal practice on a building site also to fix the tops of the profile boards at a predetermined level by using a 'dumpy' level or other levelling instrument.

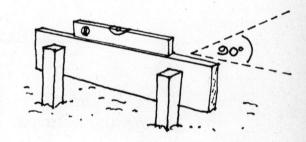

1

If no levelling instrument is available the level of the second profile board may be set to the same level as the first by using a hosepipe filled with water. On each end of the hosepipe fit a clear glass or plastic tube or funnel. Place the water level at one end against the top of the first board and the top of the second should line up with the water level in the other end of the hosepipe.

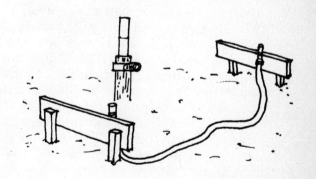

2

Drive a nail into the top of each profile board, in line with the front edge of the wall. Then drive in a second pair of nails in line with the rear face of the wall. At 100 mm from each of the first nails drive in nails to mark the front and rear of the foundation strip. This will give a foundation strip 450 mm or slightly wider. Tie a line between the nails marking the front edge of the foundation and another marking the rear edge of the foundations.

3

Repeat this process for each wall to be built. Check that walls are at right angles by checking that diagonals are equal, if building a rectangle or by measuring 4 units down one wall line, three units down the other wall line and then checking that the diagonal between these two points is 5 units.

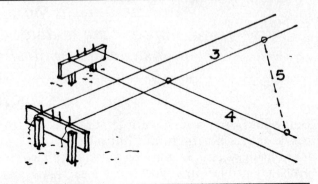

4

B Foundations

Once the setting out is complete, work can start on the foundations.

Since most soils are subject to expansion and contraction movement, resulting both from thermal variations and changes in moisture content to a depth of about 600–900 mm, it is necessary to have the bottom of the foundation 1.000 m below ground level. The exact depth and width of foundations should be agreed with the local building inspector or district surveyor. To simplify levelling and measuring the bottom of the foundation trench, take a piece of 50×50 or 75×25 mm softwood, cut it so that its length equals the required depth of the foundation plus the distance from the top of the profile board to the ground level. Across the top of this piece of timber, nail a piece of plank at right angles, with its top edge level with the end. This is called a boning rod and will be used to sight between the two profile boards, the trench being at the required depth when the top of the boning rod lines up with the top of the two profile boards.

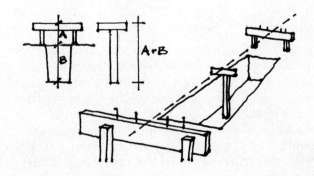

1

The trench for the foundations can be dug by machine or by hand. When digging foundation trenches, string lines between the nails on the profile boards which mark the front and back line of the foundation and dig to the lines. A wider trench will waste concrete or else require unnecessary formwork to be constructed. In weak or crumbly soil the sides of the trench may need to be shored to prevent collapse.

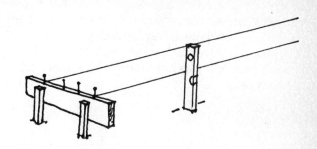

2

Dig down so that the sides of the trench are vertical and check on the depth from time to time with the boning rod. The bottom of the trench should not be left exposed to the weather or else it could dry out or become wet, causing abnormal movement after the concrete has been placed. Therefore stop digging 50 mm from the bottom of the trench and only dig out the last 50 mm when the concrete is to be laid. The building inspector or district surveyor will often wish to inspect the trench bottom prior to the pouring of the concrete foundation and should be informed in advance. The bottom of the trench should be free from any loose material, must be dry and any soft areas should be dug out.

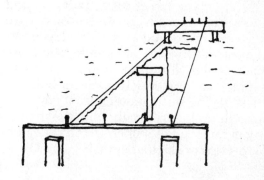

3

Where the ground slopes the foundation bottom must be level, but it can step as long as it remains 1.000 m below ground level. The top of the foundation must step accordingly and steps should be in multiples of 75 mm to correspond with brick coursing. Steps in foundations should be cast working down the hill with formwork constructed across the trench to contain the lowest end of each section. Wait for the initial set of the concrete, i.e. about 1–2 hours before casting the next section of the stepping.

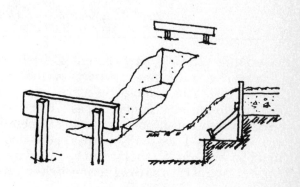

4

Unless a very small amount of foundation is to be laid, it is simplest to use ready-mixed concrete. This is delivered by lorry and if the lorry is to be taken onto the building site it will be necessary to provide a firm surface so that it does not become bogged down. If not, the ready mix can be barrowed from the point of delivery to the trench. A concrete mix of 1:2:4 with a water to cement ratio by weight of 0.5 to 0.6 should be ordered. When mixing by hand or a mixer add 1 volume of cement to 2 volumes of

sand to 4 volumes of coarse aggregate and turn over dry two or three times. Add water using a watering can with a rose and mix thoroughly so that cement is completely mixed in. No more than 2 to 3 minutes mixing at medium speed in a mixer is necessary, otherwise the mix will begin to separate.

5

Fill the trench to 150 mm below ground level and compact the concrete by poking a rod or vibrator down into it to eliminate air pockets or voids. Level off the top of the foundation and tamp down with a board. Use concrete as soon as it is mixed and do not add water to make it more workable, since this will weaken it. The tops of new concrete foundations should be covered with a damp sacking or polythene for 3 days to prevent it drying out too quickly in warm weather and up to 10 days in winter. When the covering is removed the concrete can take light loads and brickwork can begin.

6

C New Brickwork

Once the foundations are complete, bricklaying can begin. It is normal practice to build up corners, then to fill in-between.

Mix up a mortar of 1 part cement to 1 part hydrated hydraulic lime to 6 parts of fine sand. For work below the damp-proof course in certain soil conditions and with some types of bricks it is necessary to use a sulphate-resisting cement in the mortar mix. Load mortar onto a spotboard; it should be wet enough that it can be rolled into a firm 'sausage' with a sawing action of the trowel.

1

Stretch strings between the nails on the profile boards marking the front and rear faces of the wall. Spread a thin layer of mortar on top of the foundation running approximately 800 mm in either direction from the corner. Using a spirit level held vertically, drop down the position of the lines at 100 mm and 700 mm from the corner, taking care not to bend the strings and marking the positions on the mortar with the point of a trowel. Lay a straight edge on the mortar bed and join up the marks by cutting

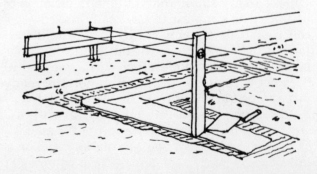

lines in the mortar with the trowel point, crossing lines at the corner. Repeat this procedure at all corners taking care to be accurate since these marks will determine the positioning of the building lines. Once the foundations have been marked the strings may be removed from the profile boards to leave room for bricklaying.

2

Much of the art of good bricklaying lies in the way the trowel is used to pick up the mortar. Do not just scoop up a trowel load of mortar from the spotboard since this will give an uncohesive, badly distributed load which will drop everywhere and, more importantly, will not give an even mortar bed when placed. Instead, cut off a piece of mortar, roll it across the spotboard with a sawing action, curving the back of the slice until it has formed a firm 'sausage' shape. Scoop up this 'sausage' in one clean sweep of the trowel, the point of the trowel moving from end to end of the sausage with the blade flat to the spotboard.

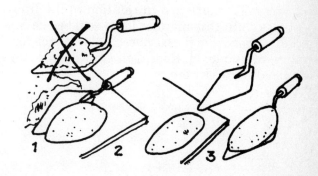

3

Lay the mortar onto the marked screed by holding the trowel along the line, tipping the mortar off and at the same time pulling the trowel back down the line. Be careful not to obscure the lines and spread the mortar using the point of the trowel to make a series of 'V' shaped depressions. When spread, the mortar course should be about 10 mm thick.

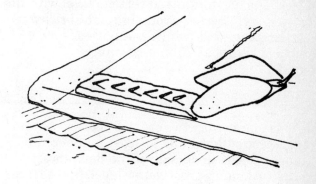

4

Place the corner brick frog upwards making sure that it sits level and that its faces coincide with the two corner lines. The position of the corner brick becomes the reference point for all later brickwork so that it is important that it is accurately placed.

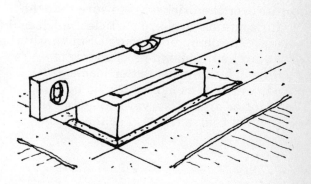

5

Take a brick in the left hand, scoop up about ⅓ of a trowel-full of mortar, keeping the trowel flat, shake it once with a sudden up/down movement to compact the mortar and shake off any excess. Now press or strike the mortar onto the end or face of the brick which will abut the first brick and spread the mortar to about 10 mm thick using the point of the trowel.

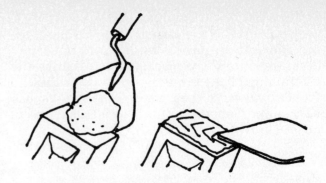

6

Press the brick firmly into place and check that it is correctly positioned in relation to the line and is level. In this manner lay 4 to 6 bricks in each direction from the corner, checking each for alignment and level. Repeat the process for the inner leaf of brickwork.

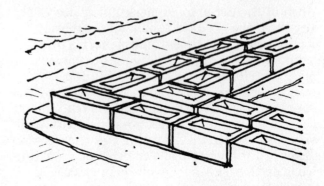

7

Fill the frogs in the first course of bricks flush with mortar, then lay down a trowel load of mortar, corner brick and then other bricks to the second course of each leaf of brickwork, stopping half-a-brick length shorter on each course. Check the horizontal and vertical level with the spirit level. Check the coursing of the brickwork with a gauge rod, which is a piece of wood marked across at 75 mm spacings.

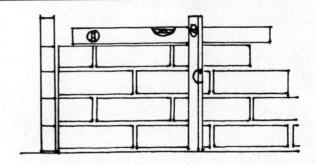

8

In this manner lay two courses of bricks to come up to ground level and at least another two courses to the underside of the damp-proof course. At damp-proof course level, fill the frogs in the bricks flush, and smooth a thin layer of mortar over the bricks. Make sure that the mortar contains no sharp particles which could puncture the damp-proof course. Starting at the corner, roll out a damp-proof course of polythene, bituminous felt or lead-cored bituminous felt, as agreed by the building inspector or district surveyor, lapping the damp-proof course (D.P.C.) at the corner.

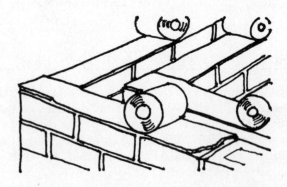

9

Lay a mortar bed on top of the D.P.C taking care not to puncture it and place two more courses of bricks (or blockwork to the inner leaf, see **12** below), checking with the level and the gauge rod. Build up the other corners in the same way.

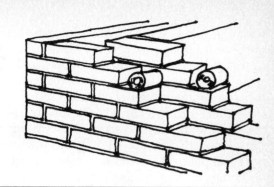

10

Take a line and two bricklayer's pins, and stick the pins, one at each corner of the wall, in a vertical mortar joint around the corner and just above the first course of bricks to be laid. Hold the line taut, just clear of the face of the brickwork and in line with the top of the course of bricks to be laid, with a loose brick placed on top of the step back to each course to be laid.

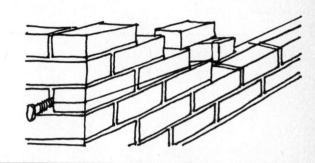

11

Using the line as a guide, lay in the course of bricks and repeat the procedure for each course, until the height of the corner has been reached. Galvanised metal wall ties of either butterfly or fish tail design should be incorporated to tie the two leaves of brickwork together. Starting on top of the first course above the D.P.C., they are placed at 900 mm intervals, alternately at every third brick course, i.e. the ties are vertically above each other at the first and sixth course with ties 450 mm away horizontally above each other at every third and ninth course. Where concrete blocks are to be used for the inner leaf, they should be laid above the D.P.C. only and

ties placed above the first course of blockwork with spacing as before. Extra brick ties should be used around openings and at corners.

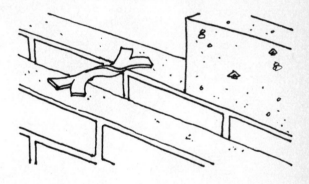

12

When laying bricks, cut off any mortar which squeezes out of the bed joint or the vertical joint with the edge of the trowel. Minor adjustments to the position or level of the brick can be made by striking it with the end of the trowel handle – major adjustments should be made by removing the bedding course and starting again. In cavity brickwork it is important to keep the cavity free of mortar. This is most efficiently done by laying a batten, 50 mm wide with a wire loop at each end, into the cavity. When the first line of wall ties is to be laid in place, the batten is withdrawn, cleaned off and laid on top of the wall ties. Bricklayers are not over-keen on using

cavity battens because it is easy to build one into the wall, but provided they are withdrawn before each row of ties is placed, they are the simplest and most effective method of preventing mortar build-up on the wall ties which can cause damp penetration.

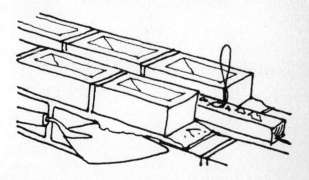

13

Before the mortar hardens any excess should be cleaned off the brickwork and the external face of the brick should be pointed. One of the simplest forms of pointing is 'rubbed' or 'bucket handle' which traditionally was executed with a piece of rounded galvanised bucket handle, but a curved piece of pipe can also be used. Rub the metal up and down the vertical mortar joints to form a smooth, curved, slightly hollow joint, repeat the process for the horizontal joints and then brush off any excess mortar.

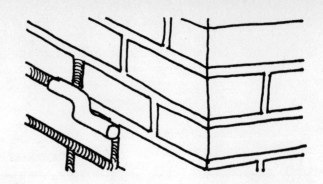

14

REPLACE STRUCTURAL TIMBER

Many old houses have structural timber beams within the plane of the external brick walls. They are most common where there is a bay window or a large opening through into a back addition, but also occur where flat-roofed rear additions join the main building. Because they are built into solid brickwork which often has failed pointing or bad detailing, these beams are frequently rotten.

Above a failed beam, cut through holes that are 2 brick courses deep by one brick wide at 900 mm centres.

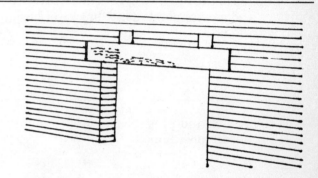

1

Feed 2 No. 150×50 mm or 1 No. 150×100 mm timbers (referred to as needles) through each of these holes and support the ends on 'Acrow' props. The needles should not exceed 2.5 m in length and should be close to the external face of the wall to allow working space inside. Where a beam occurs on first floor level or higher, the loading must be taken down to the ground and the props should stand on scaffold boards laid across floors and ceilings to spread the load. Externally it may be necessary to construct a scaffolding structure to take the load to ground and expert advice should be sought.

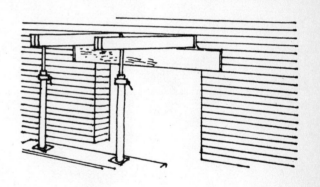

2

With the wall now adequately supported, take out the rotten beam. Having determined, with professional help, the size and number of rolled steel 'I' section joists necessary to support the load, cut out brickwork below each end of the beam so that a concrete bearing pad, 300 mm long by 150 mm deep by the width of the beam can be cast. Make up a temporary timber formwork at each end and cast concrete bearing pad in 1:2:4 mix concrete, chopping concrete down into the formwork to ensure that it is evenly distributed and trowel top surface flat.

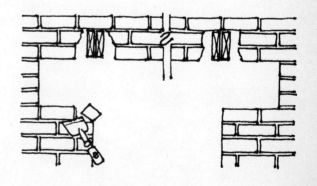

3

After 2 days remove the formwork. Wire brush the rolled steel joists (R.S.J.) to remove any rust, paint with one coat of red-oxide paint and two coats of bituminous paint.

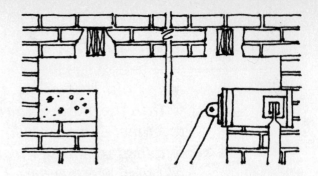

4

Four days after removing the formwork, the bearing pads should be strong enough to take the load, so slide R.S.J.'s into place. Lay a polythene or lead-core bituminous damp-proof course on top of the R.S.J.'s, overlapping to front and back and mortar pointed into brickwork and onto bearing pad.

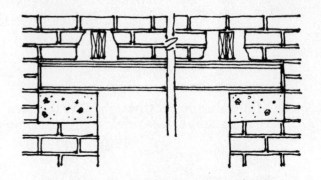

5

Remove needles and props. Relay and repoint bricks to needle positions.

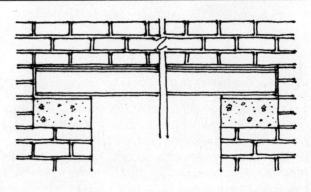

6

3
DOORS

MAKE EXISTING DOOR HALF-HOUR FIRE CHECK

A   Doors more than 44 mm thick

A solid timber door which is 44 mm thick or more, needs no cladding to achieve a half-an-hour fire check, but will require alterations to the door stops and to be fitted with a closing device. However, a panel door, having stiles and rails 44 mm or more thick, does need modification.

(i) Remove beading from around panelling on room side of door.
OR
(ii) Where panel is slotted into a flat frame door, or into a frame with integral mouldings then leave.

   In both cases fill in any old lock holes in the door with timber plugs.

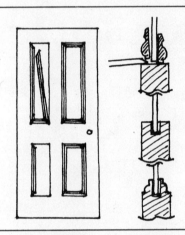

1

(i) Cut a panel of 4·5 mm non-combustible board, such as 'Masterboard' and fit tightly into the panel, push in place over the existing timber panel and replace mouldings.
OR
(ii) Cut a panel of 4 mm non-combustible board such as 'Masterboard' to fit into the extremities of the door frame and flat to the panel. Hold new panel in place with quadrant beading to a flat framed panel, or an 'L' shaped rebated bead to moulded framed panels.

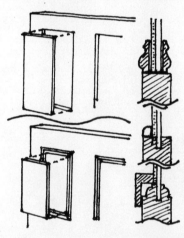

2

The door stop to the frame should be 25 mm deep. Where this is not the case, take off the existing doorstop if a separate 'plant' on to the frame, but leave moulded doorstops. Replace doorstop with a 25 (finished size) ×38 mm P.A.R. timber screwed in place. For moulded doorstops, clean off surface paint and then screw a batten to the moulded doorstop so that the total depth of doorstop is 25 mm.

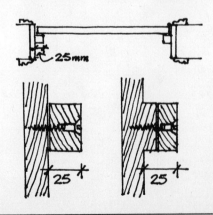

3

Fire doors must be self-closing and this can be achieved in a number of ways. When a door is to be rehung it can be hung on rising-butt hinges. However, if the door is being fire-proofed in position, the cheapest and simplest method of self-closing is to fit a tensioned-spring closer. Alternatively a patent door closer may be fitted to the door and frame.

The additional weight of fireproofing will frequently mean that the door requires rehanging.

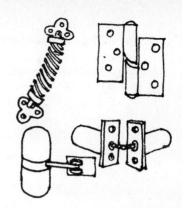

4

In some areas the authorities will accept an 'intumescent' paint or varnish finish to the existing door as being adequate protection. In these areas, simply strip off all old paint, fill in any holes, paint the door with the 'intumescent' paint or varnish, in accordance with the manufacturer's instructions, and fit new door stops and door closers.

5

B   Doors less than 44 mm thick

Modern 'flush' doors which consist of two plywood or hardboard faces separated by a cellular core should be replaced with a new fire door. Panel doors with solid timber 'stiles' and 'rails' less than 44 mm which have not warped can be fire-proofed as follows:

Fill in panel with offcuts of 4·5 mm non-combustible board such as 'Masterboard' or plasterboard. Fill old lock holes with plaster and cover on non-fireproofed side of door with an offcut of Masterboard, held in place with annular nails.

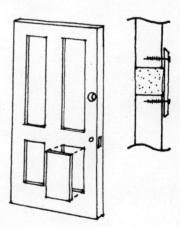

1

Cut a sheet of 'Masterboard' to the size of the door and fix in place with annular nails at 100 mm intervals, nailed into stiles and rails of door.

Doors are fire-proofed to the room side of doors on basement, ground and intermediate floors, to both sides on the top floor.

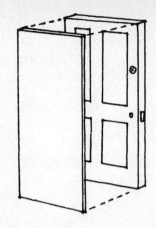

2

The door stop to the frame should be 25 mm deep. Where this is not the case, take off the existing doorstop if a separate 'plant' on to the frame, but leave moulded doorstops. Replace doorstop with a 25 (finished size)×38 mm P.A.R. timber screwed in place. For moulded doorstops, clean off surface paint and then screw a batten to the moulded doorstop so that the total depth of doorstop is 25 mm.

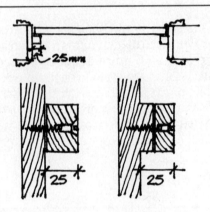

3

Fire doors must be self-closing and this can be achieved in a number of ways. When a door is to be rehung it can be hung on rising-butt hinges. However, if the door is being fire-proofed in position, the cheapest and simplest method of self-closing is to fit a tensioned-spring closer. Alternatively a patent door closer may be fitted to the door and frame.

The additional weight of fireproofing will frequently mean that the door requires rehanging.

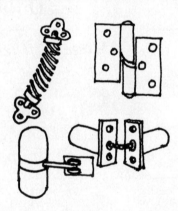

4

REPAIR DOOR FRAME

Door frames may be repaired in a number of ways dependent on the extent of the damage and whether or not the door is to be rehung or replaced.

Small sections broken out of the edge of the frame, for example, when hinges have been broken off, can be repaired by cutting horizontally at an angle above and below the damaged section, cutting down vertically between the saw cuts with a sharp chisel to remove the damaged sections. Cut new sections of timber to fit tightly into holes thus formed. Pin, glue and then screw into place. Re-hang door on the other side of frame, where replaced sections coincide with hinge positions.

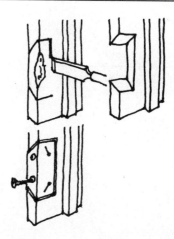

1

Where the bottom of the frame has rotted in contact with a damp floor, remove the doorstops and cut off the rotten sections of the frame. If the rotten sections do not extend as high as the bottom hinge position, fix the frame back to the wall by drilling a screw clearance hole through the frame and then drill the brickwork. Enlarge the outer face of the hole to the timber frame and plug the brickwork with a fibre plug and screw the frame back with a screw passing through a washer, recessed until flush with the face of the frame.

   Sheet the face of the frame with 6 mm plywood treated with wood preservative, replace door stops and trim sides of door and re-hang. Replace architraves.

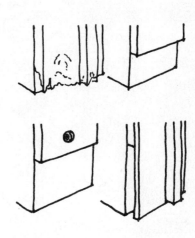

2

Where a door frame is damaged to one side it is often possible to remove one side of the frame, clean out the mortice in the head of the frame and cut a new side for the frame with a tenon to match the existing mortice. The new side can be fixed back to existing blocks or screwed into plugs in the brickwork.

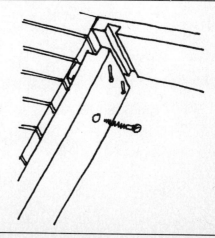

3

Small recesses which have been previously cut into door frames for hinges, lock striking plates, etc. can be filled with pieces of plywood cut to sizes and pinned and glued in position. When the glue has set, recess the pins with a punch and plane the patch flat to match the existing frame. Fill any gaps or small holes with a filler such as Polyfilla, Tetrion or Plastic Wood.

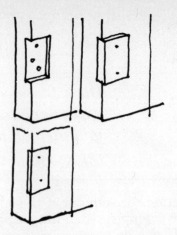

4

ARCHITRAVES

Architraves are primarily used to hide the junction between a door or window frame, and the surrounding plaster. They may be plain or moulded.

Where a section of moulded architrave is missing it will be easier to replace the complete architrave than to attempt to match up modern architrave sections. If the remaining sections of moulded architrave are carefully removed, they can be used to repair the architraves to other doors in the same house.

An architrave is normally set slightly back from the edge of the door frame, say 6 mm. When measuring for the size of an architrave, measure the height of the frame and add 6 mm so that this margin is continued across the top of the frame.

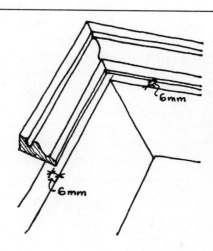

1

Cut 45° mitres to the top of each side architrave and tack architraves in place with 25 to 38 mm pins, or oval nails. Do not hammer nails fully home.

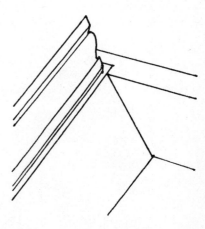

2

Measure distance between door-side edges of architraves and then wall-side edges. Before cutting mitred corners make sure that top sections of architrave will match these dimensions. Where this does not happen check that the sides of the frame or architrave have been fitted vertically and if not, adjust. Where an existing frame is out of square, then cut the top section of architrave to the longer dimension and adjust the mitre with a plane to fit. Finally nail top and side pieces of architrave, recessing and filling the nail heads.

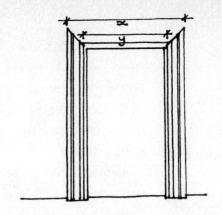

3

Where a section of architrave has been broken or cut out and a matching architrave is available, then cut through to either side of the damaged section at right angles to the architrave and carefully prise it off the frame. Cut a piece of the matching architrave to fit, nail to the frame and skew pin the back edge of the architrave to the back edge of that existing to ensure alignment, recessing and filling both nail and pin heads.

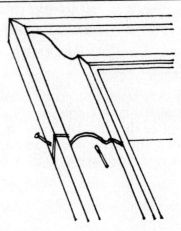

4

REPAIR INTERNAL DOOR

Damaged internal doors may be worth repairing rather than replacing, if they are not badly warped and the joints are intact.

Panels

When a panel is held in place by beading, the beading may be taken off, the broken panel removed, a new panel of 6 mm plywood put in its place, and the beading replaced.

Where a panel is held in place by rebates in stiles and rails it is simplest to glue a plywood or hardboard panel to both faces of the damaged panel. If the rebates to the frame do not include any mouldings, and the panel is too badly damaged to face as above, then the panel can be cut out with a pad saw, a new 6 mm plywood panel inserted flush with the frame and held in place with quadrant beading. The beading can also be added to non-damaged panels to match. Damaged flush door panels can be covered with hardboard or plywood.

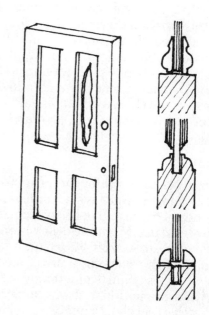

1

Where the stiles or rails have had sections broken out of the sides, the damaged area should first be cut out to give a regular shape. Cut across the grain using a tenon saw. Along the grain drill a series of holes to the waste side of the line to be cut, join the holes with a pad saw, and work down the line with a sharp chisel. Or alternatively, cut out the damaged area between the two saw cuts with a sharp chisel, working alternately from both sides. Cut a piece of timber to be a tight fit, glue and screw, countersinking the screws, into place, trimming finally with a plane. Fill any remaining crevices and the screw heads.

Holes from old night latches are most easily filled with plaster or Polyfilla, held in position by small hardboard patches pinned to both sides of the door. Where a better finish is required, shape a plug of wood to fit the hole tightly, remembering that the end of the wood grain should not be exposed on the faces of the door. Glue and press the plug into place. When the glue has set, trim the plug level with the faces of the door, using a plane, and fill any small holes that remain.

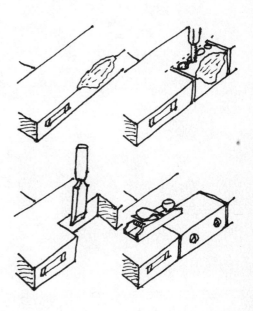

2

Shimming

Doors which fit badly within their frames, with large gaps at the tops, bottoms, or even the sides can be 'shimmed'. A door should have a 3 mm gap to the top and sides, 6 mm to the bottom, more if passing over carpet.

Measure the gap between the frame and the door at each end and the middle of the top and lock side, and deduct 3 mm from each measurement. This will give the size of the required 'shim'. Do the same for the bottom between the door and the floor, deducting 6 mm. Cut the required shims out of a suitably sized timber batten, glue and pin them in place, recessing the pin heads with a punch. Check door to ensure that it now fits and take off any 'high' areas of the shim with a plane. Plane the faces of the shim to match the door and fill any joint lines.

Easing

Doors which are too large for their frames can be 'eased'. The door should have a 3 mm gap to the top and sides, a 6 mm gap to the bottom, unless passing over carpet. Mark the door where it does not fit and plane or saw off the extra. If taking 6 mm or more off the door, use a saw, finishing off with a plane; if less than 6 mm, remove all of the excess with a plane. Flush doors have only 30 mm wide stiles and should not be eased by more than 10 mm to each stile.

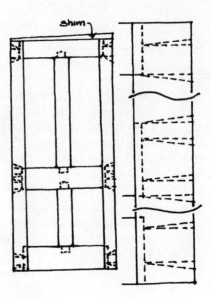

3

MODIFY AN INTERNAL DOOR

A second-hand internal door may be modified to fit an existing opening, providing that the modification does not necessitate cutting-off large sections of the side stiles or rails, which will damage the stability of its jointing.

Shimming

Doors which fit badly within their frames, with large gaps at the tops, bottoms, or even the sides can be 'shimmed'. A door should have a 3 mm gap to the top and sides, 6 mm to the bottom, more if passing over carpet.

Measure the gap between the frame and the door at each end and the middle of the top and lock side, and deduct 3 mm from each measurement. This will give the size of the required 'shim'. Do the same for the bottom between the door and the floor, deducting 6 mm. Cut the required shims out of a suitably sized timber batten, glue and pin them in place, recessing the pin heads with a punch. Check door to ensure that it now fits and take off any 'high' areas of the shim with a plane. Plane the faces of the shim to match the door and fill any joint lines.

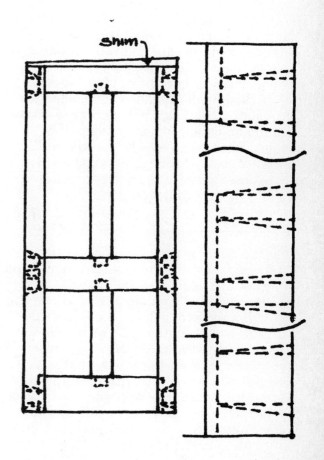

Easing

Doors which are too large for their frames can be 'eased'. The door should have a 3 mm gap to the top and sides, a 6 mm gap to the bottom, unless passing over carpet. Mark the door where it does not fit and plane or saw off the extra. If taking 6 mm or more off the door, use a saw, finishing off with a plane; if less than 6 mm, remove all of the excess with a plane. Flush doors have only 30 mm wide stiles and should not be eased by more than 10 mm to each stile.

Where a door is larger than the opening, stand it against the frame (if working alone use a piece of cord looped around the door to pull it into position), and mark the size of the opening onto the face of the door. Using a pair of compasses set to the required gap. This saves time when marking since the gap does not then need to be labouriously transferred by measurement.

For hanging doors see Sheet 3.11.

*Damaged external doors may be worth
repairing rather than replacing if they are not
badly warped. Any repair should be done so that
the security offered by the door is not impaired.*

Panels

When a panel is held in place by beading, the
beading may be taken off, the broken panel
removed, a new panel of 6 mm plywood put in its
place, and the beading replaced.

Where a panel is held in place by rebates in
stiles and rails it is simplest to glue a plywood
panel to both faces of the damaged panel. If the
rebates to the frame do not include any
mouldings, and the panel is too badly damaged
to face as above, then the panel can be cut out
with a pad saw, a new 6 mm plywood panel
inserted flush with the frame and held in place
with quadrant beading. The beading can also be
added to non-damaged panels to match.
Damaged flush doors may be covered with a
panel of exterior quality plywood, screwed and
glued to the external face, plywood or hardboard
pinned to the internal face.

1

Where the stiles or rails have had sections
broken out of the sides, the damaged area should
first be cut out to give a regular shape. Cut
across the grain using a tenon saw. Along the
grain drill a series of holes to the waste side of
the line to be cut, join the holes with a pad saw,
and work down to the line with a sharp chisel. Or
alternatively, cut out the damaged area
between the two saw cuts with a sharp chisel,
working alternately from both sides. Cut a piece
of timber to be a tight fit, glue and screw,
countersinking the screws, into place, trimming
finally with a plane. Fill any remaining crevices
and the screw heads.

Holes from old night latches are most easily
filled with plaster or Polyfilla, held in position
by small hardboard patches pinned to both sides
of the door. Where a better finish is required,
shape a plug of wood to fit the hole tightly,
remembering that the end of the wood grain
should not be exposed on the faces of the door.
Glue and press the plug into place. When the
glue has set, trim the plug level with the faces of
the door, using a plane, and fill any small holes
that remain.

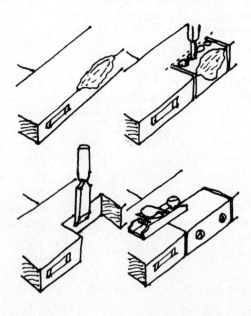

Shimming

Doors which fit badly within their frames, with large gaps at the tops, bottoms, or even the sides can be 'shimmed'. A door should have a 3 mm gap to the top and sides, 6 mm to the bottom, more if passing over carpet.

Measure the gap between the frame and the door at each end and the middle of the top and lock side, and deduct 3 mm from each measurement. This will give the size of the required 'shim'. Do the same for the bottom between the door and the floor, deducting 6 mm. Cut the required shims out of a suitably sized timber batten, glue and pin them in place, recessing the pin heads with a punch. Check door to ensure that it now fits and take off any 'high' areas of the shim with a plane. Plane the faces of the shim to match the door and fill any joint lines.

Easing

Doors which are too large for their frames can be 'eased'. The door should have a 3 mm gap to the top and sides, a 6 mm gap to the bottom, unless passing over carpet. Mark the door where it does not fit and plane or saw off the extra. If taking 6 mm or more off the door, use a saw, finishing off with a plane; if less than 6 mm, remove all of the excess with a plane. Flush doors have only 30 mm wide stiles and should not be eased by more than 10 mm to each stile.

3

A damaged external door may be given more strength by screwing a sheet of 8 mm exterior quality plywood to the external face. Internally joints may be strengthened with 100 mm 'L' shaped metal plates screwed in place.

For hanging doors see Sheet 3.11.

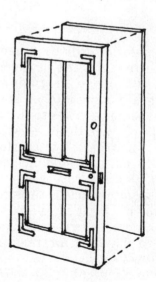

4

A second-hand external door may be modified to fit an existing opening provided that the modification does not necessitate cutting off large sections of the side stiles or rails, as this will damage the stability of its jointing.

Damaged internal doors may be worth repairing rather than replacing, if they are not badly warped and the joints are intact.

Panels

When a panel is held in place by beading, the beading may be taken off, the broken panel removed, a new panel of 6 mm plywood put in its place, and the beading replaced.

Where a panel is held in place by rebates in stiles and rails it is simplest to glue a plywood or hardboard panel to both faces of the damaged panel. If the rebates to the frame do not include any mouldings, and the panel is too badly damaged to face as above, then the panel can be cut out with a pad saw, a new 6 mm plywood panel inserted flush with the frame and held in place with quadrant beading. The beading can also be added to non-damaged panels to match. Damaged flush door panels can be covered with hardboard or plywood.

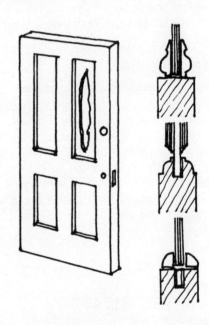

1

Where the stiles or rails have had sections broken out of the sides, the damaged area should first be cut out to give a regular shape. Cut across the grain using a tenon saw. Along the grain drill a series of holes to the waste side of the line to be cut, join the holes with a pad saw, and work down to the line with a sharp chisel. Or alternatively, cut out the damaged area between the two saw cuts with a sharp chisel, working alternately from both sides. Cut a piece of timber to be a tight fit, glue and screw, countersinking the screws, into place, trimming finally with a plane. Fill any remaining crevices and the screw heads.

Holes from old night latches are most easily filled with plaster or Polyfilla, held in position by small hardboard patches pinned to both sides of the door. Where a better finish is required, shape a plug of wood to fit the hole tightly, remembering that the end of the wood grain should not be exposed on the faces of the door.

Glue and press the plug into place. When the glue has set, trim the plug level with the faces of the door, using a plane, and fill any small holes that remain.

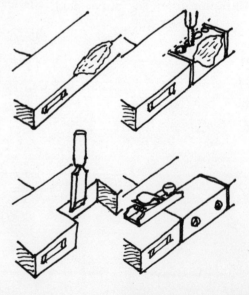

2

Shimming

Doors which fit badly within their frames, with large gaps at the tops, bottoms, or even the sides can be 'shimmed'. A door should have a 3 mm gap to the top and sides, 6 mm to the bottom, more if passing over carpet.

Measure the gap between the frame and the door at each end and the middle of the top and lock side, and deduct 3 mm from each measurement. This will give the size of the required 'shim'. Do the same for the bottom between the door and the floor, deducting 6 mm. Cut the required shims out of a suitably sized timber batten, glue and pin them in place, recessing the pin heads with a punch. Check door to ensure that it now fits and take off any 'high' areas of the shim with a plane. Plane the faces of the shim to match the door and fill any joint lines.

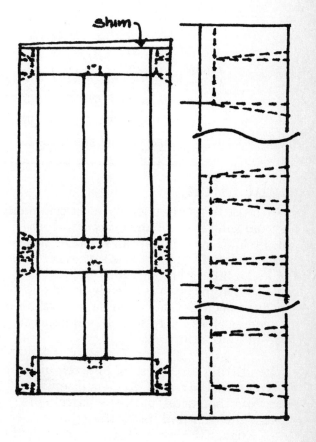

shim

Easing

Doors which are too long for their frames can be 'eased'. The door should have a 3 mm gap to the top and sides, a 6 mm gap to the bottom, unless passing over carpet. Mark the door where it does not fit and plane or saw off the extra. If taking 6 mm or more off the door, use a saw, finishing off with a plane; if less than 6 mm, remove all of the excess with a plane. Flush doors have only 30 mm wide stiles and should not be eased by more than 10 mm to each stile.

For hanging doors see Sheet 3.11.

3

Ironmongery is the collective name given to handles, hinges, bolts, letterboxes, latches, locks, knobs, knockers and other fittings, traditionally made of metal, associated with doors and windows. Some typical pieces of ironmongery are fitted as follows:–

Night latch

Night latch locks are possibly most commonly used and consist of a barrel section which contains the lock tumblers and is fitted through the door, a latch which is fitted to the rear of the door and a latch retainer which is fitted to the frame. If a night latch is already fitted but the keys have been lost it is possible to purchase a replacement lock barrel which will accept a different key pattern.

When fitting a replacement barrel, unscrew the latch from the rear of the door, disengage the lever from the barrel, push the barrel out through the door and insert the replacement barrel. Engage the lever of the new barrel in the latch and screw the latch back onto the door.

A new night latch is normally supplied with a paper template showing the position of the hole through the door. If a large enough drill bit or

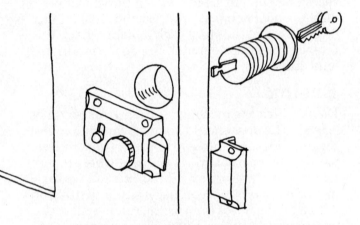

hole cutter is not available then mark the size of the hole required. Drill a series of holes around the inside of the circumference of the hole. Using a pad saw or key hole saw join up the holes and cut out the central plug of wood. Finish off the barrel hole using a half file.

1

Mortice Lock

A mortice lock is one which is fitted into the side of the door. It may have a latch attachment or simply be a 'dead lock' i.e. a key-operated lock with no latch action. Mortice locks cannot normally be fitted to doors which are less than 38 mm ($1\frac{1}{2}''$) thick.

On the side of the door, mark the size of the body of the lock. Using a drill marked with a depth stop made of a piece of plastic tube or insulation tape, drill out as much of the area to be removed as possible. Complete the slot for the lock using a sharp chisel. Once the body of the lock can slide into the side of the door, mark the size of the end plate onto the door and carefully cut out a recess with a chisel to accept the plate. Carefully mark the position of the key hole and any handle-spindle hole on the face of the door and cut and drill out appropriately-sized holes.

Slide the lock into place and secure it in position by screwing the end plate into the side of the door. A lock plate is fitted into the side of the frame in a similar manner.

Rim Lock

A rim lock is fitted to the back of a door and is most commonly found on old doors less than 38 mm (1½″) thick. It may or may not incorporate a latch mechanism. Rim latches without a lock or incorporating a sliding bolt are also available and are fitted in the same way. Although the body of the lock is fitted to the back of the door many have a metal flap which is fitted to the side of the door.

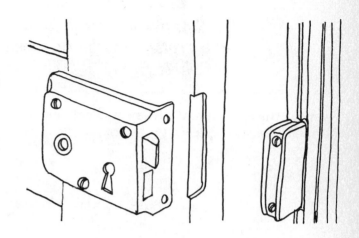

Mark the side of the door and cut a recess to accept this flap. Mark the face of the door and drill and cut out holes for the keyhole and handle spindle. Screw the lock to the door with dome-headed screws.

The striking plate is screwed to the side of the door frame and it may be necessary to cut out part of the architrave to align the striking plate with the tongues of the latch and lock.

3

Ball Catch

Ball catches are normally used for cupboards but can be used in place of latches and are less obtrusive than a rim latch on thin doors. Use a nylon ball catch with an adjustable spring tensioning the ball. Mark the side of the door and drill out a hole large enough to take the barrel of the ball catch and long enough to allow adjustment of the spring. Cut a recess in the side of the door with a sharp chisel to take the end plate of the ball catch so that it sits flush with the surface. Screw the ball in place. With a sharp chisel cut out a recess in the door frame so that the striking plate sits flush and screw it in place.

Push the door shut and check that the ball engages and that it is not too stiff. To adjust the action unscrew and remove the ball catch and adjust the tension on the spring.

4

The timber threshold on an external door which is rotten can be replaced without removing the whole frame.

Remove the door from the frame and cut down through the sill adjacent to the frame.

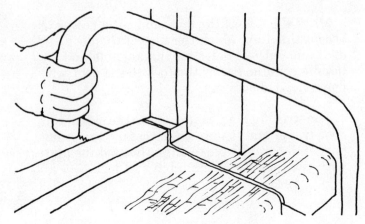

1

The frame will either be housed into the sill or a tongue of the frame may pass through the sill. Using a sharp chisel, remove the remains of the sill to expose the bottom of the frame.

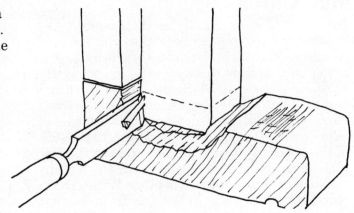

2

Cut off the bottom of each side of the frame level with the top of the sill. Cut out a section of the frame, 150 mm (6″) long and half the depth of the frame to the bottom of each side. Remove the door stop if detachable, or, if integrally moulded, then cut it off 300 mm (12″) from the bottom.

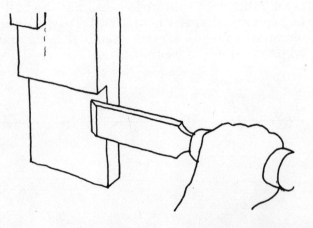

3

Cut a length of sill section timber, long enough to fit below the frame on both sides. Temporarily locate the threshold and mark the position of the removed sections of the frame onto the threshold. Cut out a slot in each position with a sharp chisel to within 12 mm of the bottom of the sill. Treat the sill with wood preservative and place it on a polythene or bituminous felt damp-proof course.

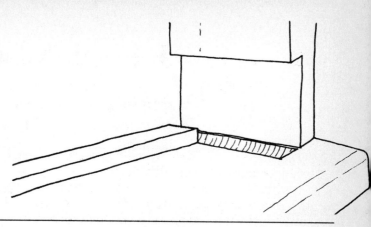

4
_____

Cut out and shape two side pieces to fit into the cut-outs in the sides of the frame and into the slots in the sill. Glue and screw the side pieces into position, screwing down into the sill at an angle. Countersink the screws and fill the screw heads with an inert filler such as Tetrion.

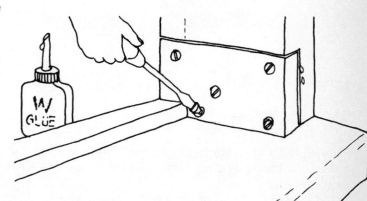

5
_____

Replace the door stops or piece into the moulded doorstop, screwing the stop to the new side pieces and the remainder of the frame to increase stability. Fill all joins, prime, undercoat and paint the frame and sill.

6
_____

RE-GLAZE DOORS

Glazing in doors is normally secured by wooden glazing beads.

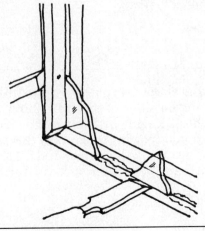

Unscrew or prise off the glazing beads surrounding the broken pane of glass. Carefully remove pieces of broken glass, tap out, or prise out, any pieces that are firmly bedded in putty.

1

Clean out old putty using an old chisel or a glazier's knife, taking care not to damage the timber frame.

Measure the size of the opening, top and bottom, left and right hand sides, since it may not be square. Deduct 3 mm from each measurement to allow for tolerance.

Glazing in external doors must often provide a degree of security and 6 mm wired glass may be the most appropriate. Order or cut glass to fit.

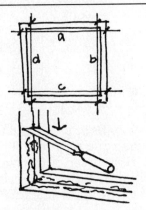

2

Squeeze a thin layer of putty into the rebate of the frame, using the thumb and forefinger. Press the glass into place, pressing the edges only and working around the pane so that some putty is squeezed out of the rebate, and the pane of glass is evenly bedded. Do not press the centre of the glass since this could cause uneven stresses which will break it. Squeeze a little putty around the front edges of the glass.

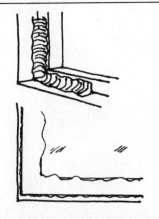

3

If the glazing beads are intact they can be used again. If not, carefully measure each side of the opening and cut glazing beads with mitred corners. Press glazing beads into position, squeezing out some of the putty. Nail or screw glazing bead into position. Trim off excess putty, filling any slight depressions so that the glass is surrounded by a thin strip of putty flush with the faces of the glazing beads and rebates.

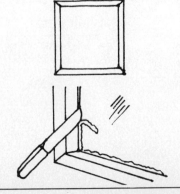

4

HANGING OR RE-HANGING OF DOOR

Measure door opening and allowing a 3 mm gap to the top and sides of the door, and a 6 mm gap to the bottom, mark the door. Take off any excess with a plane, or saw and plane if more than 6 mm needs to be removed.

Add any 'shims' that are necessary to bring the door up to size. Cut two wedges from a piece of scrap wood. Support the door in the frame on the wedges and check that it fits. Make further adjustments as necessary.

1

If existing hinge recesses in the frame are to be re-used then support the door in the frame on the wedges and mark the top and bottom of each recess on the side of the door. If new hinge recesses are to be made, position the hinges about 150 mm from the top, 200 mm from the bottom of the door.

Place a 100 mm butt hinge in position on the side of the door with the pin casing overhanging, but hard up against the edge and check that it is at right-angles to the door with a square. Mark the position of the hinges with a pencil, and the thickness of the hinge plate on the side of the door. Using a chisel cut along the lines on the edge of the door to approximately the depth of the hinge plate, with the bevel of the chisel blade facing into the hinge recess. Cut across the hinge area at 6 mm intervals and then cut out the chips so formed, working from the side of the door into the recess. Check for depth against hinge plate and deepen if necessary. The hinge recess should be flat and square to the side of the door so that the hinge plate lays flush to the edge of the door. If recess is too deep, pack the hinge out with sand or glass paper. Drill guidance holes and screw hinge into place. Repeat for second hinge.

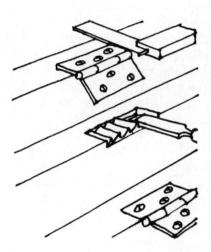

2

Support the door against the frame in an open position on the wedges and mark out the hinge outline. Take away the door and check that the hinge positions are vertically above each other. Mark depth of hinge plate on side of frame and cut out hinge recess in the same way as for the door edge. Support door in place and check that hinges fit flush to recesses, adjust as necessary and when a flush fit has been obtained screw hinges onto frame.

3

Door should now close and open without catching or binding on the frame. If the side of the door rubs at the top of the frame, but has more than a big enough gap at the bottom, then ease off screws to frame hinge plates, pack out bottom hinge with glass or sand paper and re-tighten screws. If the door still rubs the frame then check gap to hinge side; if gap is parallel all the way up, then shave some more off the lock side of the door with a plane. If the bottom of the gap is smaller than the top gap, and less than 3 mm, then pack out the bottom hinges some more. If the bottom of the gap is 3 mm, but the top gap is larger, then take the door off and deepen whichever of the two top hinge recesses is not deep enough. If the side of the door binds at the bottom, apply the same adjustment procedure, but to the top hinges.

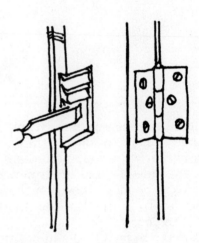

4

NEW INTERNAL DOOR FRAME

Whether fitting a new door frame to a brick, block or timber stud wall, the basic procedure is the same.

Measure thickness of wall to include depth of plaster. Where plaster is to be applied once the door frame is in position, allow 15 mm to either side for plasterwork. 12·5 mm to either side for plasterboard and skim, 9 mm either side for plasterboard only. Timber for the frame should be ex 25 mm by the width determined above. Measure the width of the opening and subtract the thickness of the two frame sides to give the size of the door required. Where a standard, or known-size door is to be used, the sides of the frame can be packed out by up to 38 mm to each side. Decide on the amount of packing, if any, required. Measure height of opening and decide on the amount of packing to be introduced, if any, to bring top of frame down to the height of the door.

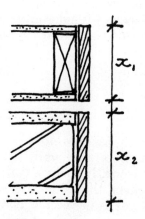

1

Having decided on size of frame, cut sides of frame to height of door, plus 9 mm tolerances, plus 10 mm to allow for housing onto head of frame. Cut head of frame to width of door, plus 6 mm tolerances, plus thickness of the two frame sides, plus any extra made available by the packing of the sides, since this will make the housings stronger.

   To each side-piece mark out a line 10 mm from the top and mark half the depth. Cut across this line with a tenon saw, cut down the grain to meet the first cut and trim with a sharp chisel.

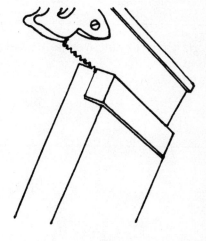

2

Mark the width of the door plus 6 mm onto the head of the frame with a square so that marks are equidistant from the ends. Draw a second set of lines the width of the 'tongues' formed on the top of the sides, apart from and parallel to the first.

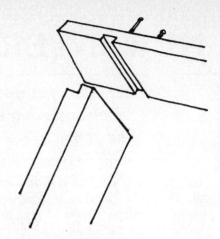

Mark the depth of the tongues on the side of the head-piece. Cut down to the depth of each pair of lines with a tenon saw and cut out the groove using a chisel, working from the edges into the middle. Check that tongues on sides fit tightly into grooves in the head, and trim with a chisel, if necessary. Fit sides and head of frame together, and glue and nail through the top of the head-piece.

3

Nail any packing pieces into the side of an opening in a timber-stud wall, or screw into plugs in brickwork. Introduce frame into opening and check that sides are vertical and parallel. Pack out as necessary. Nail to packing pieces, or studwork, with oval nails, screw to plugs in brickwork, screw-heads being countersunk, and in the line of the door-stop. Cut door-stop of ex 38×25 mm, nail to sides and head.

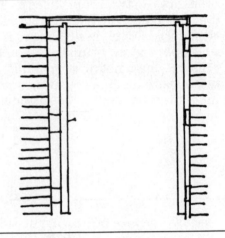

4

Attach architraves to cover joints between frame and wall.
(See Sheet 3.03).

5

4
WINDOWS

NEW WINDOW TO EXISTING FRAME

Where the sashes and weights are missing from a sash window it can be coverted to a casement window.

Remove the sash pulleys, parting and staff beading from the sash box. Line the sides and head of the sash box with ex 100×25 mm softwood, nailed into place with 38 mm ovals. Nail on an ex 25×19 mm batten to all sides to act as a window stop, placed so that its outer edge lines up with the step in the timber sill.

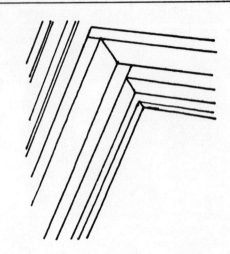

1

Make up a casement to fit the opening, allowing 3 mm tolerance to each side using ex 38×75 mm bottom rail sash section. Cut two side-pieces the full height of the casement and to top and bottom cut a mitre in the moulded glazing bead 75 mm minus the depth of the glazing bead in from the end, and cut off the moulding between the mitre and the end. Cut top and bottom members for the casement and cut mitres to the mouldings. Butt the sides and ends of the frame together and clamp them with corner clamps. Drill two 9 mm dowel holes to each corner making sure that the dowels will pass a minimum of 25 mm into the top and bottom rails. Cut 9 mm dowels, approximately 25 mm longer than required; with a file, chamfer one end, and with a chisel or craft knife carefully cut two 'V' shaped grooves down the length. Using an adhesive based on 'Urea Formaldehyde', glue the butt joints and re-clamp. Brush adhesive on to the dowels and gently tap them into place. When the adhesive has set, saw off protruding ends of dowels and plane flush with sides of frame.

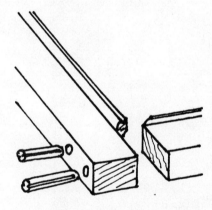

2

Place two 75 mm butt hinges, 150 mm from the top and the bottom on the edge of the frame, with the pin casing overhanging but hard up against the face. Check that it is at right angles with a square. Mark the position of the hinges with a pencil and the thickness of the hinge plate on the face of the frame. Using a chisel with the bevel facing into the recess, cut along the lines on the edge of the frame to approximately the depth of the hinge plate and deepen until the hinge plate lays flush to the edge of the window frame. If the recess is too deep, pack the hinge out with sand or glass paper. Drill guidance holes and screw hinge in place and repeat for second hinge.

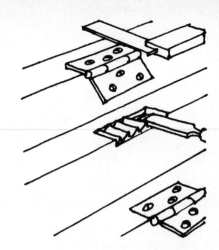

·3 _____

Hold the frame in position and mark the position of the hinges onto the frame. Check that hinge recesses are vertically in line and positioned so that the window will close against the window stops. Cut the hinge recesses as previously described for the window. Paint the frame and casement, attach a casement stay and casement fastener. Glaze casement (See Sheet 4.18) with 3 mm glass, 4 mm if the glass is more than 1·200 m in any direction. Hang the window by screwing the hinges into recesses in the frame. Fix a peg for casement stay and a latch for casement fastener to frame.

N.B. Large openings are best subdivided into a number of casement, or a combination of casements and fixed panels (See 4.03).

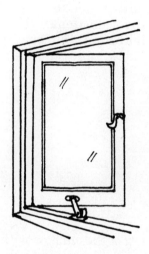

4 _____

A missing window can be replaced with a ready-made window if one can be found to match the opening, or if appearance is not important, the opening may be reduced to fit a suitable window.

Measure the opening and find the nearest-sized standard window manufactured by a local joinery manufacturer. Alternatively find a suitable second-hand window. If the size of the opening is to be reduced, then cut out a half-brick to either side to give a key to new brickwork. Any reduction in the height of the window should be built up from the sill, not above the window, unless a new lintel is also introduced.

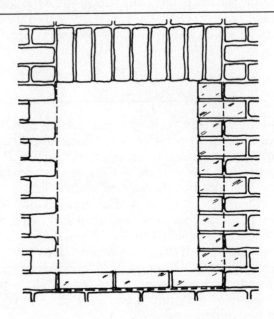

1

The positioning of the window within the depth of the wall will be determined by the sill. If there is no sub-sill and the height of the window matches the opening, then the window will sit in the front of the wall with its integral sill overhanging the edge of the brickwork by 25 mm. If there is a sub-sill, or if the height of the opening is to be reduced and a sub-sill can be constructed, then the window can be placed anywhere within the opening. If the opening has solid sides, then placing the window at the back of the opening, flush with the plasterwork, will simplify the internal plaster detail. However, if the front leaf of the brickwork is independent, or the window is to fit into an unreduced opening, which previously held a sash window, then the window should sit to the front of the opening and the frame should overlap the outer leaf of brickwork.

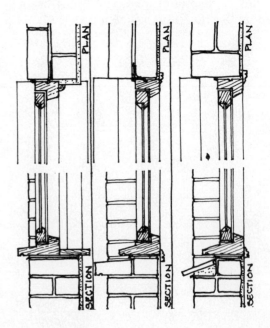

2

A new sub-sill can be constructed in a number of ways, including casting an in-situ concrete, or reconstituted stone sill. The techniques for this are similar to the repair of a stone sub-sill as described in sheet 4.17. A simpler method is to create a quarry tile or slate sub-sill.

First build up the bricks to the inner leaf of brickwork until the opening is reduced to the required depth. Spread a thin layer of mortar to the cleaned-off bricks to the outer brickwork and bed a polythene D.P.C. so that it overhangs the front face of the brickwork by 15 mm, is continued up the face of the new brickwork and is bedded in mortar on top of the new brickwork. Build up the front face of the brickwork so that it is one brick lower than the rear leaf.

Lay a sloping mortar-bed and place on a row of quarry tiles, or two layers of slates with staggered joints so that they touch the face of the new leaf of brickwork and project 25 mm past the face of the wall. Flush point the tiles or slates.

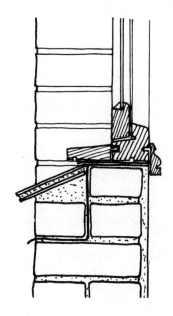

3

A window that is a tight fit into an opening with solid sides can be screwed and plugged to the brickwork. If the window is to be fitted into an opening which previously contained a sash, nail a D.P.C. to either side of the frame and place it against the back of the front leaf of brickwork. Screw two galvanised-metal brick ties to each side of the frame and build these in with the brick courses. If the opening is to be reduced, the sides may either be built solid, in which case no D.P.C. is necessary, or a vertical course may be left for a D.P.C. In either case secure the window with ties screwed to the frame and built into the brickwork.

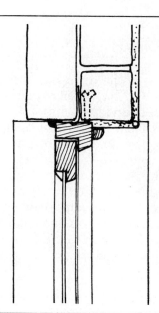

4

Where sashes and weights are missing from a sash window, it can be converted to a fixed glazed pane with opening louvres.

Remove the sash pulley, parting and staff beading from the sash box. Line the head and bottom of the sash box with ex 100×25 mm softwood nailed into place with 38 mm ovals. Cut two side-pieces of ex 100×25 mm softwood to fit between the head and the base. Select a louvre set i.e. 3, 4, 5 or more blades, and mark off the depth of the louvres from the top of each side. With a square draw a line across the side and draw a second line below and parallel to the first, the distance between the lines being equal to the thickness of a piece of ex 100×25 mm timber. On the edge, mark half of the depth of the ex 100×19 mm side pieces.

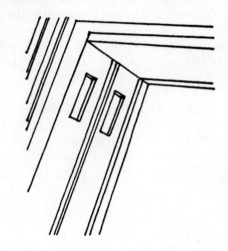

1

Cut down each of the lines with a tenon saw to the depth line. With a chisel cut across between the two saw cuts and then shave off the chips so formed. Work from the sides of the timber into the middle so that the sides are not damaged. When the groove is to the required depth, check for width against piece of ex 100×25 mm. Repeat for other side-piece and then nail sides into sash box using 38 mm ovals. Measure between bottom of grooves and cut a piece of ex 100×25 mm softwood to fit. Slide this into place to form a 'transom' and skew-nail into position.

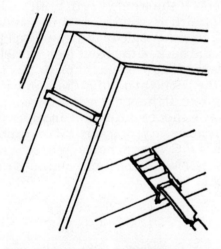

2

Screw louvre holders in position above the transom and towards the outside of the frame, and pin a piece of 9 mm-square beading on top of transom to act as a draught-stop to the lowest louvre. Nail on a 15 mm-square bead to all the sides of the opening below the transom. Run mastic between the bottom of the frame and the window-sill and paint the frame. Glaze the frame, using glazing beads on the interior of the window. (See Sheet 4.18), and clip glass into the louvre frames.

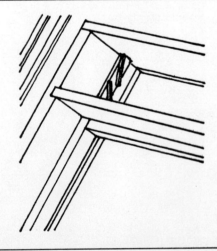

3

A similar technique can be used where the sash box is missing or there is an opening in an external wall. In this case the linings should be made of ex 150×25 mm softwood, the sides carrying through with the corners and transom glued and skew-nailed in place. Before assembling plane a chamfer onto the front edge of the bottom lining. Tack a damp-proof course to the sides of the frame and bed the base in mastic.

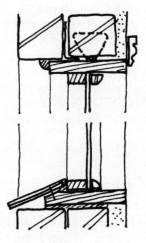

Position frame so that it overlaps the inside edge of the front leaf of the brickwork, and the back is flush with the plaster line. (In walls more than 225 mm thick this will necessitate a deeper lining or a different plaster to frame detail.) Where brickwork steps back for sash box, screw two galvanised brick ties to each side of the frame and build frame into brickwork. Where opening has flush sides, screw and plug frame to brickwork. Run mastic around frame at junction with brickwork and pin a sill of 9 mm exterior-quality plywood, bedded and pointed in mastic onto the chamfered front of the base of the frame to oversail the outside edge of the brickwork, and act as a sill. Both frame and sill should be painted to prevent wet rot.

4

RE-HANGING A SASH

Carefully prise off staff bead to sides and bottom of sash box and parting bead to sides.

Swing sash clear of frame and gripping the sash cord, prise out the nails from the side of the frame. Tie a knot in the cord and gently let it return against the pulley. Placing a piece of stick in the knot will stop it tightening too much thus making it difficult to undo.

Repeat for other sash cords and remove the two sashes.

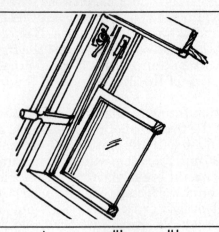

1

Prise off cover to the weight box by gently levering from below. Remove weights and take off broken sash cord. When replacing missing weights, weigh the glazed sash on a spring balance and select weights so that the two equal the weight of the sash. Minor additions to the weights can be made with offcuts of lead pipe or lead sheet.

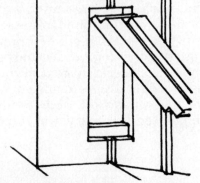

2

Feed new sash cord over pulley and down through to weight-box opening, and pull out. Sometimes the sash cord will have a tendency to stay tangled at the top of the box. This can be overcome by lashing a piece of fine twine to the end of the cord, weighting the twine with a nut small enough to pass over the pulley and then passing nut and twine through the pulley before feeding in the sash cord. The twine is then used to pull down the cord. Pull cord out of the weight box, tie on sash weight and place back in sash box. Pull sash cord so that weight rises to the top of the box, cut cord about 75 mm above the sill. Knot and return gently to allow the knot to rest against the pulley. When sash cords and weights have been renewed, replace the covers to the sash weight boxes.

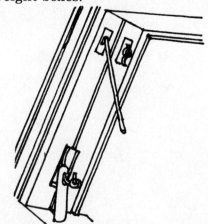

3

Place the top sash on 25 mm blocks placed on the sill and, using galvanised clouts, nail the sash cord into the groove to the side of the sash, placing the top nail the distance from the head of the frame to the underside of the sash pulley from the top of the sash. Trim off any excess sash cord. Swing sash into position and check that both sash and weights run freely. Nail back the parting beads and hang the lower sash in the same way. Nail on staff beads.

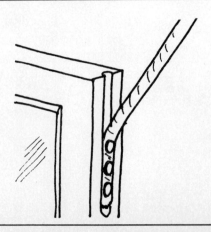

4

REPAIRING A SASH

A sash which has been badly maintained may be repaired to prolong its useful life if the damage is not too severe. A repaired sash should be well-painted to prevent further decay.

Clean out paint, old putty and any filler that has been introduced into joints in the frames which have opened up.

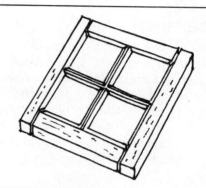

1

Using sash cramps, slowly cramp up the frame to close up joints, placing a piece of sacking or polythene over the frame to catch any glass which may shatter if the frame has been reglazed since the joints opened. Reinforce each joint with a 75×75 mm 'L' shaped mild steel angle screwed to both faces of the frame.

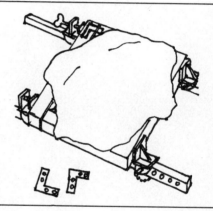

2

If the bottom rail of a sash has badly rotted it may be replaced provided that the sides of the frame have not rotted above the depth of the rail. Cut off the ends of the sides of the frame, level with the bottom of the mitre to the moulded glazing bead. Cut a new piece of 'bottom rail sash stuff' the width of the frame, mark the position of the mitres to each side and cut mitres to the glazing beads, removing the beading between the ends and the mitres. Cramp bottom rail in place and drill two 9 mm diameter holes to each side, through the bottom rail and at least 25 mm into the sides. Cut 9 mm dowels approximately 25 mm longer than required; with a file, chamfer one end and with a chisel or craft knife carefully cut two 'V' shaped grooves down the length. Using a glue based on 'Urea Formaldehyde', glue butt joints and re-clamp. Brush adhesive on to the dowels and gently tap them into place. When the adhesive has set, saw off protruding ends of dowels and plane flush with bottom rail.

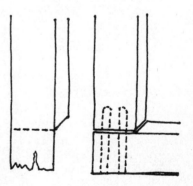

3

If frame has settled out of true then the sash will not fit and will require to be 'eased' or 'shimmed'.

'Easing'

Where the sash is too tight a fit, close both sashes so that middle rails are matching. Mark the sashes and plane to size. When planing across the end grain of a side piece then always plane into the centre of the frame so that the sides do not split.

'Shimming'

Close the sashes so that the middle rails are aligned and measure from the sashes to the frame to determine the size of the gap to top and bottom. Cut out pieces of timber to fit the gap and screw or pin to the top or bottom of the sashes, planing flush to the faces. Stand sashes in frame to check that they fit and 'ease' as necessary before re-hanging.

4

NEW SASH

The method of construction described here is not a traditional method but is perfectly adequate if the frame is painted.

1 Measure up opening in sash frame, allowing 3 mm tolerance to each side, i.e. 6 mm on the width, but only 3 mm on the height of each sash. Determine the size of the sashes, remembering that the top of the bottom rail of the upper sash and the top of the top rail of the lower sash should be level. Some Timber Merchants stock 'sash stuff' i.e. the appropriate timber sections for top rails, bottom rails, sides and glazing bars and sufficient of each should be selected to make up the new sash. Reject any that is warped or twisted.

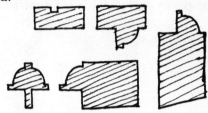

2 Cut the side rails to the full height of the sash and on each, mark the depth of the top and bottom rails, excluding the moulded glazing bead. From the mark, saw a 45° mitre through the moulded glazing bead and remove the glazing bead between the mitre and the end, with a sharp chisel. Cut the top and bottom rail so that they will fit between the sides at the points where the moulded beading has been removed. Cut mitres at the end of the beading on the top and bottom rails to match those on the side pieces.

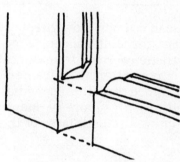

3 Butt the sides and top and bottom rails together with corner clamps and at each corner drill two 9 mm diameter holes through the sides at least 25 mm into the rails. Cut 9 mm dowels, approximately 25 mm longer than required, with a file, chamfer one end and with a chisel or craft knife carefully cut two 'V' shaped grooves down the length. Using an adhesive based on 'Urea Formaldehyde' glue the butt joints and re-clamp them. Brush adhesive on to the dowels and tap them into place. When the adhesive has set, cut off the protruding ends of the dowels and plane flush with the side of the frame.

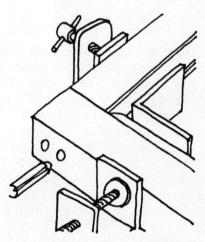

4 Using a rebating attachment, a rebating plane, or a saw and chisel cut a 9 mm square rebate down the side of each sash from the top to ²/₃ of its height. Paint, glaze and hang the sashes. (See Sheets 4.04 and 4.18.)

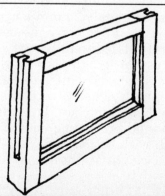

A casement window which has been badly maintained may be repaired to prolong its useful life, if the damage is not too severe. A repaired casement should be painted to prevent further decay.

Clean out paint, old putty, and any filler that has been introduced into joints in the frames which have been opened up.

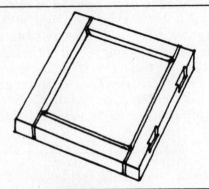

1

Using sash cramps, slowly cramp up the frame to close up the joints, placing a piece of sacking, or polythene over the frame to catch any glass which may shatter if the frame has been reglazed since the joints opened. Reinforce each joint with a 75×75 mm 'L' shaped mild-steel angle screwed to both faces of the frame.

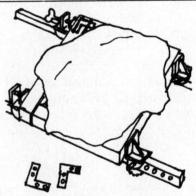

2

If the bottom rail of the casement has badly rotted, it may be replaced, provided that the sides of the frame have not rotted above the depth of the rail. Cut off the ends of the sides of the frame, level with the bottom of the mitre to the moulded glazing bead. Cut a new piece of 'bottom rail sash stuff' the width of the frame, mark the position of the mitres to each side and cut mitres to the glazing beads, removing the beading between the ends and the mitres. Cramp bottom rail in place, and drill two 9 mm diameter holes to each side, through the bottom rail and at least 25 mm into the sides. Cut 9 mm dowels approximately 25 mm longer than required, with a file chamfer one end and with a chisel or craft knife carefully cut two 'V' shaped grooves down the length. Using a glue based on 'Urea Formaldehyde', glue butt joints and re-clamp. 'Brush' adhesive on to the dowels and gently tap them into place. When the adhesive has set, saw off protruding ends of dowels and plane flush with bottom rail.
Re-hang casement as Sheet 4.08.

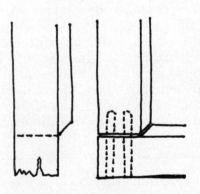

3

RE-HANGING A CASEMENT

Take off old hinges. Cut out pieces of plywood to fit tightly into the hinge recesses. Glue and pin the plywood into the hinge recesses in the casement and frame. Recess the pin heads below the level of the casement and frame surfaces, with a counter-sink punch. Plane the plywood infill pieces down level with the surface of the casement and frame.

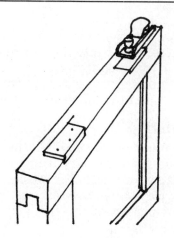

1

Place two 75 mm butt hinges 150 mm from the top and the bottom on the edge of the frame, with the pin casing overhanging but hard up against the face. Check that it is at right angles with a square. Mark the position of the hinges with a pencil and the thickness of the hinge plate on the face of the frame. Using a chisel with the bevel facing into the recess, cut along the lines on the edge of the frame to appoximately the depth of the hinge plate and deepen until the hinge plate lays flush to the edge of the window frame. If the recess is too deep, pack the hinge out with sand or glass paper. Drill guidance holes and screw hinge in place and repeat for second hinge.

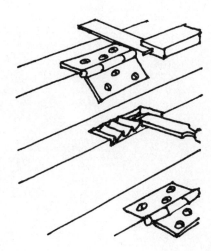

2

Hold the frame in position and mark the position of the hinges onto the frame. Check that hinge recesses are vertically in line and positioned so that the window will close against the window stops. Cut the hinge recesses as previously described for the window. Paint the frame and casement, attach a casement stay and casement fastener. Glaze casement (see Sheet 4.18) with 3 mm glass, 4 mm if the glass is more than 1·200 m in any direction. Hang the window by screwing the hinges into recesses in the frame. Fix a peg for casement stay and a latch for casement fastener to frame.

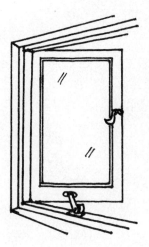

3

If the frame is out of true then the casement may not fit and if so it should be 'eased' or 'shimmed' to fit with a 3 mm gap to each side.

'Easing'

Where casement is too tight a fit, mark it and plane to size. When planing across the end grain of side pieces, plane into the centre of the casement to avoid splitting.

   If more than 6 mm needs to be removed, use a saw before finishing off with a plane.

'Shimming'

If the casement is too small for the frame, measure the distance to the frame and deduct 3 mm for a tolerance gap. Cut pieces to fill the gaps, known as 'shims' and screw or nail them to the casement. Plane shims flush with the faces of the casement.

4

NEW CASEMENT

The method of construction described here is not a traditional method, but is perfectly adequate if the casement is painted to protect it against water.

Measure up the size of the opening in the frame and allow 3 mm tolerance to each side, i.e. 6 mm on the width and 6 mm on the height. Some timber merchants stock moulded casement window section or 'sash stuff' side piece section is also suitable. Select enough to make the casement, rejecting any that is warped or twisted.

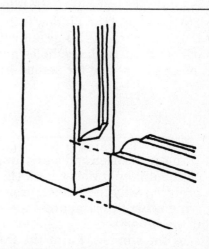

1

Make up a casement to fit the opening, allowing 3 mm tolerance to each side using ex 38×75 mm bottom rail sash section. Cut two side-pieces the full height of the casement and to top and bottom cut a mitre in the moulded glazing bead 75 mm minus the depth of the glazing bead in from the end, and cut off the moulding between the mitre and the end. Cut top and bottom members for the casement and cut mitres to the mouldings. Butt the sides and ends of the frame together and clamp them with corner clamps. Drill two 9 mm dowel holes to each corner making sure that the dowels will pass a minimum of 25 mm into the top and bottom rails. Cut 9 mm dowels, approximately 25 mm longer than required; with a file, chamfer one end, and with a chisel or craft knife carefully cut two 'V' shaped grooves down the length. Using an adhesive based on 'Urea Formaldehyde', glue the butt joints and re-clamp. Brush adhesive on to the dowels and gently tap them into place. When the adhesive has set, saw off protruding ends of dowels and plane flush with sides of frame.

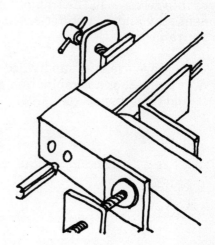

2

Place two 75 mm butt hinges, 150 mm from the top and the bottom on the edge of the frame, with the pin casing overhanging but hard up against the face. Check that it is at right angles with a square. Mark the position of the hinges with a pencil and the thickness of the hinge plate on the face of the frame. Using a chisel with the bevel facing into the recess, cut along the lines on the edge of the frame to approximately the depth of the hinge plate and deepen until the hinge plate lays flush to the edge of the window frame. If the recess is too deep, pack the hinge out with sand or glass paper. Drill guidance holes and screw hinge in place and repeat for second hinge.

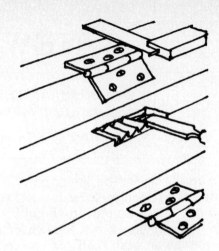

3

Hold the frame in position and mark the position of the hinges onto the frame. Check that hinge recesses are vertically in line and positioned so that the window will close against the window stops. Cut the hinge recesses as previously described for the window. Paint the frame and casement, attach a casement stay and casement fastener. Glaze casement (see Sheet 4.18) with 3 mm glass, 4 mm if the glass is more than 1·200 m in any direction. Hang the window by screwing the hinges into recesses in the frame. Fix a peg for casement stay and a latch for casement fastener to frame.

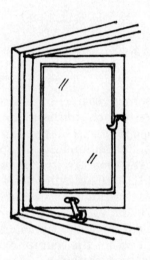

N.B. Large openings are best subdivided into a number of casement, or a combination of casements and fixed panels (see 4.03).

4

Sash-box frames have a removable section to enable the weights to be re-hung. These sections are normally sited in the side of the sash boxes, although they are sometimes sited in the room side-faces.

Sash-box covers which are situated in the sides of the box are normally held in place by the parting beads, relying on rebates, or shaping at the ends for accurate alignment.

Measure the width, height and the locating details at the top and bottom of the sash-box cover. Cut out a new sash-box cover, making sure that it is a tight fit.

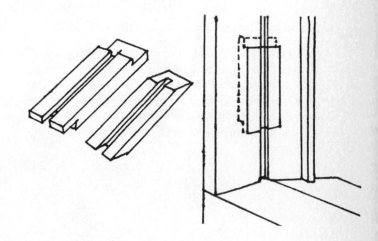

1

Where the sash-box cover is located by the parting bead, mark the width of the locating rebate onto the top and bottom of the sash-box cover. Mark the depth of the rebate on the ends of the cover. Cut a rebate to take the bead, using either a rebating plane, or by sawing along the edges of the rebate with a tenon saw and then shaving out the groove with a sharp chisel.

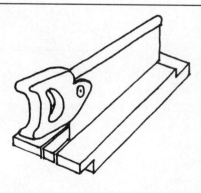

2

Paint the sash-box cover with preservative or paint and press into position. Replace parting bead but do not nail directly into the sash-box cover.

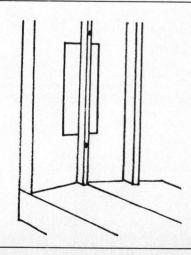

3

Architraves are primarily used to hide the junction between a door or window frame, and the surrounding plaster. They may be plain or moulded.

Where a section of moulded architrave is missing it will be easier to replace the complete architrave than to attempt to match up modern architrave sections. If the remaining sections of moulded architraves are carefully removed, they can be used to repair the architraves to other windows in the same house.

Architrave is normally positioned so that it half overlaps the edge of the window frame or sash box. The margin of frame left uncovered by the architrave should be carried across the top of the frame and should be included in the measurements for the side sections of the architrave.

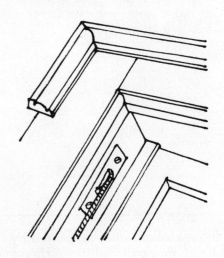

1

Cut 45° mitres to the top of each side architrave and tack architraves in place with 25 to 38 mm pins, or oval nails. Do not hammer nails home fully.

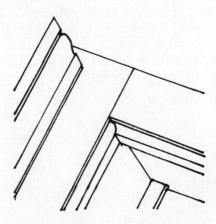

2

Measure distance between window-side edges of architraves and then wall-side edges. Before cutting mitred corners make sure that top sections of architraves will match these dimensions. Where this does not happen check that the sides of the frame or architrave have been fitted vertically and if not, adjust. Where an existing frame is out of square, then cut the top section of architrave to the longer dimension and adust the mitre with a plane to fit.

Finally nail top and side pieces of architrave, recessing and filling the nail heads.

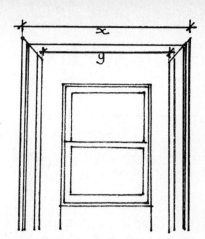

3

Where a section of architrave has been broken or cut out and a matching architrave is available, then cut through to either side of the damaged section at right angles to the architrave and carefully prise it off the frame. Cut a piece of the matching architrave to fit and nail to the frame and screw pin the back edge of the architrave to the back edge of that existing to ensure alignment, recessing and filling both nail and pin heads.

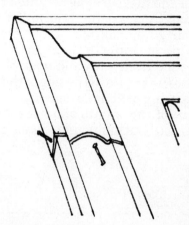

4

4.12
RENEWING STAFF AND PARTING BEADS

Staff and parting beads are parts of a sash window and are still sold by most timber merchants.

The parting bead is the thin wooden strip which separates the front and rear sashes in a sash window. To replace parting bead, prise off any old bead and measure the height of the window. Cut a length of parting bead to fit the height. Drill four guide holes for nails through the longest dimension of the bead, and then paint it. Replace the front sash and push the parting bead into the rebate in the side of the frame. Nail in place using oval nails, moving the sash up or down out of the way to allow a swing of the hammer without damaging the sash or breaking the glass.

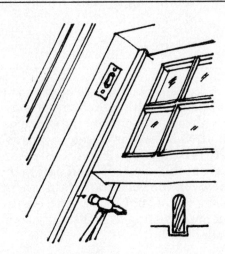

1

Staff beading is the beading which surrounds the inside of a sash window, holding the internal sash in place and stopping draughts at sill level. Prise off any broken lengths of staff bead and measure the height to both sides and the width to top and bottom of the window. Cut lengths of beading with a mitre at each end so that the bulbous portion of the staff beading faces into the room and is on the window side of the frame. Paint the beading and with both sashes in position nail the beading onto the frame so that it is tight against the bottom sash but allows it to move freely up and down the full height of the window. Move the sash up and down out of the way when nailing, to allow a swing of the hammer without damaging the sash or breaking the glass.

2

4.13
REPAIRING A TIMBER SILL

A timber sill which has not been painted will often start to rot. If this process is not too far advanced, adequate short-term repair may be possible.

For a sill which has just begun to suffer from the wet, scrape off any defective paintwork to the sill. Clean out any soft 'pith' wood with a wire brush and allow the sill to dry out.

Paint the sill with a wood preservative. Using a palette knife, fill the fissures in the top and front surface of the sill with 'Tetrion' or a similar inert filler. Prime, undercoat and gloss paint the timber sill. Run a bead of mastic around the junction of the sill and the brickwork and the sub-sill.

1

Where a sill has a section missing from the front edge due to wet rot, but the sill itself remains firm, cut out the defective timber, allow the sill to dry out and paint with wood preservative. Cover the front edge of the sill with 6 mm exterior-quality plywood, and then cover the top face with 6 mm exterior-quality plywood, oversailing the front edge by 10 mm. Prime, undercoat and gloss paint the plywood. Run a bead of mastic sealant around the junction of the plywood with the sill, brickwork and sub-sill.

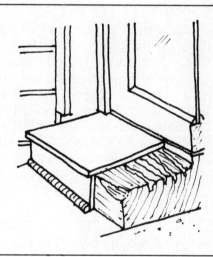

2

If a timber sill is beyond repair it is possible to replace the sill by itself, as long as the remainder of the sash box is sound. Where parts of the sash box are also rotten it is usually better to replace the box, rather than spend a lot of time replacing small parts.

Remove the sashes, staff and parting beads and the weights. If the sash box is wedged in place, remove the architraves, take out the wedges and pull the box from the wall. Where this is not possible the sill can be replaced with the box in position, but the operation is more awkward. The sill will normally be recessed to front and rear to fit between the faces of the sash box, and be rebated to accept the sides of the sash box. The pieces will normally be nailed together.

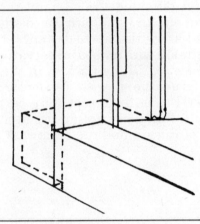

1

Cut downwards through the sill with a bow saw hard up against the sash boxes and take out the centre of the sill. Saw through the rear faces of the sash boxes 150 mm above the sill and retain the pieces removed. Using an old but sharp chisel chop off the top of the stubs of the sill to reveal the 'housed' ends of the side frames. Using the chisel and a mallet, split out the stubs of the sill until they have been removed. Cut off all nails flush to the frame with a pair of snips.

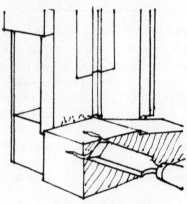

2

If the bottom of the side frame has rotted, cut it off square with a pad saw and extend the slot for the sash-box cover downwards. Take a piece of timber to match the side of the sash box (often ex 4″ × 1″) and cut a rebate to match the rebate for the parting bead. Cut a piece to replace the rotted bottom of the side frame and the 'tongue' to the bottom of the slot for the sash box. Glue and screw into place with two screws passing through both the first prong of the side frame and the tongue of the new piece, and screwing into the second prong of the sub-frame. Insert a third screw passing through the first prong and screwing into the tongue.

If the edge of the front frame is rotten, cut it off flush with the side frame and up to sound wood. Soak the exposed timber in wood preservative.

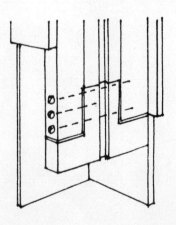

Cut the sill section so that it will fit between the front and back of the sash box and between the brickwork to the front of the box. Cut a rebate to each side to take the ends of the sides of the frame and treat the finished sill with clear wood preservative.

Slide the sill into place locating and skew nailing the sides of the frame in the rebates. Replace the bottom sections of the rear faces of the frame previously removed. Point around the new sill and the sides of the frame where they meet the brickwork, or the sub-sill with mastic.

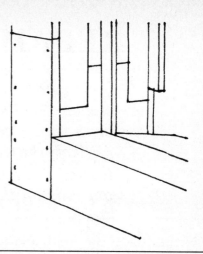

4

4.15
REPAIRING A SUB-SILL

Most stone, or, more commonly, reconstituted stone sub-sills which have been broken, chipped or in some cases eroded, can be repaired. It is unlikely that a colour match will be achieved for the replacement, since the colour of concrete depends on the aggregate.

Clean off the face of the break and the surrounding area of sub-sill with a wire brush. If the missing section projects over the face of the wall by more than 25 mm, seek professional guidance on the size of reinforcement to be used, if any.

1

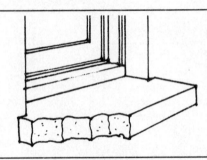

Using a masonry bit, drill holes into the face of the break at least 25 mm away from any surface, to take the reinforcing rods and grout the rods into the sill using a 1 part cement to 6 parts fine sand mix.

2

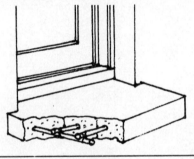

Construct a timber form to the side and underside of the section to be replaced, with the top of the sides level with the top of the sill. Although this formwork can be fairly crudely constructed, care should be taken that it is strong enough to support the weight of the concrete to be cast. Where the sill is to overhang the wall by more than 25 mm, nail a piece of waxed sash cord to the bottom of the formwork, 15 mm from the front edge. This will form a 'drip' in the sill.

3

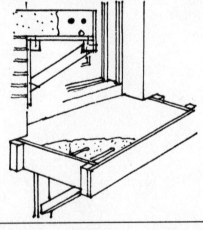

Place any additional reinforcement that is required and wire it to the protruding rods already fixed into the remains of the old sub-sill. Mix up concrete of 1 part cement to 2 parts sand, to 4 parts graded aggregate, less than 15 mm in size.

Add a P.V.A. adhesive to the mix and paint the broken face of the sill with P.V.A. Add enough water to the mix to make the concrete workable and pour it into the formwork. Prod the concrete with a stick to compact it, remove air bubbles and ensure that the formwork is full. Tamp the top level with the existing sill and

trowel with a steel float to give a smooth finish. Cover with polythene, or a damp sack for 7 to 10 days before removing formwork.

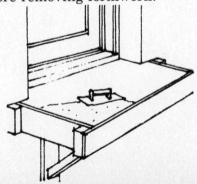

4

Remove old putty from the rebate to the frame, with an old chisel, pull out any metal 'sprigs' or pins with pliers. Take care not to damage the timber frame. If pieces of glass are still embedded in the putty, then gently tap them out with the handle of the chisel. Clean out the last of the putty in the rebate by running the chisel, bevelled edge upwards, down the rebate, applying even pressure with both hands.

1

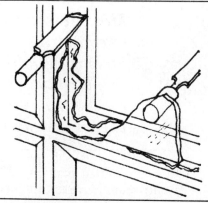

Measure the opening top and bottom to left and right, since it may not be square. Deduct 3 mm from each measurement to allow for a tolerance.

Apply putty to the rebate, either by rolling the putty into a ball and then forcing it into the rebate, using the thumb and forefinger, or by rolling the putty into a thin sausage, and then pushing this roll into the rebate with the thumb. If the putty is too wet it can be rolled on a clean stone or paper to remove some of the oil. If too dry, linseed oil can be added.

2

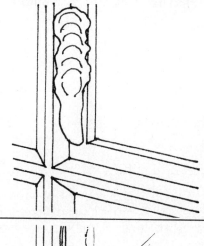

Press the glass into place, pressing the edges only and working around the pane so that some putty is squeezed out of the rebate and the glass is evenly bedded on a 2–4 mm bed of putty. Do not press the centre of the glass, since this could cause uneven stresses which will break it. Using the side of the chisel with the bevel flat against the glass, tap in 'sprigs' (headless glazier's pins) or panel pins at 300 mm spacings, so that the tops are below the level of the rebate on the other side of the glass.

3

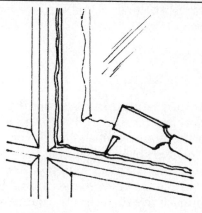

Using the same technique as before, squeeze putty into the angle between the glass and the frame. Using a glazier's, kitchen or palette knife, smooth off the surface of the putty to form an angled slope, flush with the frame and level with the rebate on the other side of the glass. Trim off the putty which has squeezed out at the back of the glass.

The putty should be left for two weeks and then painted.

N.B. The procedure for glazing metal window frames is similar except that instead of sprigs the glass is secured by spring metal clips. Normal putty will not stick to metal frames, but a special putty is available.

4

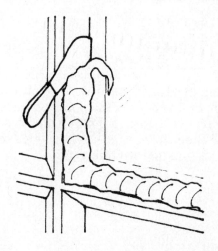

4.17
RE-POINTING A WINDOW

*Most timber windows are pointed into
surrounding brickwork with mortar, although
modern windows are normally pointed with a
flexible mastic. The technique described here is
for the repointing of a sash-box frame, although
it could apply to other types of window.*

Hack out remains of failed pointing. If gap is
more than 10 mm then move frame forward to
butt against the brickwork if possible.

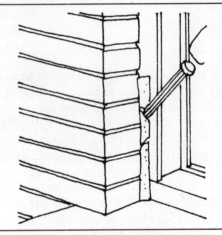

1

Mix up a mortar of 1:6 cement to sand with an
added waterproofer and add sufficient water so
that the mortar can be rolled across a spot board
with a bricklayer's trowel.

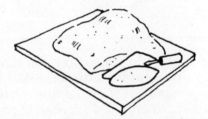

2

Point up the opening using a small pointing
trowel, forcing mortar well into the joint
between the frame and the brickwork. Bring
mortar surface slightly proud of the face of the
brickwork, and then cut a straight edge using
the point of the trowel with a straight batten as a
guide. Smooth the surface of the pointing with a
trowel to give an even finish.

3

When the mortar is stiff run the point of the
trowel down the edge of the pointing next to the
window frame to form a 6 mm wide 'V' shaped
groove. When the mortar has hardened squeeze
a 'bead' of mastic into this groove.

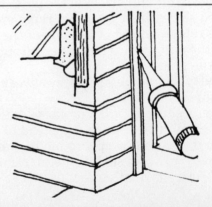

4

RE-FIXING A WINDOW FRAME

Windows are often wedged or badly fixed within a wall and become loose.

Prise off the architraves, remove any fixing wedges to the top and sides of the window and carefully remove the window from the wall opening. Clean out the old pointing and any debris from behind the brickwork.

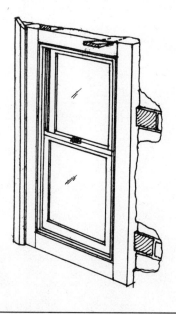

1

Where window was wedged in position, reposition the window and replace the wedges.
   Where a window was fixed to wooden blocks in the brickwork, remove the block, screw a galvanised metal tie to the back of the window and build this into the wall, replacing the wooden blocks with bricks.

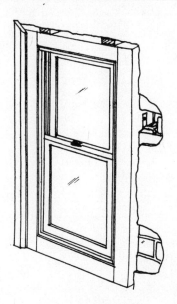

2

Repoint around the window, repair the plasterwork and replace the architraves.
(See Sheets 4.17, 4.11 and 2.02.)

3

5
CEILINGS

5.01
REPLACING A CEILING WITH PLASTERBOARD

Old plaster and lath ceilings have a tendency to fail due to the plaster losing its 'key' or hold, on the laths. Often the plaster can separate from the laths and act as a separate skin which can dramatically collapse if disturbed by an unusual deflection of the floor above, or attempts to cut holes for electrical wiring, or even the slamming of a door. Visible signs of failure are usually cracking or bowing of the ceiling, or both. Where such signs exist the ceiling should be firmly pressed to determine how much it will move, a ceiling which is still keyed to the laths should not deflect more than 3 mm, with no deflection under ceiling joists, a failed ceiling will deflect under ceiling joists as well as elsewhere. When a ceiling has failed it is easier to replace it than to attempt a patch repair.

Take down the ceiling plaster and laths. Once an initial hole has been made in the ceiling break down the laths, pulling down the nearest ends so that plaster adhering to them will be brought down away from the body. When all the laths have been broken down run the forked end of a crowbar or large claw hammer along the underside of each joist, pulling out or breaking off flush the nails used to hold the laths in place. Make sure that all the nails have been removed.

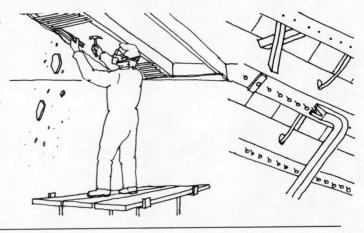

1

Measure the spacing between the joists from centre line to centre line. If the joists are more than 450 mm apart, then 12.5 mm thick plasterboard is necessary, if less, then 9 mm is adequate. Plasterboard can be purchased in two sizes 1,830×900 mm (6'–0"×3'–0") and more commonly 2,440×1,200 mm (8'–0"×4'–0") and the board size should be chosen to minimise wastage.

When boards are fixed so that they are joined under a ceiling joist, calculate where the edges at right angles to the ceiling joists will meet and mark these positions. Cut 'noggin' pieces of 50×50 or 50×75 mm softwood so that they fit tightly between the joists. Skew nail these noggins between joists so that their centre lines

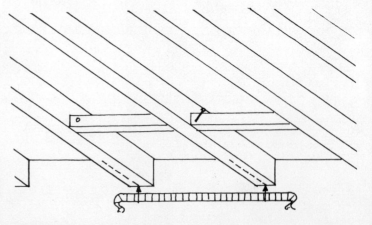

coincide with the joints to the board edges, and to each end of the room. No plasterboard edge which oversails the edge of a joist by more than 200 mm should be unsupported.

2

To cut plasterboard lay it flat, cut through the ivory surface and score the plaster core using a craft knife against a straight edge or batten. Lift the board, tap along the reverse of the cut so that the remainder of the plaster core snaps along the cut and the board bends. Cut through the grey surface using the cut plaster core as a guide.

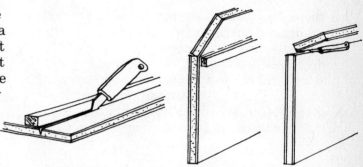

3

Using galvanised clout nails, nail boards to the ceiling joists and noggins with the ivory face of the board facing downwards and with joints no more than 5 mm wide.

This operation is best carried out by three people, two standing on the floor supporting the board, using 'T' shaped wooden supports, while the third standing on a platform, or using a box, stool or step ladder, nails it in place. Two people can nail boards in place, but they both need to work off a platform, supporting and nailing the board at the same time.

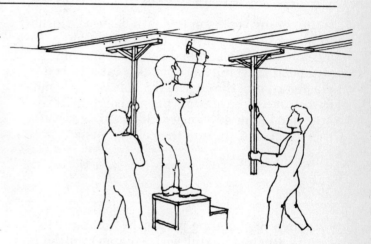

4

When nailing the board in place take care not to hit or damage it with the hammer, and do not break the surface with the nail heads. Recess the heads of the nails with a punch, so that they are below the level of the board, but do not break the surface. Fill the nail heads using some filler such as pollyfilla and a palette knife. Cover the joints with 50 mm wide paper adhesive tape. N.B. The noggins are not essential in short-life houses, except at edges, where there is no support to a board which oversails by more than 300 mm.

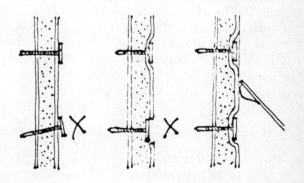

5

5.02
PATCHING A CEILING

Where a small area of ceiling has been damaged but the remainder is firm then it can be patched.

If the ceiling is a plasterboard ceiling, remove the damaged board, or cut out part of it so that the new section can butt-joint to it under a ceiling joist or noggin. Cut a piece of plasterboard of the appropriate thickness to fit the hole, and, using galvanised clout nails, nail it in place. Grey face down if it is to be plastered, or texture finished, ivory face down if not.

1

If the ceiling is plaster and lath, leave the laths in place, taking out only those which have already been broken and can be removed without disturbing more plaster. Take down any plaster around the edge of the hole which is not firm. Cut a piece of 9 mm plasterboard to fit the hole and using galvanised clout nails, nail it over the laths, up into the ceiling joists.

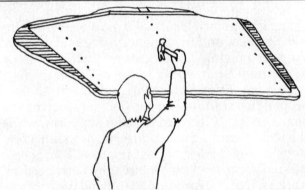

2

Mix up some bonding plaster by adding it to clean water and mixing with a plunger until it is of even consistency, capable of forming and holding peaks when the plunger is removed. Wet the surface of the plasterboard patch and the edges of the firm ceiling plaster. Using a trowel, fill in between the edges of the plasterboard patch and the ceiling. Bring out the level of the patch to 3 mm below that of the ceiling, using the bonding plaster and checking the level against a straight edge held across the patch. Scratch the plaster to give a key.

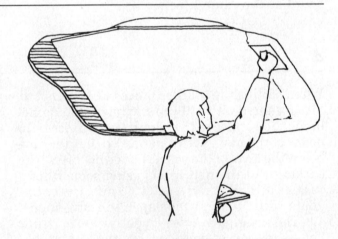

3

Mix up finish, or board-finish plaster, whichever is appropriate to the patch, by adding it to clean water and mixing with a plunger until it has the even consistency of soft butter. Brush off any loose plaster to the patch and brush clean water over it and the edges of the surrounding ceiling. Apply a skim coat approximately 3 mm thick to the patch with broad sweeping strokes of the trowel level it out to match the surrounding ceiling. Flick with water and polish with a clean trowel, again using sweeping strokes.

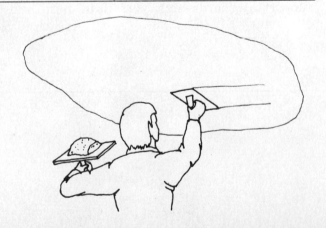

4

PARTIAL CEILING REPLACEMENT

*Where a large area of ceiling has been damaged,
but the remainder is firm, then a partial
replacement is adequate, particularly where cost
is more important than the look of the job.*

Cut back the damaged area of the ceiling to give
a firm regular edge, supported below a ceiling
joist. If the ceiling was lath and plaster, leave
laths in place, removing only those which are
already broken, or can be removed without
disturbing the edge of the plaster.

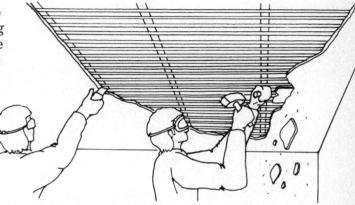

1

Measure the spacing between the joists from
centre line to centre line. If the joists are more
than 450 mm apart, then 12.5 mm thick
plasterboard is necessary, if less, then 9 mm is
adequate. Plasterboard can be purchased in two
sizes, 1,830×900 mm (6′–0″×3′–0″) and, more
commonly, 2,440×1,200 mm (8′–0″×4′–0″) and
the board size should be chosen to minimise
wastage.

When boards are fixed so that they are joined
under a ceiling joist, calculate where the edges
at right angles to the ceiling joists will meet and
mark these positions. Cut 'noggin' pieces of
50×50 or 50×75 mm softwood so that they fit
tightly between the joists. Skew nail these
noggins between joists so that their centre lines
coincide with the joints to the board edges, and
to each end of the room. No plasterboard edge
which oversails the edge of a joist by more than
200 mm should be unsupported.

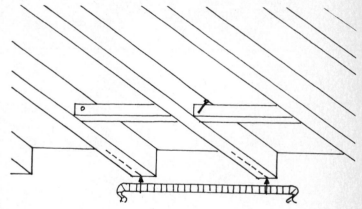

2

To cut plasterboard, lay it flat, cut through the
ivory surface and score the plaster core using a
craft knife against a straight edge or batten. Lift
the board, tap along the reverse of the cut so that
the remainder of the plaster core snaps along the
cut and the board bends. Cut through the grey
surface using the cut plaster core as a guide.

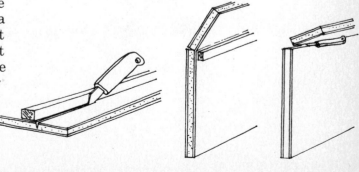

3

Using galvanised clout nails, nail the boards to the ceiling joists and noggins, if any, over the laths, with the ivory face of the board facing downwards, and with joints no more than 3 mm wide.

This operation is best carried out by three people, two standing on the floor supporting the board, using 'T' shaped wooden supports, while the third, standing on a platform, or using a box, stool or step ladder, nails it in place. Two people can nail boards in place, but they both need to work off a platform, supporting and nailing the board at the same time.

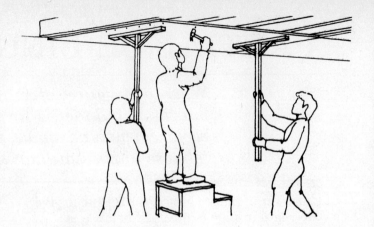

4
_____

When nailing the board in place take care not to hit or damage it with the hammer, and do not break the surface with the nail heads. Recess the heads of the nails with a punch, so that they are below the level of the board, but do not break the surface. Fill the nail heads using some filler, such as polyfilla and a palette knife. Cover the joints with 50 mm wide paper adhesive tape.

Grade the junction with the existing ceiling using a filler or bonding plaster.

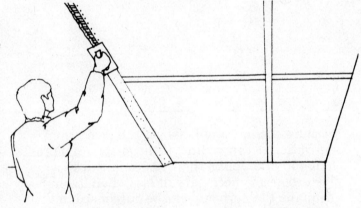

5
_____

The underside of a staircase known as the 'soffit' is normally plastered or plasterboarded to hide the construction, and more importantly to provide fire protection. The soffits of stairs should be plasterboarded or plastered even when hidden by a cupboard, for example in a basement, or at the bottom level of the stairs.

Take off the damaged soffit covering, both plaster and laths.

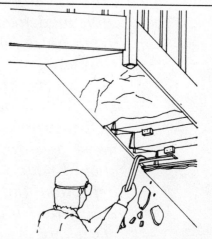

1

The underside of the stairs should be covered with a sheet of 9 mm plasterboard; nailed in place with galvanised clout nails.
The fixing will depend on the construction of the staircase.
(a) If the staircase has two structural sides or strings the plasterboard may be nailed to the edges of the strings with a piece of beading pinned to the side of the outer string to protect the exposed edge of the plasterboard.
(b) If the staircase is supported on two timbers running below the steps (carriages) then the plasterboard can be nailed to the carriages with its edges in between the strings.
(c) If neither of the above solutions is suitable, nail a batten or a series of wooden blocks to the inside of each string and 9 mm in from the edges. Cut plasterboard to fit tightly between the strings and nail on to the battens or a series of wooden blocks to the inside of each string and 9 mm in from the edges. Cut plasterboard to fit tightly between the strings and nail onto the battens or blocks.

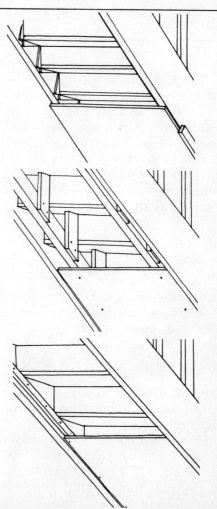

REPLACING A CEILING WITH PLASTERBOARD AND A PLASTER OR TEXTURE FINISH

Old plaster and lath ceilings have a tendency to fail due to the plaster losing its 'key' or hold, on the laths. Often the plaster can separate from the laths and act as a separate skin which will dramatically collapse if disturbed by an unusual deflection of the floor above, or attempts to cut holes for electrical wiring, or even the slamming of a door. Visible signs of failure are usually cracking or bowing of the ceiling, or both. Where such signs exist, the ceiling should be firmly pressed to determine how much it will move; a ceiling which is still keyed to the laths should not deflect more than 3 mm, with no deflection under ceiling joists, a failed ceiling will deflect under ceiling joists as well as elsewhere. When a ceiling has failed it is easier to replace it than to attempt a patch repair.

Take down the ceiling plaster and laths. Once an initial hole has been made in the ceiling break down the laths, pulling down the nearest ends so that plaster adhering to them will be brought down away from the body. When all the laths have been broken down, run the forked end of a crowbar or large claw hammer along the underside of each joist, pulling out or breaking off flush the nails used to hold the laths in place. Make sure that all the nails have been removed.

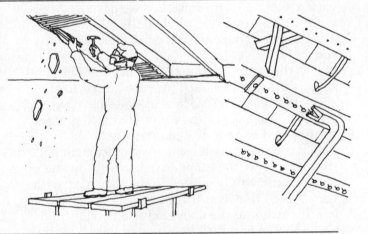

1

Measure the spacing between the joists from centre line to centre line. If the joists are more than 450 mm apart, then 12.5 mm thick plasterboard is necessary, if less, then 9 mm is adequate. Plasterboard can be purchased in two sizes 1,830×900 mm (6'–0"×3'–0") and more commonly 2,440×1,200 mm, (8'–0"×4'–0") and the board size should be chosen to minimise wastage.

When boards are fixed so that they are joined under a ceiling joist, calculate where the edges at right angles to the ceiling joists will meet and mark these positions. Cut 'noggin' pieces of 50×50 or 50×75 mm softwood so that they fit

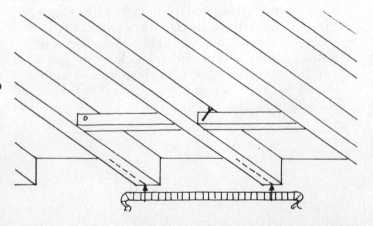

tightly between the joists. Skew nail these noggins between joists so that their centre lines coincide with the joints to the board edges, and to each end of the room. No plasterboard edge which oversails the edge of a joist by more than 200 mm should be unsupported.

Boards should alternatively span along and perpendicular to ceiling joists, so that there are no straight joints longer than one board length.

2

To cut plasterboard, lay it flat, cut through the ivory surface and score the plaster core using a craft knife against a straight edge or batten. Lift the board, tap along the reverse of the cut so that the remainder of the plaster core snaps along the cut and the board bends. Cut through the grey surface using the cut plaster core as a guide.

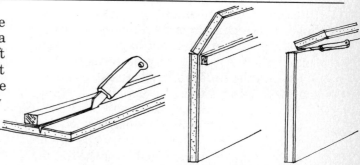

3

Using galvanised clouts nail boards to the ceiling joists and noggins with the grey face of the board facing downwards and with joints no more than 5 mm wide.

This operation is best carried out by three people, two standing on the floor supporting the board, using 'T' shaped wooden supports, while the third, standing on a platform, or using a box, stool or step ladder, nails it in place. Two people can nail boards in place, but they both need to work off a platform, supporting and nailing the board at the same time.

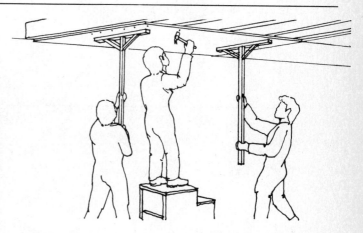

4

For a plaster finish, mix up 'board finish' plaster by adding it to clean water in a bucket or galvanised metal tub and mixing with a plunger until it has an even consistency like soft butter. Run a thin layer, say, 1 mm of this plaster down the joints and lines of nail heads to the boards in the first working area, an arm's length in any direction from the first corner. Bed 75 mm wide linen-scrim tape into this plaster so that it covers the joints, and nail heads laying flat against the boards. Using the trowel, apply a 3 mm thick coat of plaster to the boards and tapes in the working area and using broad sweeping movements of the arm level out the surface. Flick with clean water and give the plaster an initial polish with the trowel, using broad sweeping strokes, keeping trowel and plaster wet. Complete the ceiling in this way taking particular care to polish the junctions between working areas.

5

For a textured finish, mix up 'Artex' or 'Texit' until it has the consistency of thick, non-drip, emulsion paint. Using either a trowel, or a broad emulsion brush, run a thin layer of the finish down the joints in the working area, an arm's length in any direction, starting in one corner of the room. Bed 75 mm wide linen-scrim tape into this so that it covers the joints and sits flat. Using the brush or trowel apply an even coat to the boards, covering about one square metre at a time before texturing. Texture can be added by pulling the surface down using a flicking action of the end of the brush, or by dabbing it with a sponge wrapped in a polythene bag, or by using a textured roller. Alternatively patterns may be 'combed' into the finish; a swirling pattern may be achieved using a twisting action of the bag and sponge, or experimentation can produce other textures. Margins at the junction with the wall or around light fittings or stairwells can be achieved by drawing a wet brush over the finish. Working in this way cover the whole ceiling, taking care to match the pattern of the texturing as the work progresses.

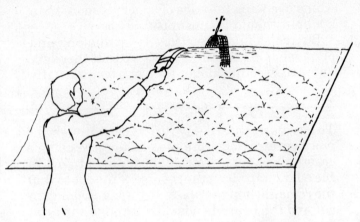

6 _____

6

FLOORS

6.01
RENEWING A FLOOR JOIST

(a)   Take out the damaged joist, measure it and obtain new or second-hand timber of the same section. Paint with a timber preservative and stand the ends in a bucket of preservative.

(b)   If the end of the joist was previously let into the wall, take out the end and clean out the hole in the brickwork. If the end had been affected by dry-rot play a blow lamp over the surrounding brickwork and in the socket. Spray with a suitable dry-rot inhibiting fungicide and leave to dry.

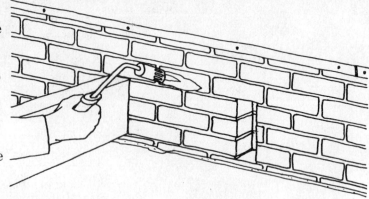

1

Purchase a galvanised metal joist hanger slightly less deep than the floor joist. Mark the depth of the bottom of the joist hanger onto the bottom of the end of the joist and cut a notch so that the hanger will be flush with the bottom of the joist. Using a 1:3 cement sand mortar lay a cut semi-engineering or dense brick into the socket in the brickwork so that its top surface supports the joist hanger at the right height for the floor. Point in the joist hanger.

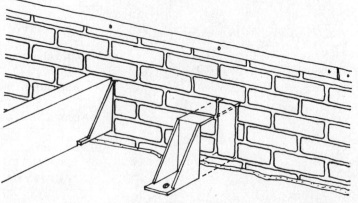

2

If the end of the joist was previously supported on a timber wall plate laid on top of the brickwork, remove the wall plate, or section supporting the joist. Play a blow lamp over surrounding brickwork and spray with fungicide. Replace the section of wall plate with timber of similar section treated with wood preservative and laid on polythene or bituminous felt which also runs up between the wall plate and the brickwork. Notch the new joist end so that it sits onto the wall plate at the correct level.

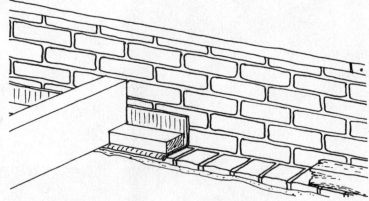

3

Place the new joist in position. Replace any 'herring-bone strutting' i.e. the criss-crossed timber battens which separate the joists. If the strutting is missing cut two lengths of 50×38 mm s.w. with 45° angles at each end and skew nail to both joists.

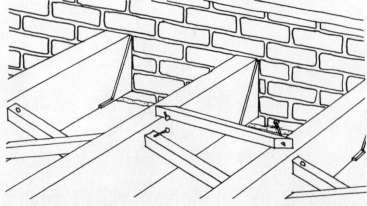

4

REPAIRING A JOIST

Where the end of a floor joist has rotted it may be replaced providing that the section to be replaced is less than ⅓ of the total span (distance between supports) of the joist.

Support the joist, or joists to be repaired from below using 'Acrow' props with planks or boards to spread the load at floor and ceiling level. If a number of joist ends are to be replaced, then the load should be carried down to the ground.

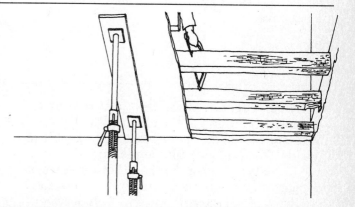

1

Cut off the rotten end of the joist so that sound timber is left. Treat the remaining section of joist with a combined fungicide and timber preservative. Obtain new or second hand timbers of the same section as the joist, paint it with timber preservative and stand the end that is to abutt the wall in a bucket of preservative.

2

If the end of the joist was previously let into the wall, take out the end and clean out the hole in the brickwork. If the end had been affected by dry rot play a blow lamp over the surrounding brickwork and in the socket. Spray with a suitable dry rot inhibiting fungicide and leave to dry.

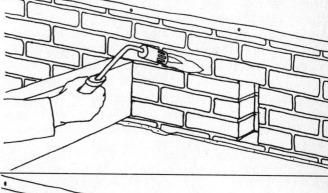

3

Purchase a galvanised metal joist hanger slightly less deep than the floor joist. Mark the depth of the bottom of the joist hanger onto the bottom of the end of the joist and cut a notch so that the hanger will be flush with the bottom of the joist. Using a 1:3 cement sand mortar lay a cut semi-engineering or dense brick into the socket in the brickwork so that its top surface supports the joist hanger at the right height for the floor. Point in the joist hanger.

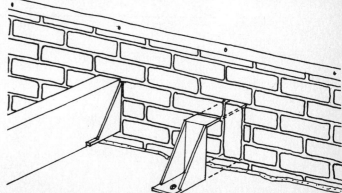

4

If the end of the joist was previously supported on a timber wall plate laid on top of the brickwork, remove the wall plate, or section supporting the joist. Play blow lamp over surrounding brickwork and spray with fungicide. Replace the section of wall plate with timber of similar section treated with wood preservative and laid on polythene or bituminous felt which also runs up between the wall plate and the brickwork. Notch the new joist end so that it sits on to the wall plate at the correct level.

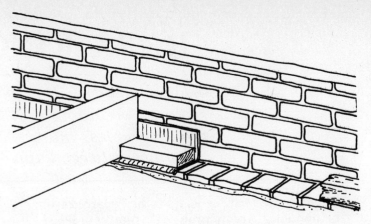

5

Either Cut a length of the new joist so that it overlaps the cut end of the old joist by 900 mm and using 12 mm diameter coach bolts, bolt it to the side. The bolts should be placed alternatively in the top third and bottom third of the joist and no nearer the end of each section than the depth of the joist. On each bolt between the two pieces of wood, there should be a toothed washer called a timber connector, and the head and nut of each bolt should tighten down on to a 38 mm diameter washer. There should be four or more bolts to each overlap.
Or

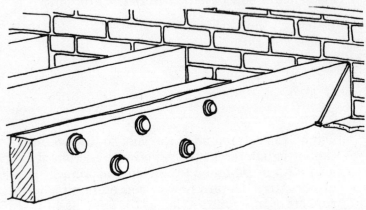

6

Cut a section of the new joist so that it fits between the cut end of the old joist and the wall. Cut two pieces of 25 mm thick timber or plywood the depth of the joist and 1·500 m long and paint them with preservative.

Place one of these 'splints' either side of the butt jointed joist and its new end. Using 12 mm diameter coach bolts bolt through the splints and joists, three times to each side of the joint, alternately to the top and bottom third of the depth of the joist with no bolt nearer than the depth of the joist to the end of each section.

7

RENEWING FLOORBOARDS

Before lifting floorboards, switch off the electricity, since cables may be positioned under boards and could be cut by tools.

Lift straight-edged floorboards by inserting a 100 mm flat cold chisel or bolster between the boards next to the end of the board to be lifted and lever end of board upwards. If the board is difficult to lift work alternatively on each side until it comes free. Insert the claw of a sturdy claw hammer under each side of the board, levering upwards and working down the length of the board, until all the nails are free and the board can be lifted free. Break off or pull out any nails or flooring 'brads' which are left in the top of the joist.

1

Lifting tongued and grooved floorboards is more difficult, involving cutting off the board's tongue, since the boards are 'secretly' fixed, i.e. the nails are hidden. Before cutting off the tongue of a board, check that there are no boards which have already been lifted or that there is not a board which has been screwed down so that services can be easily reached.

To cut the tongue off a tongued and grooved board a 'floorboard saw' or a pad saw will be necessary. With a pad saw, drill a row of small diameter holes along the join of the boards, join them together and insert the pad saw. Saw along the full lengths of the board with the saw as nearly horizontal as possible to avoid damaging pipes or cables below the sawcut.

A floorboard saw is used in a similar manner, but no starter holes are necessary. Insert a bolster into the saw cut and lever up whichever board lifts more easily. Subsequent boards can be levered up using a bolster and a claw hammer.

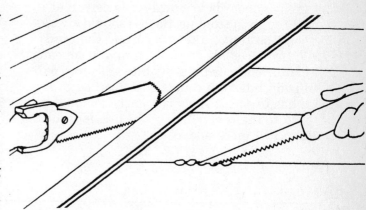

2

When replacing large areas of floor, the boarding should be cramped together to reduce problems caused by the timber drying out and shrinking. Cramping can be done using special devices which are clamped onto the floor joist and exert pressure on the side of the board to be nailed.

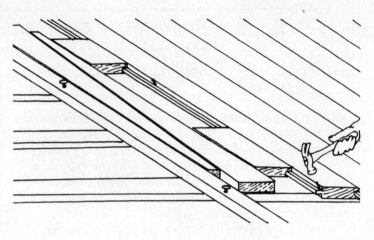

If these cramps are not available, take a length of floorboard and cut it diagonally down its length, crossing from 25 mm in from its bottom side to 25 mm from its top side, if the board is viewed standing on edge, thus forming two wedges. Nail a batten to the joists, parallel to and one wedge deep, plus 10 mm away from the board to be nailed. Place the wedges between the batten and the floorboard and tap them together until the board is tightly wedged against its neighbour. Nail the board in position, pull up the batten and renail it ready for the next board.

When cramping tongued and grooved boards, use off-cuts to protect the tongue of the board.

3

When nailing down straight-edged floorboards, always use cut steel flooring brads. For tongued and grooved boards use oval nails driven at a skew through the tongue. Boards should always butt joint on top of a floor joist and the brads should be placed about 10–15 mm in from each side of the floorboard, since cables and pipes will often run under the centre of a floorboard. If a board has been cut short of a joist, it should be cut back to the centre line of the previous joist and an infill piece added.

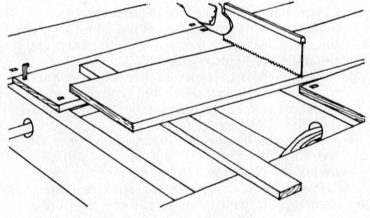

4

6.04
CHIPBOARD FLOOR

When replacing a large area of timber flooring it is sometimes cheaper and certainly a lot quicker to use flooring grade, tongued and grooved chipboard.

The flooring should pass under the skirtings. The chipboard may either be slipped under the skirtings to three sides of the room, or it may be simpler to remove all of the skirting and to replace it after the floor has been laid.

Lay down a section of the flooring grade chipboard, tongue facing outwards and countersink screw, once to each joist, adjacent to the tongue.

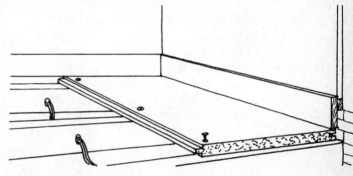

1

Slot the next section of chipboard in place and cramp it up tightly against the first. Cramping can be done using special devices which are clamped onto the floor joist and exert pressure on the side of the board to be nailed.

can be hired

If these cramps are not available, take a length of floorboard and cut it diagonally down its length, crossing from 25 mm in from its bottom side to 25 mm from its top side, if the board is viewed standing on edge, thus forming two wedges. Nail a batten to the joists, parallel to and depth of one wedge, plus 10 mm away from the board. Place the wedges between the batten and the chipboard and tap them together, until the board is tightly wedged against its neighbour. Countersink screw it in place, remove the batten and repeat the procedure.

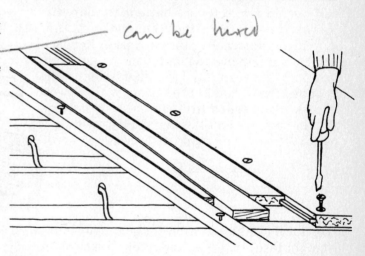

2

To lay the last board, remove the skirting, lay the board and replace the skirting.

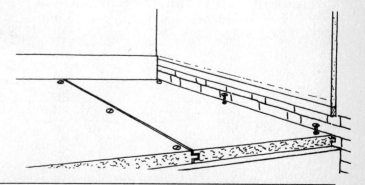

3

CHIPBOARD FLOORING ON A SOLID FLOOR

A solid floor which is both damp and cold can be made more comfortable by covering it with a damp barrier and a floating chipboard floor.

Take off skirting and hack off the plaster to 150 mm above floor level all round the room. Brush clean the solid floor and fill in any cracked or chipped pieces with 1:3 cement: sand: mortar. If the floor is rough then cover it with building paper, newspapers, cardboard, old lino or fine sand. Make sure there are no sharp edges, nails, or staples, which could damage the damp-proof membrane. Cover the floor with 1000 gauge polythene, lapping, folding and taping any joins that are necessary and taking the polythene 150–200 mm up the wall, or up to join up with a damp-proof course. (See Sheets 2.09 and 2.10).

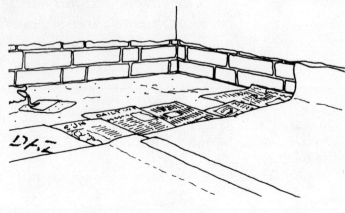

1

Cut 50×25 mm softwood battens to span the shortest dimension of the room and paint them with preservative. Lay the battens in Aquaseal 88 or a similar mastic, on top of the polythene and pack between any local depression in the floor and the bottom of the battens with plywood offcuts, also bedded in Aquaseal. The battens should be placed at 400 mm centres with a batten at each end against the wall.

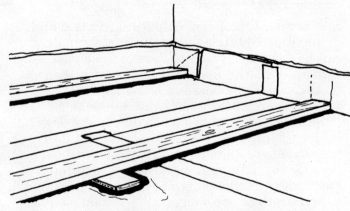

2

Lay down the first section of chipboard, 15 mm from the face of the wall and screw to each of the battens using screws which are not long enough to pass through the batten and pierce the damp-proof membrane. Lay down the next section of chipboard, press it up hard against the first and screw once to each batten. Repeat until the far wall is reached and again stop 15 mm short of the wall.

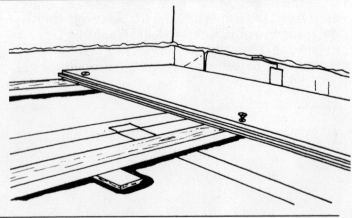

3

Lead the polythene up the wall and fix it into a mortar course in the brickwork which is 150 mm above the original floor level or connect it into the damp-proof course (See sheets 2.09 and 2.10). Fix a skirting to the wall to cover the polythene and blocked out from the wall if necessary to clear the 15 mm ventilation gap to each side of the floor. Drill ventilation holes to each section of skirting and cover them with an insect screen or fixed grille or cowl. This ventillation is to allow any water which might collect on top of the polythene due to condensation, to evaporate.

If the room is to be used as a bathroom or kitchen, mastic point the junction between the skirting and the chipboard, and seal the chipboard with three coats of polyurethane varnish.

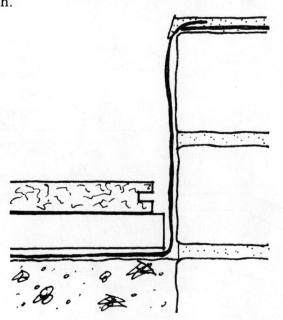 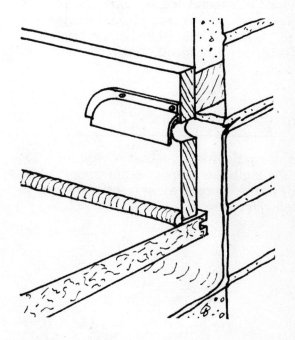

4

6.06
REPAIRING A SOLID FLOOR

A solid concrete floor which is damaged but is dry is worth repairing. However a damp concrete floor should only be repaired where the house has a short life, otherwise it should be replaced.

In either case, clean off the surface of the floor. Using a hammer and cold chisel chip out any cracks and chip the surface of any depressed areas to form a key. Paint the cracks and low points with Unibond or a similar adhesive. Fill the cracks with a 1:6 cement:sand mortar containing some Unibond and mixed fairly dry. Trowel the surface smooth. Allow the mortar to dry.

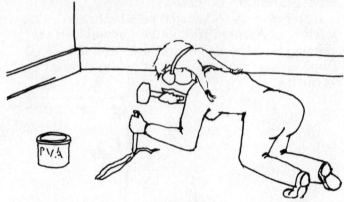

1

For a damp floor apply a coat of Aquaseal 10 which is a pitch and epoxy sealant. Spread it evenly on the floor and allow it sufficient time to harden before use.

2

A dry floor can be finished either with a resin sealer or a self-levelling screed, either of which will give a hard surface which should protect the patches from breaking up. A sealer is painted on with a brush but a self-levelling screed is mixed with water and then roughly travelled over the floor. It will then level out to give a hard smooth surface.

3

LAYING A NEW CONCRETE FLOOR

*Laying a new solid floor is a relatively simple,
but back-breaking task!*

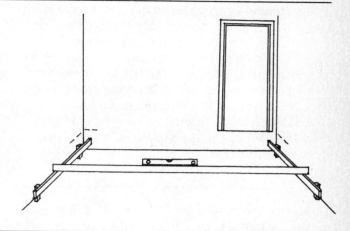

Break out any existing solid floor and dig out the
area of the floor to 250 mm below the intended
finished floor level. Next to each of two walls of
the room set up level boards with the top edges
125 mm below the required floor level. First
drive two pegs of 50×50 mm softwood into the
ground next to the wall at each end. Measure
down from the proposed floor level and nail a
plank to the pegs, using a spirit level to check
that it is level. Repeat for the second wall and
level across between the two boards to ensure
that they are at the same level.

1

Fill in the floor area, level with the tops of the
boards, with hardcore. Hardcore can be broken
bricks, broken concrete, stones, pebbles, glazed
or fired clayware, e.g. old pipes, or other hard,
inert materials. It must not contain metals,
which corrode, timber which rots, clay soil
which expands and contracts with changes in its
moisture content, or other materials which will
rot, dissolve or move when wet. The hardcore
must be compacted so that it will give a firm
base for the floor; pneumatic or mechanised
devices can be used or more simply a sledge
hammer and hand tamper. Check the level of
the hardcore by placing a plank across between
the two level boards. Take the time to compact
the hardcore evenly. When the hardcore is level,
pull out the level boards and fill in against the
walls with hardcore, compacting and levelling
to match the rest.

2

Cover the hardcore with a layer of fine sand,
raking and smoothing the sand to ensure that
there are no sharp protrusions which could hole
the polythene damp-proof membrane. Lay a
damp-proof membrane (D.P.M.) of 1000 gauge
polythene, taking it up the wall by 150 mm, or
until it laps into the damp-proof course (D.P.C.)
in the wall. Overlap any joints in the polythene,
by at least 200 mm and seal it either by twice
folding both pieces together, or by glueing, or by
sticking together with a plastic adhesive tape.

Once the polythene has been laid be very
careful not to puncture it. Keep it clean, avoid
walking on it unless absolutely necessary and

check that there are no nails or stones sticking
out of the soles of boots or shoes, before doing so.

3

Concrete should be laid, starting at the end of the room furthest from the door and working back and out of the room via the door. If there is more than one door, it may be advisable to block off all but the one to be used for access to prevent accidental damage to the new floor, caused by someone absent mindedly walking over it. A concrete mix of 1 part cement, to 2 parts sand to 4 parts coarse aggregate to a maximum size of 20 mm will normally be suitable for floor laying. This can either be delivered ready-mixed, hand-mixed or mixed with a mixer on site. It is not economical to order less than three cubic metres of ready-mix, which is enough to cover 24 square metres at 125 mm thick. Lay down boards, which are free from nails or splinters, from the door to the working area, as a runway for a wheelbarrow.

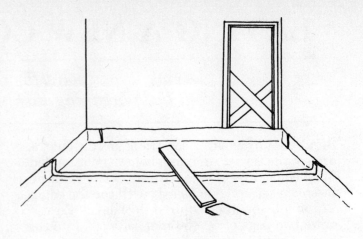

4

Take two lengths of 50×125 or 75×125 mm timber which are free from nails, splinters or any other sharp projections and are 1,200 to 2,000 mm long. Place them with one end against the end wall, parallel to and spaced approximately 450 mm from each side wall. Fill in between these forms and between them and the side walls with concrete, coming out a comfortable arm's span from the end wall, and no more than one metre. Using a piece of floorboard approximately 150 mm shorter than the width of the room, compact the concrete level with the tops of the forms. Use the board to rake off excess concrete.

5

Lift the forms out of the concrete and move them back to the start of the compacted concrete. Fill in the holes left by the removal of the forms with concrete, using a trowel. Compact and level the infilled sections so that they match the surrounding floor. Polish the concrete with a metal float to give it a hard 'shiny' finish, or with a wooden float for a matt finish. A matt finish is most suitable if additional floor finishes such as floor tiling or levelling screed are to be laid.

6

In this manner fill in between the forms, level and finish the floor, working down the room towards the door. For the last section, change direction so that the forms are parallel to the area of floor already laid. The final area adjacent to the door is laid with the forms going through the door.

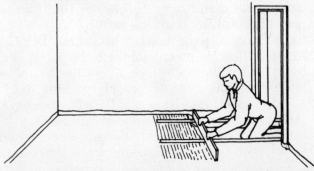

7

6.08
HARDBOARD SHEETING TO A FLOOR

Covering timber floors with hardboard is sometimes necessary to ensure that smoke cannot enter a room from the one below. It is also useful when a level working surface is required; for example when laying floor tiles, fitted carpets, etc.

Hardboard can also be stuck to a concrete floor as a floor finish or a basis for a finish.

On a timber floor use standard hardboard if it is to be covered with a carpet, otherwise use an oil-tempered hardboard which is both harder and more water resistant. First check that there are no nails, pins, tacks, etc. sticking up from the floorboards, removing or recessing any that are found. Nail down any loose floorboards. Lay the sheets smooth face upwards and stagger the joints between sheets where possible. Pin to the floor with hardboard pins at 150 mm centres along the edges and at 300 mm centres over the remainder of the board.

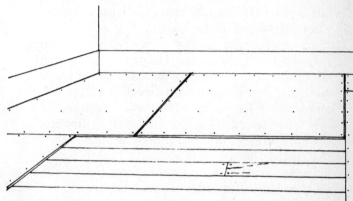

1

On a concrete floor, first check that there are no sharp irregularities that will damage the sheeting and fill in any cracks, holes, or localised depression with 1:3 cement:sand:mortar. Clean off the surface of the concrete and spread a rubber resin or synthetic latex adhesive over the area to be covered by the first board. Lay a sheet of 6 mm oil-tempered hardboard, smooth face upwards, bedded into the adhesive. In this way cover the whole of the floor, butting the edges of the hardboard sheets and where possible staggering the joints between sheets.

2

INSECT TREATMENT

When a floor has been attacked by wood-worm or beetle, but the timber still has adequate strength, it can be treated with an insecticide. Remove any timber boards or sections of joist that have been badly weakened by insect attack and burn them. Replace the missing sections as appropriate. (See Sheets 6.01, 6.02, 6.03 and 6.04).

Lift every third floorboard and inspect the joists and undersides of the boards. Fill a hand-pressurised garden spray with a suitable insecticide, e.g. Rentokil. Using the spray, soak the underside of the boards and both sides of each joist, working in both directions from each lifted board. Leave for a few days before nailing down floorboards to allow the smell to disperse. N.B. Spraying should only be done in a well ventilated room, while wearing protective clothing, goggles and a respirator. Read and observe the safety instructions on the insecticide container.

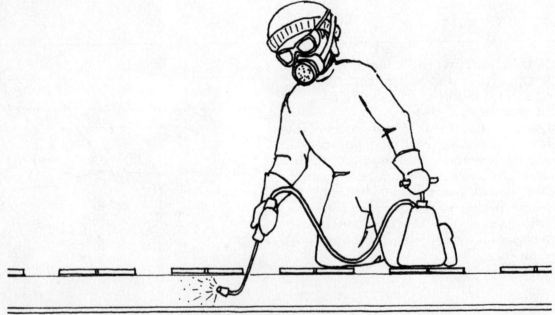

6.10
REPLACE WALLPLATE

The joists to timber floors are frequently supported on timber 'wallplates' or 'nailing plates'. Since these pieces of timber usually sit directly on brickwork they are often rotten.

The rotten 'nailing plate' or 'wallplate' can be replaced in small sections if no other work is required to the floor, or in complete lengths if the joists are being removed, repaired or temporarily supported.

Remove the rotten section of nailing/ wallplate. If dry-rot is suspected, play a blowlamp over the surrounding brickwork to burn off any spores (these may not be visible), and when the brickwork is cool, spray it with a fungicide. Lay polythene or bituminous felt on top of the brickwork and up the wall in the case of a wallplate. Replace the rotten wall/nailing plate with timber of similar size, treated with a wood preservative.

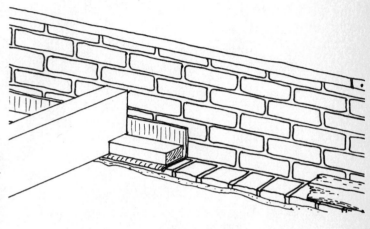

1

6.11
SLEEPER WALL

Timber ground floors are frequently supported on 'sleeper' walls or on secondary joists carried on brick piers to reduce the spans and thus reduce the thickness of the floor joists. When replacing or relaying a ground floor it may be necessary to rebuild these, either because they have failed or are no longer level, or to provide better ventilation.

Take down the defective sleeper wall or brick pier and if the bricks are to be reused, clean off the old mortar. Using a 1:1:6 mortar, and the techniques described in Sheet 2.16, rebuild the pier or the sleeper wall. When building a sleeper wall the bricks are laid with a gap of a third of a brick long between each brick, so that air is free to move beneath the floor. A damp-proof course should either be built into the wall or pier, or be placed between the brickwork and any nailing plate.

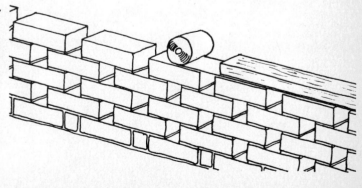

1

7
STAIRCASES

REPLACING A NEWEL POST

Newel posts are the sturdy posts at each end of a flight of stairs which support the handrails. If a house has been left empty, they are often broken off.

The exact method of replacement will depend on the construction of the staircase, and the positions of the post. Since the handrails, which are supported by the newel posts, exist partly to prevent people falling, the posts must be adequately fixed. Some typical methods of fixing replacement newel posts are described here; the principles should be applied in other cases.

A newel post at the bottom of a flight of stairs which has been broken off above the top of the 'string' or side of the staircase can be simply replaced. Cut off the broken stub to give a tidy end. Then cut a length of ex 75×75 mm softwood the full height of the post. Bolt the newel post on to the stub of the old using two 12 mm diameter coach bolts.

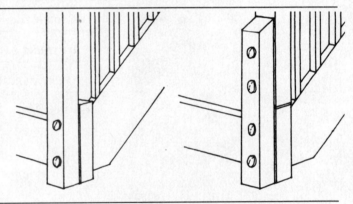

1

Where the newel post at the bottom of a flight of stairs has been broken so that an inadequate stub, or no stub is left, then fixing a replacement is more difficult.

(a)   If the staircase is constructed so that there is a timber 'carriage', i.e. a 75×50 mm or larger timber supporting the stairs, directly behind the string, then the newel post can be bolted to it, using two 12 mm diameter coach bolts. Again, for the newel post an ex 75×75 mm softwood post is cut to the height of the newel post above the floor.

(b)   Where the bottom of the flight is resting on a floor joist, take up the floorboards. Cut an ex 75×75 mm softwood newel post the height of the old newel post, plus the thickness of the floorboards and the depth of the floor joist long. Cut a section out of the side of the newel post 25 mm deep and the depth of the floor joist long. Using two 12 mm diameter coach bolts with toothed timber connectors, bolt the new newel post to the side of the floor joist. If practical or possible screw the side of the staircase on to the newel post. Cut the floorboard to fit around the newel and replace.

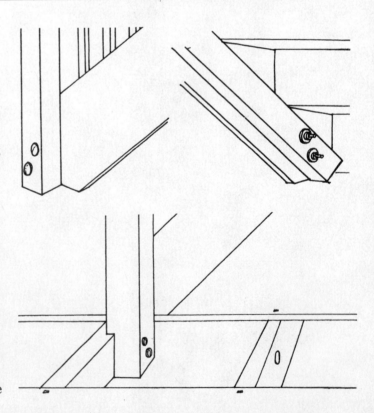

2

At the landings the top of the flight of stairs will be carried on a floor or a trimmer joist. The new newel post, ex 75×75 mm should be bolted to this joist, using two 12 mm diameter coach bolts. It may be bolted to the joist over an existing facing timber, or bolted and fitted against the side of the joist, as described in 2(b) above.

3

When fitting a new newel post against the side of the staircase or a facing to a landing, do not cut it to fit around any projecting 'nosing' since this will weaken the newel. Instead mark the position of the newel, saw through the nosing with a tenon saw until the saw cuts are flush with the face of the side. Prise off the section of nosing between the two saw cuts if it is an added nosing. If the nosing is integral to a tread riser or the edging to the landing, carefully remove the section between the saw cuts with a sharp chisel until it is flush with the face.

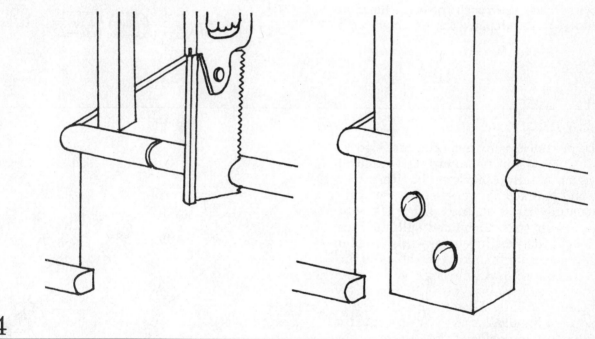

4

A NEW HANDRAIL

When providing a new handrail it is often difficult to reproduce the original staircase design which will often have incorporated curved, or specially shaped sections. Where straight sections are missing, however, it is often possible to obtain a matching or similar section handrail from a Timber Merchant.

Saw off a section of handrail timber to fit tightly between the two newel posts. At each end drill two clearance holes for No. 8 screws at an angle of approximately 30°, starting 30 mm in from the end on the underside. With a countersink bit, or a sharp chisel, cut a pocket so that the screw is recessed just below the surface of the underside of the handrail. Using two 62.5 mm long No. 8 screws, screw each end of the handrail to the newel posts. Replace the balusters as sheet 7.06.

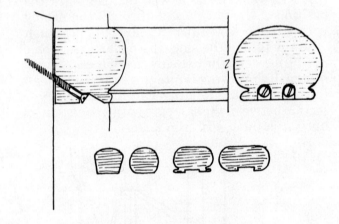

1

A handrail on the wall side of a staircase can either be provided using a special moulded handrail or by mounting an ordinary handrail moulding on handrail brackets. In either case they should be fixed at every second vertical stud to a studwork wall, or at 800 to 900 mm centres to a solid wall. A moulded wall-mounted handrail is fixed by drilling holes perpendicular to the flat face, countersinking the holes on the curved face and screwing through so that the flat face sits hard against the wall. The screw head is then normally filled flush.

An ordinary handrail is fixed by screwing the brackets to the underside of the rail, and then screwing the brackets to the wall. In both cases fixings to solid walls should be made with 50/62.5 mm No. 8 or No. 10 woodscrews, into a fibrous or plastic plug previously placed. When fixing to stud walls, a guidance hole should be drilled into the studs before screwing.

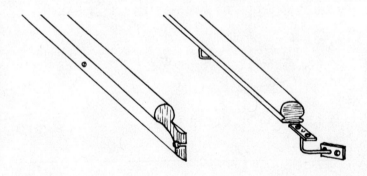

2

NEW BANNISTERS

Bannisters should be constructed so that the top of the handrail is 900 mm high at the landings and 840 mm vertically above the pitch line which is a line connecting the nosings of the treads of the steps. To comply with the Building Regulations, there should be no gap in the balustrade large enough to allow a sphere of 100 mm diameter to pass through.

In accordance with Sheet 7.01 bolt a newel post into position at the top and bottom of each flight. The newel posts should be cut from ex 75×75 mm softwood, and the tops can be shaped or capped. A simple shaping is to saw off the top from each face at a constant angle to produce a pyramidal top, finishing off with a file or sharp plane before sanding.

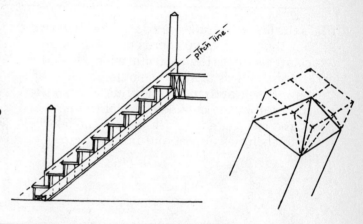

1

Two or three second-hand floorboards, depending on their width, or two pieces of ex 225×25 mm softwood are used to form the top and bottom rails. Place the top board so that it overlaps the stair-side faces of the newel posts and the top edge is 840 mm vertically above and parallel to the pitch line and mark both sides of the newel posts on the board. Cut the ends of the board so that they are flush with the outside edges of each newel post. Cut a piece of ex 50×25 mm softwood so that it fits between the marks for the inside edges of the newel posts. Screw this batten to the newel post side of the top edge of the board, so that it is flush with the top edge. Round off the top of the board and the batten so that it is smooth to form the handrail. Screw this handrail twice to each newel post, countersinking the screws.

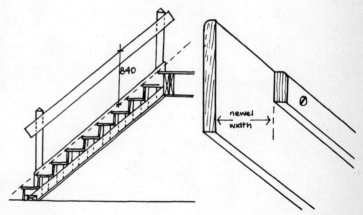

2

At 1,000 mm to 1,200 mm centres or midway
between the newel posts an intermediate
support should be introduced. The intermediate
support should be cut from ex 100×50 mm
softwood so that it completely overlaps the side
or string of the staircase and fits beneath the
handrail batten. Angle the top and bottom of the
support so that they match the batten and the
bottom of the stair side. Also cut an angle to the
top support so that it tapers into the handrail.
Screw the support to the side of the stairs with
four countersunk screws and screw the handrail
to the support with two countersunk screws.

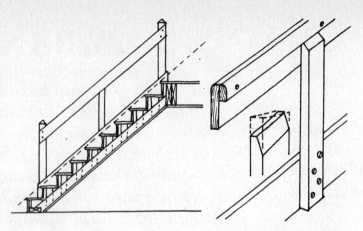

3

Place the lower board(s) parallel to the top board
so that there are equal spaces between them,
which are not more than 100 mm wide. Mark the
ends of the boards against the outside edges of
the newel posts and cut the ends flush. Screw the
boards against the outside edges of the newel
posts and cut the ends flush. Screw the boards
twice to each newel post and intermediate
support.

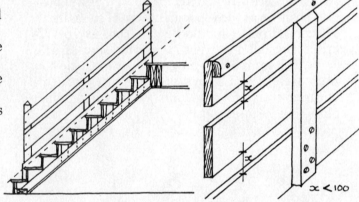

x < 100

4

7.04
RENEWING BALUSTERS

Balusters are the slim vertical members which give the handrail support between the newel posts and provide a fence against falling. They may be simply a square section, or elaborately turned pieces of wood. In some cases iron balusters may be interspersed with the wooden ones to give greater strength.

Carefully lever out the remains of a broken baluster, pulling out the nails from the underside of the handrail and the recess in the floor or step. Clean out the recess with an old chisel.

1

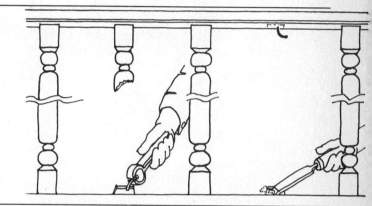

If second-hand matching balusters are not readily available, measure the height from the underside of the handrail to the bottom of the recess, both front and back if below a sloping handrail; also measure the sides of the recess. Take a square-section timber to match the size of the recess, usually ex 25×25 mm softwood and cut to the required length.

If the handrail has a recess to receive the top of the balusters, fit the top end first, then the lower end. If not, place the lower end in its recess and slide it under the handrail until the baluster is vertical. Skew nail the bottom of the baluster with lost head nails. Before skew nailing the top,

clamp an offcut of wood against one side to keep it in position while nailing. Recess the nail heads with a punch.

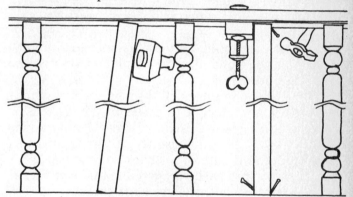

2

7.05
RE-FIXING LOOSE BALUSTERS

When re-fixing loose balusters pull out any securing nails that are visible with a pair of pincers.

Re-skew nail using lost head nails and punch heads below the surface of the baluster.

When skew nailing the tops of the balusters to the handrail hold them in position with a block of wood clamped to the handrail.

REPAIRING A STAIR NOSING

The nosing on a stair is the part of the flat tread of a stair which projects over the face of the vertical riser, and is usually rounded. Nosings are also carried round to the side of the stair or of the landing.

Cut the remains of the broken nosing off flush with the face of the riser using a pad or floorboard saw. Clean out the recesses to each side of the stair, if it is enclosed by two strings, with a chisel.

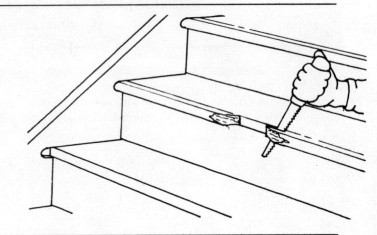

1

Measure the depth and projection of the nosing to the other steps and the width of the nosing. If the stair is enclosed by two strings the new nosing should be the distance between the two strings, plus the depth of the recess to one side only.

Cut a suitable section of timber to size and shape the front edge with a plane to match the other nosings.

Drill and countersink the new nosing in three places, and place it in position. When positioning between two strings place one end in a recess so that the nosing is flush against the tread and then move it back so that it sits halfway into each recess. Glue and screw the new nosing to the edge of the tread.

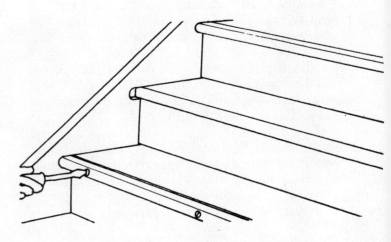

2

Where the centre of the nosing is damaged it may alternatively be repaired by cutting out the damaged section with two angled cuts back to the face of the riser and chiselling out between the cuts.

Cut a piece of batten to fit tightly in the shape so formed. Screw and glue the infill piece in position. Using a plane or rasp shape the repair to match the nosing.

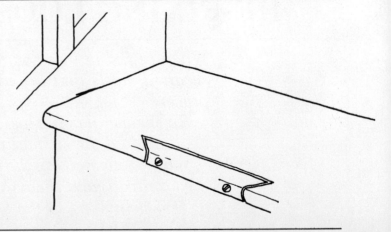

3

REPAIRING A TREAD

It is important that the rise of each step in a staircase is equal since unequal steps can cause loss of balance. If one or two treads need repair it is safer to cover all of the treads to maintain equal steps.

Cut off the nosing to the tread if damaged. Screw and glue a piece of ex 32×25 mm softwood to the face of the riser to replace the nosing.

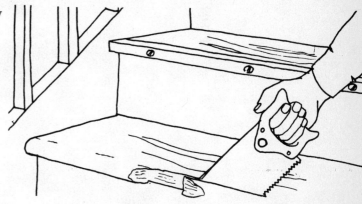

1

Cut out a piece of 9 mm plywood to cover the tread and the new batten. Glue and pin the plywood to the tread and the batten. Round off the edge of the plywood and the batten to provide a nosing.

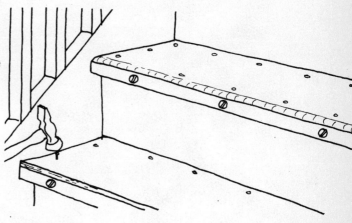

2

8
FIREPLACES

BLOCKING UP A FIREPLACE FOR A GAS FIRE

If the surround to the fireplace is damaged or no longer required it should be removed. Surrounds are normally held in place by metal brackets and mortar, or just mortar and can be levered off with a crowbar. Before removing the surround, sweep the chimney. (See Sheet 8.04).

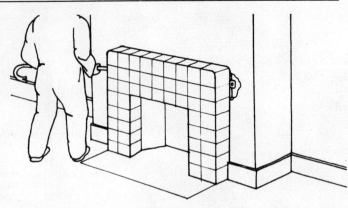

1

Construct a frame of 50×50 mm softwood to fit tightly into the opening in the chimney breast or surround if retained. The frame can simply be butt jointed and nailed at the corners. Fit the frame into the opening and wedge it in place with wedges cut from offcuts. Alternatively the frame can be masonry nailed when fitted into a brick chimney breast. The face of the frame is recessed 6 mm from the face of the surround, or the finished surface of the chimney breast.

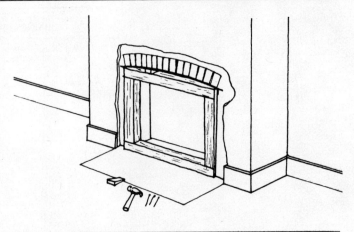

2

Cut out a piece of 6 mm thick asbestos-free fire insulating board such as 'Masterboard' to fit the opening. On it mark the position and size of the vent outlet to the gas fire. Drill holes at the corners of vent position and cut out with a pad saw. Drill clearance holes in the board and screw it to the frame using metal cups for the screws to facilitate removal for sweeping and to reduce the likelihood of cracking the board.

Make good plasterwork around board. (See Sheet 2.02).

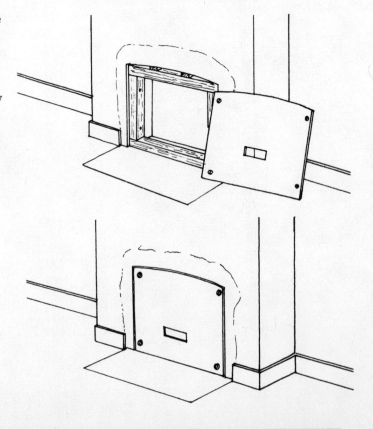

3

BLOCKING UP A FIREPLACE WITH PLASTERBOARD

If the surround to the fireplace is damaged or no longer required it should be removed. Surrounds are normally held in place by metal brackets and mortar, or just mortar and can be levered off with a crowbar. Before removing the surround, sweep the chimney. (See Sheet 8.04).

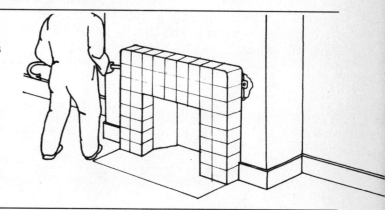

1

Construct a frame of 50×50 mm softwood to fit tightly into the opening in the chimney breast or surround if retained. The frame can simply be butt jointed and nailed at the corners. Fit the frame into the opening and wedge it in place with wedges cut from offcuts. Alternatively the frame can be masonry nailed when fitted into a brick chimney breast. The face of the frame is recessed 9 mm from the face of the surround, or the finished surface of the chimney breast, 12 mm if it is to be skim plastered to match the surroundings.

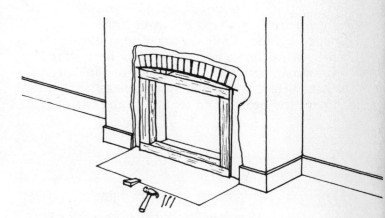

2

Cut a piece of 9 mm plasterboard to fit the opening. With a sharp craft knife cut a vent hole for a gas fire, or a 200×150 mm opening central to the sheet. Nail the plasterboard in position using galvanised clout nails, ivory face outwards if fitted in a surround, or if it is to be left unplastered, grey face out if it is to be plastered.

3

Recess the nail heads, taking care not to damage the board. Fill the nail heads or skim plaster. (As Sheet 2.04).

Fit a fixed vent incorporating an insect screen over the hole in the plasterboard to ventilate the chimney. Without this vent, condensation and rain penetration within the chimney can cause damp patches to appear.

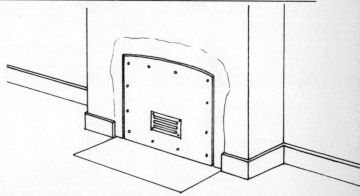

4

8.03
BRICKING-UP A FIREPLACE

Remove the fireplace surround. Surrounds are normally held in place by metal brackets and mortar, or just mortar and can be levered off with a crowbar. Sweep the chimney. (See Sheet 8.04).

1

Using the techniques described in sheet 2.16, fill in the opening, using bricks or lightweight concrete blocks, laid on top of the hearth. The brickwork should be flush with the brickwork of the surrounding chimney breast and include an opening of 225×75 mm approximately 450 mm above the hearth and central to the opening.

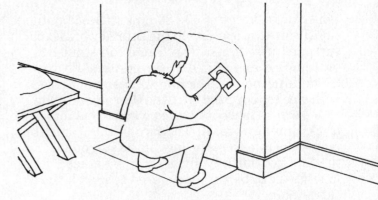

2

Using the techniques described in sheets 2.01 or 2.02, finish the bricking up to match the surrounding wall surface. Fit a fixed vent with an insect screen over the hole in the brickwork. Without this vent, condensation and rain penetration within the chimney can cause damp problems.

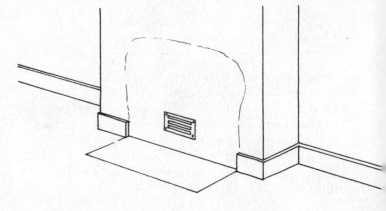

3

CHIMNEY SWEEPING

Chimney sweeping produces a lot of dust and soot. In a furnished room take care to cover up or remove the furniture.

Cover the chimney opening with an old sheet or cloth weighted down on the mantlepiece and against the fire surround. Leave enough material in the centre to gather up into a fold through which the brush can be introduced.

1

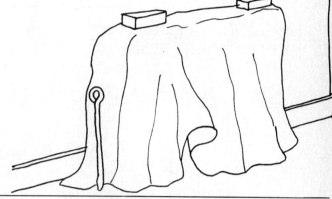

Screw the flue brush onto the first cane, place the brush in the fire place and drape the cloth around the cane, grasping it with one hand so that a tight fitting sleeve is formed through which more canes can be fed. Weight the bottom of the cloth to hold it down onto the hearth.

2

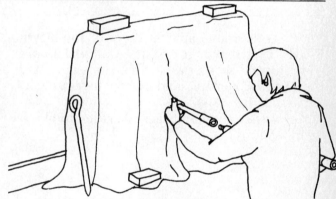

Screw on the next cane and push the brush up the chimney. Screw on each cane in succession, pushing the brush upwards. If the brush sticks at a bend in the flue, pull it back a little way and push upwards again, repeating this sawing action until the brush moves upwards. The canes must only be turned clockwise, if they are turned anti-clockwise they will unscrew and block the chimney. When the brush has passed out of the chimney pot it will move freely.

3

Pull the brush back down the chimney, taking care not to unscrew any of the sections. Unscrew each cane as it comes out of the cloth. Shovel up the soot brought down the chimney and clean up.

4

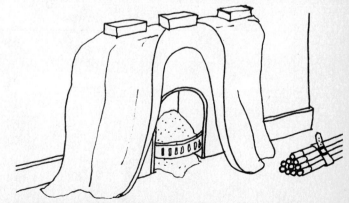

8.05
FITTING A FIRE SURROUND

Fire surrounds are available in many different forms and it is not possible to cover all types, but the techniques described are applicable in most cases.

Where a fire surround is to be fitted to a chimney breast, hack off any plaster in the area of the surround.

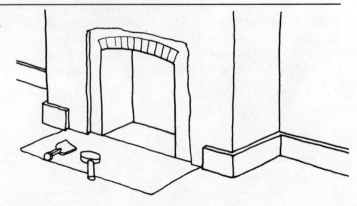

1

Place the surround against the wall and if it is fitted with fixing lugs drill the wall and secure the surround with rawbolts. If no lugs are fitted then use 1:3 cement:sand mortar to secure the surround.

Plaster fire surrounds may be stuck in place with bonding plaster.

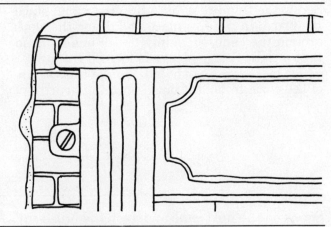

2

Replaster around the surround. (See Sheet 2.02).

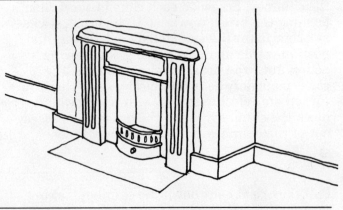

3

9
ELECTRICS

ELECTRICITY – GENERAL PRINCIPLES AND TECHNIQUES

Background

Electricity is produced all over the country in generating stations powered by coal, oil, water and nuclear fuel. It is fed into a system of distribution cables, transformer stations, sub-stations and mains, known as the National Grid. Although the power stations are administered by the Central Electricity Generating Board, the local supply is administered by regional, or area boards.

The Electricity Boards are obliged to supply electricity to potential consumers, but are entitled to make a charge for connection to their main. In remote areas the cost of connection is often prohibitive, thus relieving them of this obligation. Electricity boards have also successfully contested their obligation to supply squatters but will usually do so in return for a substantial deposit.

The electricity in the National Grid is supplied at a very high voltage (132,000 volts) to regional transformer stations, which break it down for local high voltage distribution (11,000 volts). It is further broken down by sub-stations into the supply which runs in the street main, which is a three phase 415 volt supply. An individual house will normally receive a single phase supply which is rated at 240 volts, although a house split into flats may receive two or even three phases.

Once inside the house the Electricity Board's main will terminate in a box referred to as the supply or company head. The company head is usually made of black bakelite, and will have a small lead seal, which will break if the casing is opened. Inside the head is a main fuse for each phase supplied. This company head as its name implies is the property of the Electricity Board and should not be tampered with.

Adjacent to the company head and connected to it by two wires known as tails is sited the electricity meter. This is also the property of the Electricity Board, and will have a seal to show if it has been opened. If the supply to the house has been disconnected the meter may have been removed. Other methods of disconnection are removal of the main fuse from the company head and cutting off the cable in the street. In the latter case, reconnection can cost anything from one to several hundred pounds.

Theory

Electricity will flow when there is a pathway from the source back to the source, or from the source to the earth. In order to control its flow, it is carried by conductors which are surrounded by insulation. The conductors are materials which offer little resistance, such as most metals, and in particular, copper, which is used in domestic wiring. Insulants are materials which offer a high resistance to electricity, so that it does not flow through them. These are materials such as plastic, ceramic, rubber and PVC. PVC is most commonly used as insulation in modern domestic wiring.

The two forms of wiring used in domestic installations are flex and cable. Flex is made up of conductors of thin copper strands wound together and coated in PVC. There are three, one for the 'live', one for the 'neutral' and one for the 'earth'. These three insulated conductors are then held together by an outer PVC sheathing. Flex with only a live and a neutral conductor is also available. Cable is made up of three conductors, but the earth is a single uninsulated copper wire; the 'live' and the 'neutral' are both insulated with a PVC coating. All three are bound together in an outer PVC sheathing. Insulation for the earth wire is provided separately as green, or green and yellow sleeving. Flex, as its name implies, is intended to be flexible, and is normally round in section. It is used for connections from movable appliances to plugs, or for pendant bulb-holders in light fittings. Cable is meant for fixed use in the running of circuits. It is rather flat in section and should not be used in locations where it is subject to flexing, since it can break internally, causing a fault or short circuit.

In order to provide the pathway for electricity to flow, cables are laid from a distribution point, the consumer unit, to various outlet points. When an appliance is plugged into an outlet it completes the circuit. The electricity flows to the appliance via the live wire and returns via the neutral wire.

The flow of electricity generates heat owing to the resistance provided by the conductor. The amount of heat generated is dependent on the thickness of the conductor, and the amount of electricity flowing through the wire.

This production of heat is used in electric fires and light bulbs where the thickness of the wire is reduced and it is made of a metal which provides resistance to the flow of electricity, but is able to withstand high temperatures. In a light bulb the conductor, the filament, is surrounded in an 'inert gas' to prevent oxidation and becomes so hot that it glows white, producing light.

The production of heat can be harmful to cables and flexes, since it causes insulation to break down, to become brittle, or in extreme cases to catch fire. It is therefore important to use cable or flex which is thick enough for the purpose, not to overload a circuit and to fit the correct size fuses, so that if an excessive demand for supply is placed on the cable of flex the fuse melts. A circuit breaker can be used in place of a fuse but its function is the same, to provide a weak link which will fail before the circuit becomes overloaded, or when a fault occurs.

The correct size fuses and cables for domestic wiring circuits are as follows:

Circuit	Fuse	Cable Size
Lighting Circuit	5 amp	1 or 1.5 mm²*
Radial Power	20 amp	2.5 mm²
Ring Power	30 amp	2.5 mm²
Radial Power	30 amp	4.0 mm² or 6.0 mm²*
Radial Power	45 amp	10.0 mm²
Radial Sub Main	60 amp	16.0 mm²

*N.B. The choice of cable size will depend on the length of cable.

For appliances the size of the fuse may be marked either on the body of the appliance, or a metal tag. The fuse is rated in relation to the current flow which is measured in amperes which will be abbreviated to amp, amps or A. The amount of electrical power required by an appliance is measured in watts (W). Some appliances will only be marked in watts, but it is possible to calculate the appropriate size fuse for the plug by dividing the wattage by the voltage (V) which is standardised at 240 volts,

i.e. $\text{Amps} = \dfrac{\text{Watts}}{\text{Volts}}$

therefore for an electric fire marked 3KW (one kilowatt is a thousand watts) the correct sized fuse is:–

$\text{Amps} = \dfrac{\text{Watts}}{\text{Volts}} = \dfrac{3000}{240} = 12.5$

The nearest standard fuse size is 13 amps.

Just as water has a natural tendency to flow to the lowest point if unrestrained, electricity has a tendency to take the path of least resistance to earth. The function of the earth wire is to provide a low resistance path to earth in the event of a fault developing. However, paths of less resistance may be offered, for example, by water or gas pipes, or by somebody coming into contact with a conductor. In order to eliminate danger caused by pipework becoming live, it must be earthed or bonded. (See Bonding). In order to minimise the possibility of receiving an electric shock some simple rules should be obeyed.

1 Always switch off at the mains and remove the fuses before doing any work to electrical installations.
2 Always pull out the plug before doing work on any appliance.
3 When appliances are not in use switch the socket off, or pull out the plug, or both.
4 Never take a mains power appliance, be it radio, television, tape recorder, or fire, into a bath or shower room.
5 Never switch on, plug into, or work with electricity with wet hands.
6 When working with electrical circuits:–
DO NOT touch metal pipework.
DO NOT work bare-foot.
DO use insulated tools with plastic or wooden handles and touch them only by the handles.
DO wear rubber-soled shoes, or stand on an insulating mat or a block of dry wood when working in damp conditions, or in contact with the ground.

Electric Shock

Electric shocks can vary in intensity depending on what other objects the person is in contact with, and therefore how good a path to earth they provide. A slight shock will often only be felt as a mild 'tingling' sensation or a slight numbness. More severe shock can cause burns, induce a state of shock, or stop the heart. In bad cases of electric shock the victim is often 'stuck' to the source of the shock, unable to move. In these cases:–

1 Switch off the power at the mains.
2 If it is not possible to disconnect the power, then use an insulated material to move the victim, but do not touch them, since until disconnected from the power they are 'live'. Use dry wood, plastic or rubber as an insulant; for example, a broom handle, the legs of a wooden dining chair, plastic bowl or container.
3 Once the victim is disconnected from the supply, check that they are still breathing. If they are, then call an ambulance and treat them for shock. If not send someone to call the ambulance, while artificial respiration is administered to the victim.
4 The most commonly known form of artificial respiration is mouth-to-mouth resuscitation or the 'kiss of life'. This should only be used if the casualty has stopped breathing.

(a) Lay the victim on their back and clear any obstruction such as false teeth from their mouth. If the tongue has fallen back, blocking the throat, then pull it back into position.

(b) Pull back the head, lifting the chin until the throat is clear. Pinch the nostrils closed (except when the victim is a small child).

(c) Cover the mouth (mouth and nostrils for a small child) with your own mouth and blow gently checking that their chest rises. If the chest does not rise, pull the head further back and try again.

(d) When the chest rises remove your mouth and let the chest fall before once more gently blowing into the victim's mouth.

(e) Continue in this way, repeating the blowing about every five seconds for up to four hours, until the casualty begins to breath of their own accord, or until help arrives.

5 To treat for shock lay the victim down, with the legs slightly elevated by placing a cushion under the feet. Loosen any tight clothing at the waist and collar and keep the casualty warm. Do not give them very much to drink, even if they ask for it and especially do not give them alcohol or sugary drinks, both of which will interfere with any anaesthetic that may be necessary later.

GENERAL TECHNIQUES

1 Bonding/Earthing

Bonding is a technique used to ensure that all fixed metalwork such as the bath and kitchen sink, as well as gas and water pipework all offer an equal path to earth. This prevents someone getting a shock by acting as a link on touching a piece of metal which has become 'live' due to a fault, and another piece of metal which is earthed.

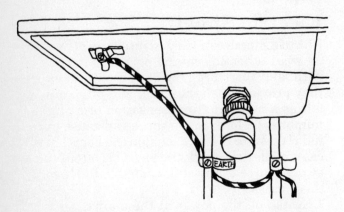

Bonding is carried out by attaching an earth clip to pipes, the underside of a sink or bath and any other fixed metalwork. A length of single insulated 16 mm² earth wire is taken from the clip and connected into the earth at the consumer unit or meter. Bonding should be carried out after the earth circuit has been completed.

The whole system may be earthed in one of three ways:

(a) The earth is connected to the incoming gas or water main. This technique is no longer favoured since both gas and water mains are now frequently replaced in plastic. The Electricity Boards will therefore not normally accept this form of earthing for new installations.

(b) The earth may be connected to the sheathing of the incoming electricity main. This is the favoured method of earthing but is not always possible and the Board should be consulted about earthing to their main if no connection already exists.

(c) Where it is not possible to earth to the Board's main, the earth may be connected to an earth rod buried in the ground. A special copper earth rod or a length of copper pipe has to be driven into or buried in the ground close to the position of the incoming main. The earth connection from the consumer unit is then attached to the earth rod.

The main earth connection should be made with a clip which will not corrode and the conductor should be insulated and protected against corrosion. Special earth clips are available which are made of a corrosion resistant alloy and which have a tag embossed with the slogan 'Earth Connection – Do not Remove!'

1 Electricity Board Connection

The Electricity Board have a right to test any electrical installation before connecting a supply or meter. The tests they are empowered to carry out are:

1 Test of Polarity. To make sure that all fittings are correctly connected.

2 Test of the Earth, for continuity and effective earthing.

3 Test of Insulation, to ensure adequate insulation.

4 Tests of Continuity of circuits.

They will also usually take off the front cover of one or two fittings to ensure that earth connections have been insulated with 'green sleeving'. It is advisable to carry out these tests before asking the Board to connect, since if the system fails they charge for each subsequent test. If an electrician has been employed to carry out the installation or modifications, then ask for a Test Certificate to present to the Board. If the installation is purely a do-it-yourself effort then the Board will carry out a more rigorous test and may make a small charge. Since a safe electrical installation is essential to personal safety it would be foolish to try to avoid having the system adequately tested.

Once the system is ready to be tested by the Board, ask them to make the connection. In practice the Electricity Boards can take rather a long time to process a request for a connection. Forward planning and early discussion with the local office is therefore always advisable. If a new supply is to be laid because there has not been a supply in the past, or the old one has been disconnected in the street, the Board will probably require payment in advance of the reconnection.

If the electrical installation is not complete but power is required to run power tools, and to provide lighting, a builder's supply may be requested. The Board will connect a meter provided that there is a piece of chipboard or blockboard to fix the meter to, and a consumer unit or a switched fuse box to which to connect the tails from the meter. Builders' supplies are charged at a high rate per unit of electricity used, so it is good sense to make the transfer from a builder's supply to a normal supply as soon as possible.

2 Stripping Cable and Flex

When stripping cable or flex it is important that the insulation is not damaged. To achieve this, score the outer sheathing of the cable or flex working from the point where the sheathing is to be stripped back towards the end with a sharp knife. At the end cut down through the sheathing.

Open the cut sheathing, grasp the inner conductors and peel back the outer sheathing. Cut off the peeled back outer sheathing by cutting parallel to the conductors.

To strip the ends of the conductors, either set the jaws of a wire stripper to the diameter of the conductor, close the jaws over the insulation, twist and pull, or using a sharp knife slice away the insulation working with the knife almost parallel to the conductor and towards the end.

Never cut around a cable or flex since when removing a sheathing the insulation to conductors may be damaged and when removing insulation from a conductor the conductors themselves can be damaged. Either can cause a fault or short circuit.

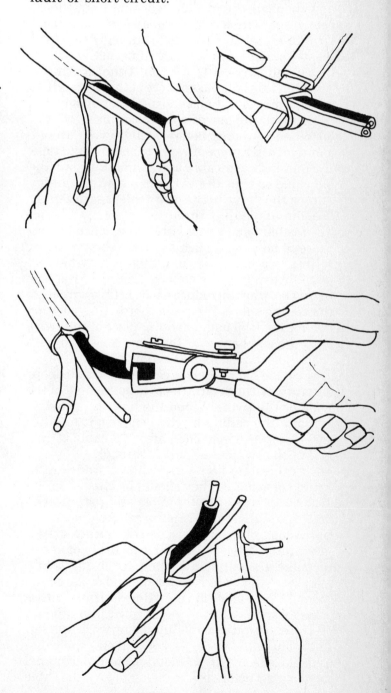

3 Concealed Wiring

Concealed wiring is run in floor or ceiling spaces, in stud walls or below the plaster on solid walls. The following points should be observed.

(a) Below floors wiring should not run alongside pipework and should cross all pipework at right angles. The cable can be left unclipped.

When crossing floor joists, the cable should not be taken through a notch in the joists, since this will weaken the joist and leave the cable vulnerable to nails when the floor boards are replaced. Instead in the middle third of the joist, about 75 to 100 mm from the top drill a hole large enough to take the cable or cables.

(b) When positioning power points above the skirting, mark the position of the mounting box and chop out the plaster, working from the centre out, with a cold chisel and club hammer. Drill or chisel downwards to cut out part of the plaster stop-batten which will normally be just below and parallel to the top of the skirting. Through this hole pass a piece of thin wire with a hook formed on the end and use it to pull a loop of cable up to the power point position.

(c) When rewiring, before withdrawing an old cable, attach a piece of twine to one end and tape the join between cable and twine. Pull out the old cable so that the twine is pulled through. Attach the twine to the new cable, again taping the join and pull it through.

(d) If cable has to pass through a space where there is no access, such as above the top floor ceiling to a back addition, then it may be possible to pull it through by 'fishing'. From one fitting position introduce a loop of thin wire into the ceiling space. From another fitting position fish for the loop using another piece of thin wire with the end bent over to form a hook and with the other end attached to some twine.

Once the hook is felt to connect with the loop, carefully withdraw the loop, keeping hold of the hook or the twine. When the hook is pulled through the ceiling by the loop, use it to pull through the twine. Then attach a cable to the end of the twine and pull it through.

(e) If cables are being run when a stud wall is being constructed they should be clipped to the studwork. However, for an existing studwork wall it is sufficient to run the cable between the plasterboard or laths. To do this, either drill down into the top of the wall from the floor above or make a small hole in the plaster and feed cable into the wall. Fish for the end of the cable from the hole made at the fitting position, with a piece of wire with the end formed into a hook.

(f) When running cable in plasterwork, chisel out a channel in the plaster and clip the cable into place. A plastic or metal protective channel can be used before replastering to give the cable greater protection from damage from wall fixings.

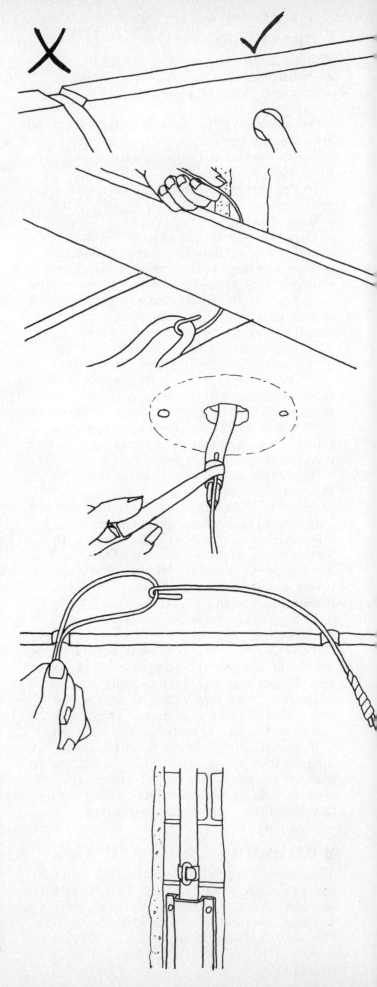

4 Surface Wiring

Surface wiring is most commonly used to run cable down walls and across ceilings where there is no access above. Much of the wiring is run below floors in the same manner as for concealed wiring.

(a) All surface wiring below 1.5 m (4'–6") should be covered by a protective capping to protect it against damage. This capping is available in one, two, or three cable widths.

(b) Surface wiring can be run in mini-trunking which is a plastic 'U' section which is attached to the wall. The cable is then run in this channel, holes being cut in the walls of the channel adjacent to fittings or at junctions. Once the cables are in position a lid is clipped into place to close the trunking.

(c) To pass surface wiring through the wall, drill a hole through the wall; do not attempt to take wires around door frames, since this can result in damage to the cable, even if the door and door stop are notched to accept the cable.

5 Clipping

There are two forms of cable clip in common usage; metal buckle clips and plastic saddle clips.

(a) Buckle clips are supplied without pins, but the one-size clip will fit most cable sizes. The clip is nailed to the wall using an appropriate pin and the cable placed over the pin. The buckle is bent up round the cable and the strap end pulled through and then bent back on itself, when the cable is securely is position. These are the best clips for use below protective capping.

(b) Plastic saddle clips are available to fit specific cable sizes, one or two cables and flexes. It is therefore necessary to have a variety of clips. The clips come complete with a steel pin which will not usually be capable of penetrating brickwork, when it must be replaced with a masonry pin. Plastic saddle clips are easier to use than metal buckle clips, but are more obtrusive.

Cables need not be clipped when they run concealed horizontally or below a floor. When cables are exposed they should be clipped at 750 mm intervals. Concealed vertical drops of cable should be clipped at the top and at 900 mm intervals, if they drop more than 5 metres.

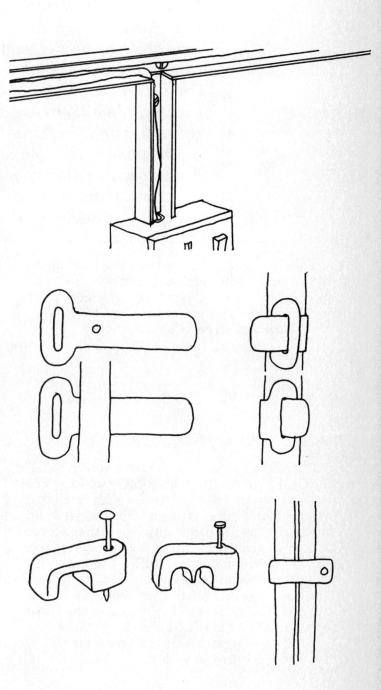

In houses divided into flats, it is necessary to run sub-mains to each flat. The electricity meters may be grouped along with the company head if this is in a communal area or easily accessible from each flat, or the meters can be placed in each flat. In either case it is important that the consumer units are situated inside each flat. The connections to the company head or the meters are the responsibility of the Electricity Board, but the sub-mains must be provided by the occupant or owner of the house.

In each flat, select the most suitable location for the incoming sub mains and fix a 600×750 mm piece of block or chipboard to the wall. Screw the board to the studwork, or drill and plug the brickwork and screw it to that.

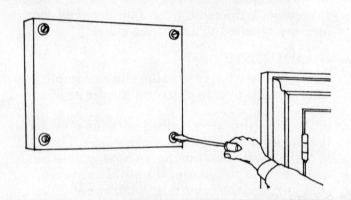

1

Sub mains may either be run in 16 mm² T and E PVC cable, or the Electricity Board may require it to be run in 'Pyro' or MICC (Mica Insulated Copper Core) cable. It is advisable to call in an electrician or the Electricity Board themselves if 'Pyro' is required, since it is very expensive to buy in short lengths and difficult to install requiring special seals and connections to keep the mica insulation free from moisture.

When using 16 mm² cable, flatten the cable, removing any kinks and clip it into place, running a separate cable from the company head to the board in each flat.

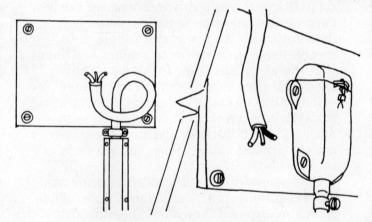

2

Whether the meters are to be positioned adjacent to the company head or in each flat, it is usual to protect the sub-mains with an isolator adjacent to the company head position. An isolator is simply a box containing an off/on switch and a suitable fuse, in this case 60 amps. To the company head end of each sub-main, connect an isolator, connecting the earth, sheathed in green sleeving, to the earth block, the neutral into the neutral terminal which is usually sited above the switch and the live into the live terminal, which is usually sited above the switch position. To the incoming side of the isolator connect live, neutral and earth 'tails' in 16 mm² single conductors, long enough for the Electricity Board to connect into the company head or the meter.

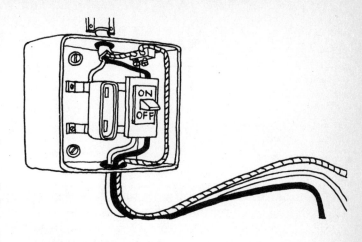

3 _____

At the flat end the sub-mains cable is either left ready for connection to the Electricity Board's meter, or connected directly into the consumer unit, in which case the live and neutral are connected to the incoming live and neutral positions on the switch and the earth is sheathed in green sleeving and attached to the earth block. When all the necessary connections have been made, request a connection of the meters and the tails by the Electricity Board.

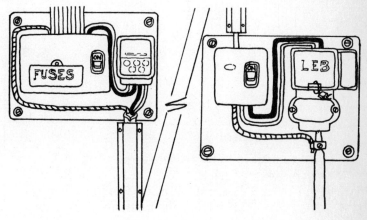

4 _____

INSTALLING A CONSUMER UNIT

The Consumer Unit is where the incoming mains supply is divided via fuse protected connections, to serve the different house circuits. It also contains the mains ON/OFF switch.

Consumer units are available in different sizes depending on the number of fuses and may be of metal, bakelite, or bakelite with a wooden base. 'Wylex' manufacture an inexpensive unit which is easy to wire. Decide on the number of fuses required by adding up the number of circuits required. An average two-storey terraced house may need the following:

30 amp ring mains	– 2 (one per floor)
5 amp lighting circuit	– 1
30 amp cooker point	– 1 (even if using gas it is sensible to run a cooker point for future use)
20 amp immersion heater	– 1 (to a fused spur)
Total	= 5

It is sensible to buy a consumer unit with at least one extra fuse way to allow for some future expansion; for example, an extra ring main. When purchasing the consumer unit you must also know the number and capacity of the fuses required, since the fuse socket and the fuse holder are different for each fuse rating. At this stage it is also necessary to select the type of fuse to be used; rewirable, cartridge or miniature circuit breakers. Although miniature circuit breakers (MCB's) are more expensive than the other two varieties they are easier to reset and cannot easily be tampered with. They are therefore the safest.

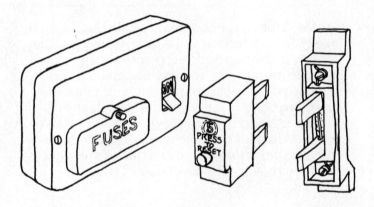

1

The consumer unit is normally mounted on a board adjacent to the electricity meter. If the consumer unit is to be fitted in a position remote from the meter, the Electricity Board may require that there is an isolator switch adjacent to the meter and that the connection between this isolator and the consumer unit is run in 'Pyro' which is difficult to use and is best avoided if possible.

Before mounting the box on the wall, cut out a slot in the wooden base or knock out the preformed holes in a metal box, for the entry cables and the tails to the metre. If using a metal box, fit rubber 'grommits' in the holes to protect and insulate the cables from the metal. Screw the base of the box to the board, or the wall.

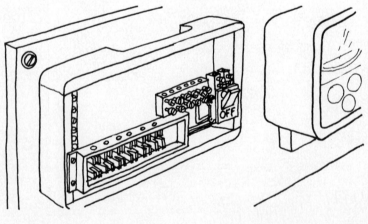

Bring the two cables for a ring main into the box and strip back the sheathing to 10 mm inside of the box. Take the live wires to the first fuse position on the left-hand side of the box. Cut to length. Strip back enough insulation on each to fit into the brass terminal, loosen the terminal screws, twist the ends together, push them into the terminal and tighten down the two screws. The terminals for the neutral bar are not opposite the fuse ways. Take the two neutral wires to the first terminal on the left-hand side of the neutral bar, cut to length, strip back enough insulation on each to fit into the terminal, loosen the terminal screws, twist the ends together and push them into the terminal and tighten down the two screws. Take the two earth wires to the lowest terminal on the earth

bar, cut to length, cover each in green sleeving, loosen the terminal screws, twist the ends of the wires together, push them into the terminal and tighten down the screws.

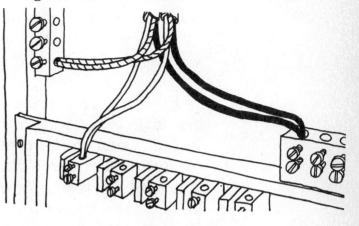

3

Screw a 30 amp fuse holder to the first fuse position. Connect each of the circuits to the consumer unit in the same way, although the lighting and other radial circuits will only have a single cable to connect. As each is connected attach an appropriately sized fuse holder to the fuse position.

When all of the circuits are connected the 'tails' may be attached to the consumer unit. If the tails are already connected to the meter it is sensible to get the Electricity Board to make the connection, since these are live. If there are no tails then connect tails of singly insulated 16 mm² conductors, a green (green and yellow) to the earth bar, a red (brown) to the live bar and a black (blue) to the neutral bar. The live and neutral tails should be long enough so that they can be connected to the meter and the earth so that it can be connected to the sheathing of the incoming main's supply cable. These connections should be made by the Electricity Board.

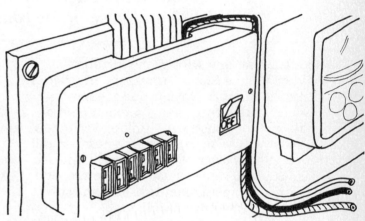

4

Once the tails are connected, replace the unit's cover and fit in the fuses. Screw on the fuse box cover and switch on. In some boxes the labelling of the main switch may seem confusing when the cover is off because it is designed to be seen through a window. The common convention is that when the switch lever points up it is 'OFF' when it points down it is 'ON'.

Before replacing the fuse cover, list the fuses and the circuits they serve, either on the inside of the cover, or on a piece of paper stuck or taped to the inside of the cover.

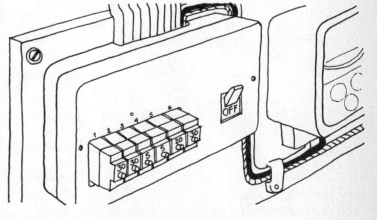

5

There are two types of power circuit, radial and ring. A radial circuit leaves the consumer unit and connects to a number of sockets, stopping at the last.

For a ring circuit the cable is continued from the last circuit back to the consumer unit. The capacity of a radial circuit is limited and modern power installations are done in the form of a ring. There may be a spur taken off the ring provided each spur has no more than two sockets on it, and there are more sockets on the ring than on spurs. Ring circuits are run in 2.5 mm² PVC sheathed cable with copper conductors and have a 30 amp fuse in the consumer unit.

Before starting any wiring, the installation should be planned to determine the number of outlets, the number of rings and the most economical cable runs. Draw a rough plan of each floor of the house and, thinking about how each room will be used, mark the number and position of the power points required. Since sockets cost the same as double adaptors, and are much safer, plan to provide enough sockets to adequately meet forseeable needs.

Regulations allow that a ring circuit can serve up to a 1,000 sq. ft. (90 sq. metres) of floor area, but some consideration should also be given to the likely load on the ring. A ring main having a capacity of 30 amps can supply 7½ kilowatts of power. If at one time a ring is expected to serve three 2 kilowatt electric fires, it has very little spare capacity for any other appliances and the fuse will blow if an electric kettle (normally requiring 3 kilowatts is plugged into the ring. In this case two rings splitting the loads are necessary. Where electric fires are not being used as the main form of heating a maximum of

1

15 outlets (double sockets counting as 2) including spurs on a ring is a reasonable guide within the 1,000 sq. ft.

Having plotted the positions of the outlets and the consumer unit, check that no sockets have been positioned in bathrooms, and that no sockets are close to the kitchen sink. Now work out the shortest route for the ring main, connecting in remote sockets with spurs and adjusting some socket outlet positions, and plot this on the plan.

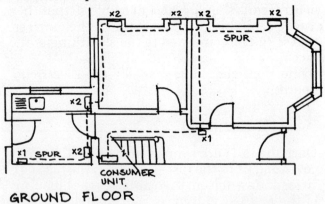

GROUND FLOOR

Having decided whether the circuits are to be concealed or surface mounted (see 9.01) proceed to run the 2.5 mm² PVC sheathed cable keeping it free from kinks. Run the cable to each power point position on the ring and leave a loop. Do not cut the cable but take it completely round the ring, excluding any spurs. As the cable run proceeds straighten the cable and clip it in place, leaving a generous loop, say 300 mm long at

each socket position. Once the ring is clipped, cut the cable and run the cables for the spurs from appropriate socket positions on the ring leaving a 200 mm tail and clipping the cable to spur socket positions.

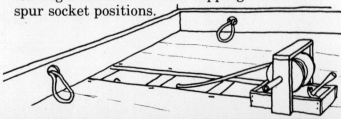

2

Fitting a surface-mounted power socket. When using surface mounted sockets a pattress or base plate will give useful extra room. Cut the loop and break out the appropriate preformed holes in the pattress, pull the cable through and screw the pattress to the skirting. If the socket is to be screwed to the wall then mark, drill and plug both the pattress and the socket-fixing holes before screwing the pattress to the wall. Strip back the PVC outer insulation to about 10 mm inside of the pattress.

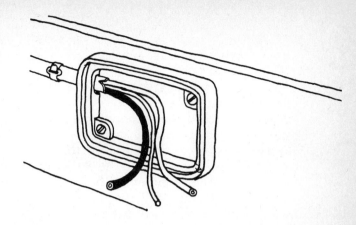

3

Hold the back of the socket up to the pattress and bend the conductors at the point that each will reach the appropriate terminal, red – live, black – neutral, copper – earth. Strip off the insulation to the live and neutral between the bend and the end. Cut a piece of green (green and yellow) earth sleeving and push it over the earth conductor and into the outer PVC sheathing so that it covers the conductor between the sheathing and the bend.

Repeat this process for the second ring cable and any spur cable leading from the socket.

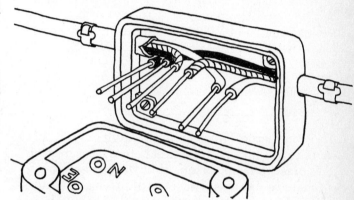

4

Twist the sets of conductor wires from each cable together
    earth to earth
    live to live
    neutral to neutral.
Loosen the terminal screws on the socket and pull the braided conductors through the appropriate terminals.

Screw the socket to the wall or skirting board. Pull the conductors to take up any slack and tighten down the terminal screws. Cut off the excess wire and screw on the top of the socket.

This technique allows very little scope for future alterations since the connections are left tight. Therefore in concealed wiring leave slack leading into the fitting, or in surface-mounted wiring a tuck of cable in the pattress to allow for future alterations.

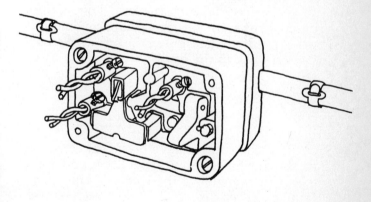

5

Fitting a flush-mounted socket. Flush-mounted sockets are normally used only with concealed wiring, and are fitted against a metal back box. Back boxes are available in two depths, one being plaster depth which gives very little room and is not really suitable for power sockets except for a spur with only one connecting cable. Knock out the metal blanks to the entry positions for the cables. Screw the box to the side of a wooden stud or chop a hole in the brickwork with a cold chisel and hammer so that the box will be flush with plaster. Drill and plug the wall and screw the box to the wall. Fit rubber 'grommits' (rings) to the holes through the box to protect the cables and pull the cables through into the back box. The wall should now be made good around the box.

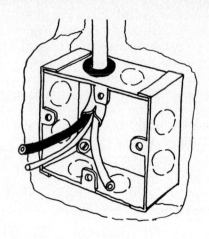

Cut back the PVC outer sheathing to 10 mm from the grommit.

6

The conductors must be left long enough to be fixed to the back of the socket before it is screwed into place, but not so long that the box becomes full of wire. Hold the socket in position and bend the conductors from the first cable so that they will connect into the socket with the minimum of slack. Cut the conductors to length and strip the insulation off the last 10 mm of the live and neutral, and cover the earth with green sleeving to within 10 mm of the end. Repeat for the other ring cable and spur if appropriate and twist together the exposed conductor ends earth to earth, live to live, neutral to neutral. Loosen the terminal screws, fit the appropriate conductors into the terminal and tighten the screws. Screw the socket back to the box.

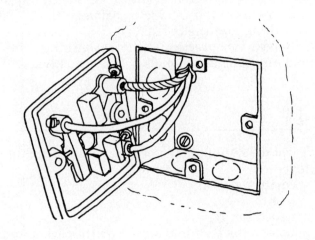

7

Once all of the sockets have been connected check the ring for continuity (See 9.10), and then connect the two ends of the ring into the consumer unit or fuse box. The conductors are twisted together, earth to earth, live to live and neutral to neutral, and then connected together into the live terminal for the fuse-way, the neutral bar and the earth bar.

A 30 amp fuse or mini-circuit breaker is then fitted into the fuse-way. (See 9.03).

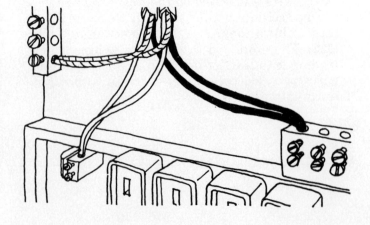

8

Lighting circuits are radial from the consumer unit and can be junction box or loop in systems. They are run in 1.5 mm² PVC sheathed cable and have a 5 amp fuse way in the consumer unit. One circuit is normally adequate for the average house with less than twelve points.

On a sketch floor plan or the plan used for the power circuits mark the positions of the lights required. Lights are normally placed in the centre of a room, but more than one light may be required, or a light placed to hang in a special position. In addition, wall points may be required for spotlights. The fittings in one room may be controlled from one switch, or several switches. Switches should be positioned so that as you enter a room they are by the opening side of the door at chest height. On stairways it is normal to switch the lighting so that it can be controlled from the top and bottom of each stair, which requires special two-way switches and wiring.

Select the system to be used; junction box wiring is easier to install since the boxes can be wired from above, and it uses less cable than a loop-in system. However, since three-way terminal ceiling roses are only marginally cheaper than four terminal roses, it is more expensive on fittings because a junction box is used for each switch. On balance a loop-in system is probably cheaper than a junction box system, although it uses more cable and does require all connections to be carried out below

the ceiling, usually on a step ladder. If, in future, it may be difficult to gain access from above, for example, where a sound-insulating floor is being laid or the upper floor is being made into a separate flat, then use loop-in wiring with unclipped cable, which will allow future rewiring to be done by pulling through first a cord, and then a new cable when extracting the old wiring, all connections for which are below the ceiling. A mixture of loop-in and junction box wiring can be used in the same circuit. Mark the cable runs on the plan.

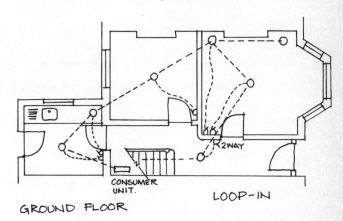

GROUND FLOOR   LOOP-IN

1

Run the 1.5 mm PVC sheathed cable to each ceiling rose, lighting point or junction box position and allow a 300 mm loop of cable at each. In old houses, floorboards above ceiling roses or lighting circuits may be loose or screwed rather than nailed. Junction boxes can be screwed to the sides of joists or to walls.

Ceiling roses should be screwed to a piece of board, nailed between the joists. First cut a piece of floorboard to fit tightly between the joists just above the ceiling. In the centre of this board drill a hole large enough to take the cables coming into the ceiling rose. Place the board between the joists just above the ceiling and nail it to the joists. Alternatively the rose can be held to the

bottom of a joist by one screw, the other screw going into the ceiling finish, but this is less satisfactory.

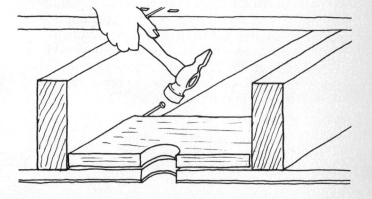

2

Wiring a 5 amp four terminal junction box. The four terminals in the junction box are:–

           Common live
           Common neutral
           Common earth
           Switched live

The incoming and outgoing cables are connected live to the common live, neutral to the common neutral and earth to the common earth terminals. The switch cable is connected earth to the common earth, live to the common live and the 'neutral' conductor is connected to the switched live terminal. The cable to the ceiling rose is connected earth to the common earth, the neutral to the common neutral and the live to the switched live terminal. The cables enter the junction box via preformed cut-outs which are broken out as needed, and the outer sheathing is cut back to within 10 mm of the junction box casing. The earth wires are sheathed with green sleeving.

    In junction box wiring three-terminal ceiling roses or bulb holders are used, the terminals being simply live, neutral and earth. The pendant flex connects into the live and neutral terminals.

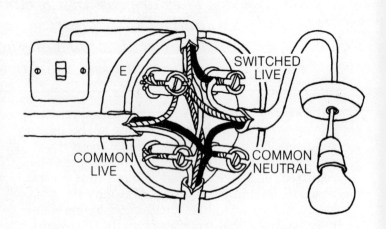

3 _____

Wiring a four-terminal ceiling rose in a loop-in system. The four terminals which are sometimes three strip terminals and one screw terminal are:–

Common live	(three holes for strip terminals)
Common neutral	(three holes for strip terminals)
Common earth	(single screw terminal)
Switched live	(two holes for strip terminals)

    The incoming and outgoing cables are connected, live to the common live, neutral to the common neutral, earth to the common earth. The switch cable is connected, earth to the common earth, live to the common live and 'neutral' to the switched live. The pendant flex is connected, live to the switched live and neutral to the common neutral. The pendant should be hooked over the restraining hooks before screwing back the top, since this takes the strain off the electric connections.

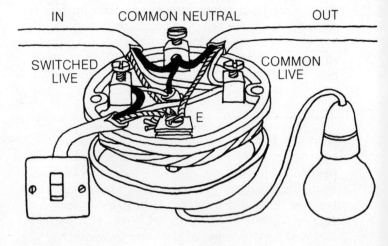

4 _____

A one-way switch is wired in the same manner for either system. If concealed wiring is being used, the metal back box can be a shallow 'plaster depth' box. Break out a cable entry hole in the box and line the entry with a rubber grommit to protect the cable. Fix the box to the brickwork or to the studwork. Sheath the earth conductor in green sleeving and attach it to the earth terminal on the back box. The live and neutral conductors are connected into the switch terminals, live to the top terminal, neutral to the bottom.

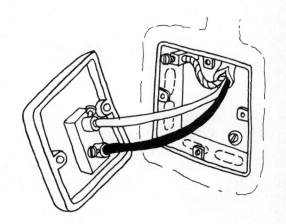

A surface-mounted switch is fitted in the same way, except that the switch is mounted on a plastic box fitted to the surface of the wall.

Switches should be positioned so that they are at chest height and can easily be found when opening the door of a darkened room. They are frequently mounted adjacent to the door frame.

A dimmer switch is connected in exactly the same way although it may require a deeper mounting or back box.

5

Two-way switching requires special two-way switches which have three terminals and either a special cable, having an earth and three other conductors, coded red, yellow and blue, or two lengths of ordinary cable run between the two switches. The ceiling rose or junction box is wired in the normal manner and the switch cable taken to the nearest of the two switches and the live and neutral are connected to two of the terminals but not the one marked 'common'. Using the special cable or two lengths of ordinary 1.5 mm² cable join the common terminal of one switch to the common on the other, the live to the live and the neutral to the neutral. The earth wires are sheathed in green sleeving and connected to the earth terminals in the mounting boxes.

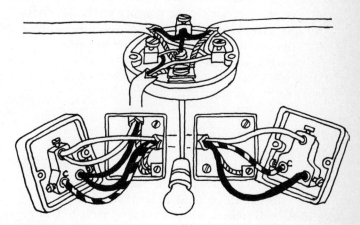

When using two strands of ordinary cable, cut back the conductor which is not used so that it cannot cause a short circuit. Screw the switches to the back boxes.

6

When the circuit is complete, check for continuity (See 9.10) and then connect the end to a 5 amp fuse in the consumer unit. (See 9.03).

7

9.06
BATHROOM WIRING

In a room containing a bath or shower, regulations and common sense demand for reasons of safety that extra precautions are taken.

Lighting in a bathroom should be controlled by a light switch sited on the wall *OUTSIDE* the bathroom, or by a ceiling-mounted switch controlled by a cord pull if sited in the bathroom. Light fittings must not be ceiling roses with pendants but bulb holders attached to the ceiling or else totally enclosed fittings. It should not be possible to touch the fitting when standing in the bath or shower.

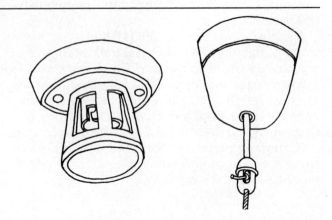

1

Power points are *NOT* allowed in bathrooms. A point for an electric shaver may be fitted but it must be isolated from both the supply mains and earth and supplied instead by a secondary circuit. The simplest way to achieve this is to install one of the many lightning units which are manufactured with a built-in shaver socket, to comply with the British Standard. The light unit must be connected into the lighting circuit with concealed or adequately protected cable. Alternatively, shaver sockets are available with built-in transformers, which can be run on a fused spur of a ring main.

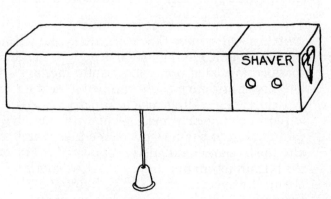

2

An electric wall heater may be fitted in a bathroom provided that it is fixed so that it cannot be touched when standing in a bath or shower, and the ON/OFF switch is operated by a cord pull. The supply cable must be adequately protected and run from a fused, switched spur. Ideally the fused spur switch should be sited by the bathroom door so that in the event of an accident the heater can be isolated before entering the room. Provided the heater demands less than 13 amp (3 kilowatts) it can be supplied by a spur off a ring main. Larger heaters will require a separate spur from the consumer unit.

(The installation of the switched fused spur box is the same as that for a water heater.) (See 9.08).

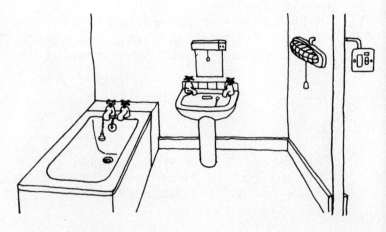

3

9.07
COOKER POINT

Although the intention may be to use a gas cooker; when rewiring a house it is worth providing an electric cooker point for future flexibility.

Cooker units are available for flush or surface mounting. Even when running concealed cables it is quite normal to use a surface-mounted cooker point since the connection is made into the underside of the box. When using a flush unit a separate cable connection pont can be fitted to the wall behind the cooker position. Most cooker points incorporate a switched power socket.

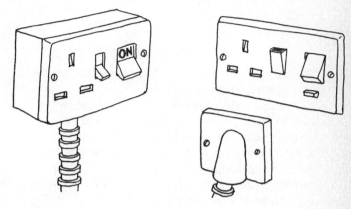

1

A flush cooker unit is mounted on a double metal back box of standard depth. Knock out the preformed holes for the entry cable and the cable to the cooker connection point and line the hole with rubber 'grommits' to protect the cables. Screw the box to the brickwork or the studwork so that the top is flush with the finished wall surface. Do the same for the cooker cable connection point which mounts on a single metal back box. For a surface mounting unit knock or break out the preformed holes for the supply cable, but only break out for the cooker connection if connecting a cooker since the hole will otherwise only allow dust and damp into the unit. Cookers are normally rated at 45 or 30 amps so the cable to use is 10 mm² T and E (Twin and Earth) PVC sheathed cable. Run the cable from the consumer unit to the cooker point as a single radial circuit. Inside the cooker point, strip back the insulation on the incoming supply to within 10 mm of the grommet. Connect the live to the live terminal, the neutral to the neutral terminal and having sheathed it in green sleeving, the earth to the earth terminal.

When a cooker cable connection point is being used, connect a further length of 10 mm² T and E cable to the cooker point, live to live, neutral to neutral and earth to earth, and connect the other end into the cooker cable connection point. Again, live to live, neutral to neutral, earth to earth, using green sleeving on both earths.

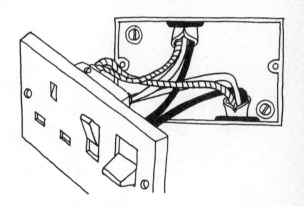

2

Connect the end of the cable into a fuseway in
the consumer unit and fit a 30 amp fuse unit.
When fitting in the list of fuseways inside the
consumer unit fuse cover, note that the cable is
capable of taking up to 45 amps if required.

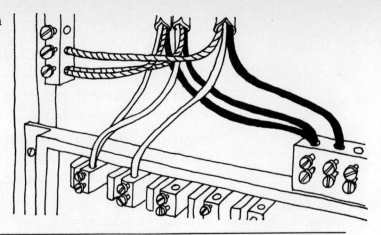

3

When connecting a cooker to the cooker point,
use a special, metal sheathed,
asbestos-insulated, flexible cooker cable, which
can withstand the heat from the cooker. Knock
or break out a blank hole in the bottom of a
surface-mounted cooker point or unscrew the
cover to a flush cooker cable connection point.
Connect the live to the live, neutral to neutral,
and earth to the earth terminals.

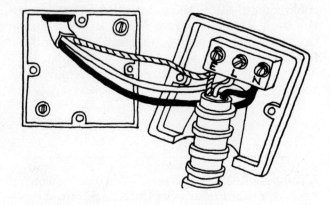

4

Electrically heated hot water may be provided in three ways, by an immersion heater in a hot water cylinder, by an immersion heater in a smaller sink point cylinder, or by an instantaneous water heater. Although their electrical rating may vary, immersion heaters are normally 3 kilowatt, while instantaneous heaters are usually 6 or 7 kilowatts. They all require a fused spur connection.

The switched, fused spur box is positioned adjacent to the water cylinder or heater. The box can be surface or flush mounted and if flush mounted has a standard single metal back box. Either break out the preformed holes in the surface box or the metal back box, fit a rubber grommit to the metal back box and screw the back box to the wall. Bring a 2.5 mm² T and E PVC cable (4 mm² if feeding an instantaneous water heater) into the box and strip back the sheathing to within 10 mm of the casing. Through the hole in the front of the casing bring the flex from the water heater (or for a wall mounted fire, a cable may be brought in through a knock-out hole in the mounting box) and strip back the sheathing to within 10 mm of the casing. Cut the conductors of the cable and the flex to length and bare the ends. Insulate the earth of the cable with green sleeving. Twist the ends of the flex and cable together, earth to earth, live to live and neutral to neutral. Fit each into the appropriate terminal and tighten down the screw. Screw the front plate onto the box.

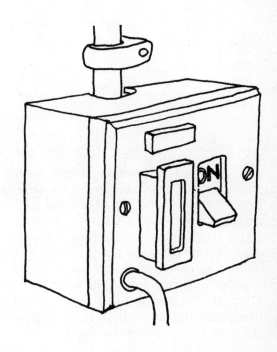

1

Connect the other end of the spur to a fuseway in the consumer unit. Fit a 20 amp fuse (30 amp for an instantaneous water heater, when 4 mm² cable is used).

2

Before re-using existing circuits carry out the following checks and repairs as necessary. If a great deal of work has to be done it may be easier to start again. Lighting circuits are usually in better condition than power and therefore more readily re-usable.

Before starting and work, switch off the mains switch and remove all of the fuses.

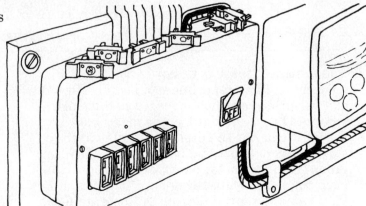

1

The cable may be PVC, rubber or lead sheathed depending on its age. Take up floorboards and examine the cable for signs of failure; rubber insulation often has a crazed surface when it has failed. Take the front cover off a number of power points and examine the insulation. If the insulation has perished then disconnect the power point, pull through some more cable, cut off the ends of the conductors and strip back the sheathing and the insulation. If the insulation has perished beneath the sheathing then the cable will need to be replaced. If not, reconnect the power point.

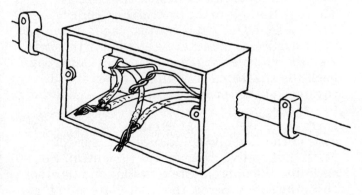

2

Take off the front cover of all the power points and wall switches. If the earths have not been insulated cover them with green sleeving. Where the cable is lead covered, the earth is the lead sheathing. Each cable should be connected to the earth terminals by an insulated (2.5 mm²) conductor (wire) attached to an earth clip on the lead sheathing. When checking the wiring of power points check that too much insulation has not been stripped back on the live and neutrtal connections, which could cause shorting. Where the insulation has perished strip it back until it is sound.

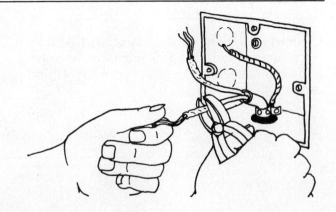

3

Unscrew the ceiling rose covers. These are often painted over and are jammed. Try running the top of a bradawl or screwdriver around the junction between the cover and the base of the rose and attempt to unscrew the cover by hand. If this fails, wrap a cloth round the cap and grasp it with an adjustable wrench or grip. There are four possible results of using force; one, the cap breaks; two, the rose breaks; three, the rose becomes loose and four, the cap unscrews. The first three will regrettably result in the need to replace the ceiling rose.

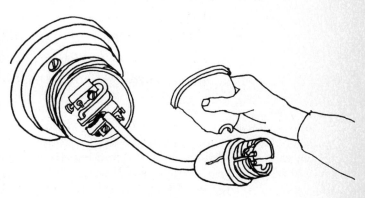

Once the cap is removed, examine the insulation and cut back any that is perished.

The flex to the pendant bulb holder will usually have perished from the heat of the bulb and the bulb holder itself may also be broken or very brittle. Replace the flex and bulb holder if necessary.

4

Having examined all of the fittings and the cables, including checking that the cables are adequately sized for their purpose, that there are not too many fittings on each circuit, and that broken fittings have been replaced, examine the fuse arrangements. If there is a variety of switched fuse and isolator boxes, or an old style fuse box with a separate mains switch, it may be worth while replacing them with a new consumer unit (See 9.03).

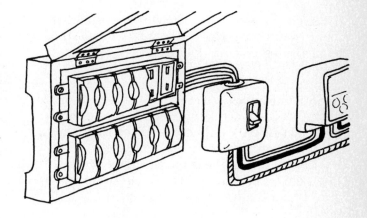

Check that the fuses are correctly wired and if in doubt rewire with the correct size fuse wire:
5 amp for a lighting circuit in 1 or 1.5 mm² cable
20 amp for a radial power circuit in 2.5 mm² cable
30 amp for a ring power circuit in 2.5 mm² cable
30 amp for a radial power circuit in 6.0 mm² cable
45 amp for a radial power circuit in 10 mm² cable

5

Before using the circuits they should be tested for earth continuity, polarity, insulation, integrity and other faults. (See 9.10).

6

9.10
TESTING EXISTING CIRCUITS

As well as testing existing circuits it is advisable to test newly installed circuits before connecting them into the consumer unit.

To construct a simple circuit tester, take a 3 volt double battery of the type used in bicycle lamps and to each terminal solder a 300 mm length of single strand insulated flex or bell wire. To the end of each piece of wire attach a crocodile clip and take care that the two clips are kept apart. The other half of the circuit tester is a torch bulb in a holder or a bell to which two or more 300 mm long wires with crocodile clips on the ends are attached. The bell has the advantage that it can be used by one person.

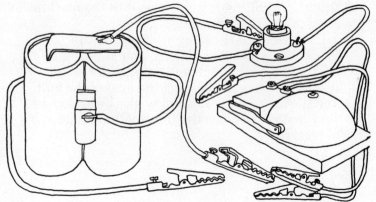

1

Polarity for power circuits can be tested by constructing a simple tester or by using a simple polarity tester manufactured by Galatrex, which is in the form of a plug with neon indicators on the back which shows which conductors have been crossed. To make a simple tester, take a piece of twin core 5 amp flex and fit one end to a 240V bulb holder fitted with a bulb, the other end is connected with the live conductor to the live connection of a plug, with the neutral conductor connected to the earth pin. Use a 3 amp fuse in the plug.

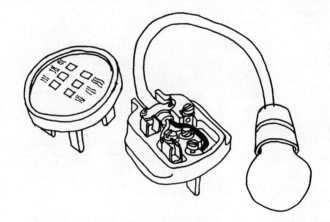

2

The quality of the insulation can only be tested by using a 'Megger', an instrument which by means of a hand generator, or a battery, subject the circuit to a high voltage and then measures any leakage; too great a leakage indicates that the insulation is perished. A 'Megger' can also be used to test circuit continuity and earth continuity.

They are expensive pieces of equipment and if one cannot be borrowed, it may be better to ask the Electricity Board to run a test.

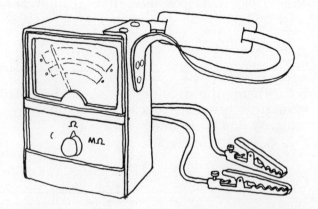

3

To test the polarity of a power circuit, simply plug in the Galatrex tester and note the reading, or plug in the home-made tester. If the wiring is correct then the bulb will light. If the bulb does not light then either the earth is not continuous, or the live and neutrals have been changed over. Test the continuity of the earth by using the circuit tester and take off the front of the power point to check the wiring. Test every socket outlet in this way.

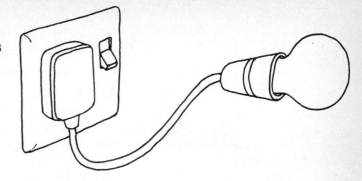

4

To test a lighting circuit for switched polarity, switch each switch to the off position, remove the bulb from a pendant bulb holder and test each terminal with a neon mains tester screwdriver.

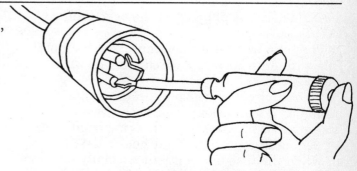

5

To test continuity, switch off at the mains and remove all of the fuses. At the consumer unit disconnect one circuit at a time for testing. Check that the battery and bulb or bell of the tester are working. For a ring main, take each conductor in turn, connect the bell or bulb to one end of the conductor with a crocodile clip, and connect the other crocodile clip from the bell or bulb directly to one terminal of the battery. Connect the other terminal of the battery to the other end of the conductor. If the conductor is continuous the bulb will light, or the bell will ring.

6

For a lighting circuit or a radial power circuit, disconnect at the consumer unit and connect the bell or bulb to the earth conductor and the live conductor. At the other end of the circuit connect the battery to the earth and the live. If the bulb lights or the bell rings then both conductors are continuous. Repeat with the tester connected between the earth and the neutral conductors. If the bell does not ring then one of the conductors is not continuous. If it does not ring when connected with the live and earth, but does ring when connected with the neutral and earth then it is the live which is not continuous. If it does not ring when switched from the live to the neutral then try connecting it across the live and the neutral. If it now rings then it is the earth which is discontinuous. If it still does not ring then more than one conductor is discontinuous.

To narrow down the area in which a fault lies,

make the test at different points on the circuit. When a faulty section has been identified, narrow it down as much as possible and then check all of the connections in the fittings. If there are no loose or broken connections then a section of cable will need to be replaced.

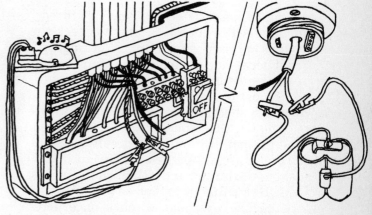

7

MENDING A FUSE

A fuse will 'blow' or a mini-circuit breaker will
trip off, if there is a fault which could cause
damage to the system. Some common causes are:
Overloading the circuit: a ring main is only
capable of supplying 7.5 kilowatts of power, and
if there are already two electric fires, each
taking 3 kilowatts in use, when the 3 kilowatt
electric kettle is plugged in the overloading
occurs.

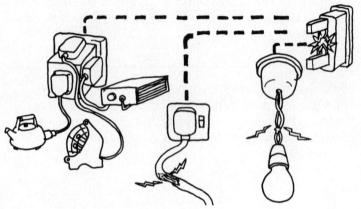

Plugging in a faulty appliance, for example,
one with an incorrectly wired plug, or with a
damaged flex.

A short circuit developing in the system, for
example, a loose connection to the back of a
socket allowing wires to touch, or the insulation
perishing in a pendant light holder flex.

When the fuse blows it will normally only
affect a single circuit unless the fault is across a
number of circuits, for example, a nail driven
into a bunch of cables, or a fire melting the
insulation to a number of cables.

1

When an appliance is plugged in and nothing
happens, first check the fuse in the plug. Unless
the plug has a built-in fuse ejector – normally a
red plastic tongue in the base marked 'FUSE'
which when pulled ejects the fuse, then undo the
screw in the centre of the base of the plug and
remove the cover. Take out the fuse; if it has
gone there will normally be a dark line down the
side. Replace the fuse with a new fuse of similar
rating, i.e. 3 amp with 3 amp. Replace and screw
on the plug top or push the fuse ejector back into
place.

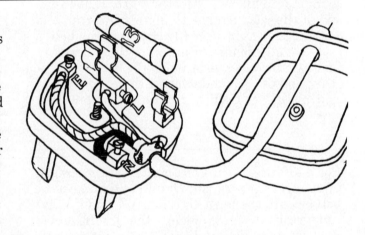

2

If nothing happens when the newly re-fused
plug is plugged in then it is time to check the
mains fuse in the consumer unit. Working with
a torch if necessary, switch off the mains switch
in the consumer unit and remove the fuse cover.
Check the list of fuses and the circuits they
serve, which should be inside the fuse cover. If
there is no list then each fuse will have to be
checked in turn. If miniature circuit breakers
(MCB) are in use, simply reset the tripped MCB
by pushing the button and switch on the mains.
If the MCB remains reset then switch off again,
replace the fuse cover and switch on once more.
If rewirable fuses are in use extract the fuse
holder(s) and examine the wire. If it is burnt

through, then undo the securing screws, remove the remains of the old wire, thread in a length of the appropriate size fuse wire through the fuse holder, wrap it around one screw, tighten the screw, pull the wire taut and wrap it around the second screw and tighten that screw. Never use wire that is thicker than the fuse rating, i.e. 30 amp in a 3 amp fuse, and always wrap the wire clockwise around the screws. Replace the fuse, switch on the mains switch, and if the fuse holds then switch off again, replace the fuse cover and then switch on once more. If the fuses are cartridge fuses use a similar procedure to replace the fuse.

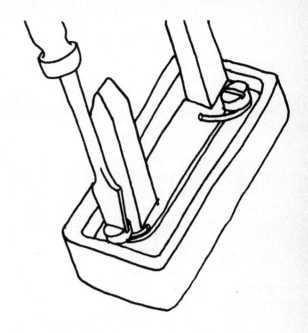

If the fuse blows when replaced, then unplug the appliance or switch off the light fitting which is suspect and try again. If the fuse blows again then unplug everything from the circuit. If the fuse then holds, either the circuit was over-loaded or an appliance was faulty. If the fuse still fails then there is a fault in the circuit and this should be checked. (See 9.10).

3

If all the circuits go dead and there is no apparent common cause and no-one has switched off the mains at the consumer unit, then telephone the Electricity Board before starting to replace fuses. The Board may have a problem which has interrupted the supply. If no such problem exists then check all the fuses. If all are intact, then there may be a fault in the company head. The fuse sometimes blows if there is a surge in the supply, so again call the Electricity Board.

N.B. **Using heavier gauge wire in fuses than appropriate can lead to over-heating of cables and electrical fires. Therefore it should not be considered even for a temporary repair.**

4

Check that the appliance to be used has an adequate flex. Built-in flexes to T.V.s, stereos, washing machines, etc. will be adequate, but home-made lamps or extended flexes may not be.

   Unless the appliance, such as an electric drill, has a concentric earthing system denoted by a ▣ marking on the casing, the flex should have an earth as well as a live and neutral. The flex should have an outer sheath surrounding the two or three conductors, each with its own insulation.

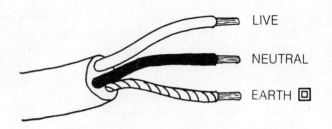

The European Colour Code is:–
Live   – Brown insulation
Neutral – Blue insulation
Earth   – Green and Yellow striped insulation
but some older appliances will have the old British Code:–
Live   – Red
Neutral – Black
Earth   – Green

1

Unscrew the top of the plug by undoing the screw in the centre of the base. If the plug is of moulded rubber, or a type in which the base fits inside the top, then thread the top onto the flex. The live terminal may be sited under the fuse; if so, remove the fuse. Carefully strip back the outer flex casing by 50 mm, loosen the cable grip screws and slip the flex under the bar and tighten the screws so that the end of the outer sheath is firmly held. Take the green and yellow (green) earth conductor to the large earth pin, cut it to length, bare enough of the end to fit into the terminal on the end of the plug, twist the strands of wire forming the conductor together, loosen the terminal screw, place the end of the conductor into the terminal and tighten down the screw. Repeat the process for the brown (red) live conductor which connects to the fuse terminal and the blue (black) neutral conductor which connects to the third pin terminal.

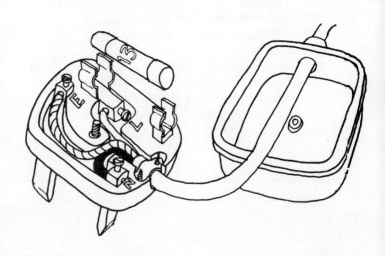

   Before replacing the cover, check that the fuse is appropriate to the appliance. A 3 amp fuse is adequate for stereos, radios, fridges, black and white T.V.s, lights, and appliances with loads of up to 750 watts. A 13 amp fuse is necessary for electric fires, kettles, washing machines, colour televisions and appliances of more than 750 watts.

   Having fitted the appropriate fuse, replace the cover and screw it in place.

2

10
CHIMNEYS & PARAPETS

LADDERS, SCAFFOLDING AND SAFETY

Working at heights can be very dangerous and a high proportion of fatal accidents on building sites are falls resulting from carelessness in the use of or faults in ladders or scaffolding.
Ladders and scaffolding are usually available for hire and should be carefully inspected before renting.

Ladders

Before using a ladder check that it is not damaged, that there are no cracked, rotten or bent rungs and no loose joints. Make sure that the ladder selected is long enough to reach the required height safely.

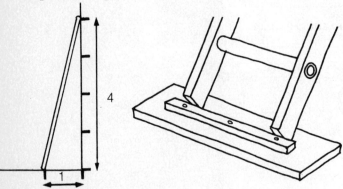

A ladder that is correctly positioned has its base one quarter of the height reached from the wall. The top should not rest on guttering, plastic or metal, glass or glazing bars. Extension pieces should overlap by at least three rungs. The foot of the ladder should be level so that each side is firmly supported. On firm ground a wedge can be introduced under one side if it is uneven, but on soft ground the ladder should be stood on a board.

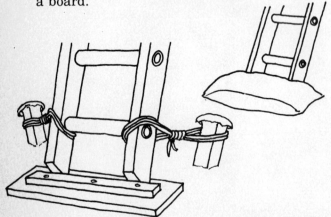

A batten nailed to the board will stop the ladder slipping. Secure the base of the ladder by driving stakes into soft ground and lashing the foot of the ladder to them or placing a sandbag at the base on hard ground. Alternatively get someone to steady the ladder if it is being used only for a straight up and down inspection.

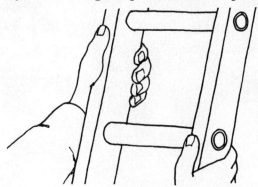

To climb a ladder wear sensible footwear; a stout pair of shoes is ideal, since while they protect the feet, the rungs can still be felt. Grasp the sides of the ladder, look straight ahead and climb the ladder, sliding the hands up the sides, keeping them in contact with the ladder at all times. Never climb higher than the fourth rung from the top. Never attempt to stretch out sideways more than a comfortable arms length since this could cause the ladder to slide.

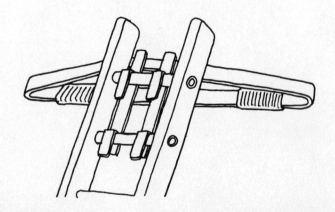

Secure the top of the ladder whenever possible, tying it to a sturdy downpipe bracket, a board placed across the inside of a window opening or an eye bolt screwed up into the underside of a roof joist. When working below an overhang fix a ladder stay onto the end of the ladder. A ladder stay should also be used to bring the ladder out past guttering when carrying out roofwork.

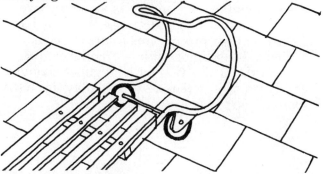

Roof Ladder

Roof ladders or crawling boards are essential when working on pitched roofs. They should not be used from a ladder but from a scaffolding tower. Before use check that none of the battens or joints are damaged and that the ridge hook is securely fastened.

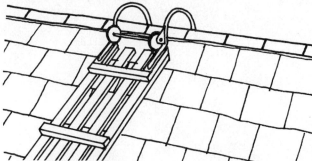

Wheel the ladder up the roof and connect extension pieces as necessary, making sure that they are firmly locked together. When the ladder reaches the ridge, turn it over and hook the end over the ridge and pull back to make sure that it is firmly located. To climb the boards, hold the cross battens and use them as steps. When working off a roofing ladder, use the cross bars to hold tools rather than attempting to leave them on the roof slope.

Scaffolding

Scaffolding is a specialist skill and because of the number of accidents which have occurred resulting from incorrectly erected scaffolding it is now difficult for the layman to simply hire a set of scaffolding to erect. The normal procedure is to hire scaffolding which the firm will erect, the initial charge covering both the erection and removal of the scaffolding, plus a set hire period, say one month. After that time a hire charge is operated on a weekly basis. It is worth seeking a number of quotations since this is a competitive field of equipment hire.

A correctly erected scaffold will be equipped with handrails and toe boards, all ladders will be fixed in place, the scaffold will include some diagonal bracing and will be tied back into the building for added stability. In addition the board platforms will be laid so that the boards are adequately supported and there are no traps caused by boards being able to see-saw.

Scaffold Towers

If access is required to only a small area of the building or to the roof, then a scaffold tower may be hired. There are a number of different systems for scaffolding towers available but they usually consist of a series of frames which slot together; cross braces; poles and boards. When erecting a scaffold tower it is important to incorporate diagonal bracing into each side of the tower and to cross brace the base. Ask the hire shop to demonstrate the type of clips used in the system and to provide an instruction manual.

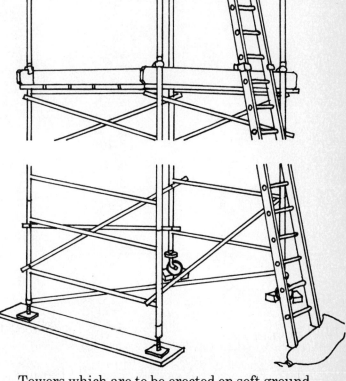

Towers which are to be erected on soft ground should be placed on scaffold boards which will spread the load and stop the feet sinking unevenly into the ground. Stepped or sloping ground can be compensated for by using adjustable base legs on the scaffold; don't try and pack up below the legs since uneven packing can cause the tower to sway or twist. If castors or wheels are fitted to the base of the tower rather than base plates, then lock the brake on each wheel and chock each wheel with a brick to either side, before using the tower.

Above two storeys the tower will be safer if tied-in to the building. A simple method of tying-in is to place a scaffold board or pole across the inside of the window opening so that it overlaps the walls and then, using rope or scaffold pole and clips to link the two together. Securely fix any ladders used with the tower either with rope or a special ladder clip. Do not climb the tower, particularly when carrying anything, since this can be very dangerous. To transfer heavy materials up or down the tower, rig up a hoist of a gallows bracket extending above the tower to which is fastened a pulley or block and tackle. Enclose the working platform with a hand rail and edge the boards with a vertical board known as a toe board, to stop things being kicked over the edge.

Use of Scaffolding

Whatever form of scaffolding is being used treat it with respect and remember that it is not a climbing frame. Where scaffolding is positioned so that it projects into a path, paint the ends of the poles or mark them with lights to draw people's attention to them. At night take up the bottom ladder so that children can't climb onto the scaffolding. Scaffolding is an 'attractive' nuisance as far as children are concerned and failure to take precautions to make access difficult, if not impossible, for children, can result in a legal action for negligence should a child hurt themself as a result of playing on the scaffold.

TAKING DOWN A CHIMNEY

If a chimney breast is removed, the chimney must not be left unsupported and although alternative supports can be introduced it is more satisfactory to take down the chimney and make good the roof.

Erect a scaffolding platform and protect the surrounding roof surface in a manner appropriate to the position of the chimney and the type of roof. Remove the chimneypots and carefully dismantle the chimney. Once the load of the pots and flaunching have been removed old chimney stacks are often very easy to pull apart, and care should be taken to ensure that large sections do not fall.

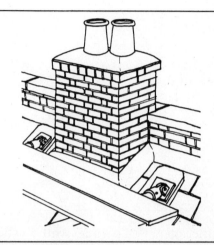

1

If a section of the roof is supported on the chimney breast, provide alternative support for the rafters with 'Acrow' props, using scaffolding boards to spread the load of the props on the floor below. Take down the chimney in the roof space leaving in position any bricks which are bonded into the party wall or parapet wall. Cut off any such bricks flush with the face of the wall using a 100 mm cold chisel or 'bolster', first lightly tapping each side and the top of the brick with the bolster and club hammer to weaken the break line before striking the bolster with the hammer on the top of the brick.

In order to support the extended rafters attach a 75×75 mm timber to the wall using 'L' shaped brackets of 50×6 mm mild steel set 100 mm into the brick courses at 600 mm centres and screwed to the timber (See Sheet 11.06).

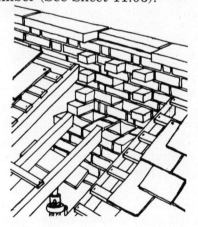

2

Using the same section timber as the rafters, bolt on extension pieces which overlap the rafter end by 750 mm and are held in place with 3 No. 12 mm diameter coach bolts with toothed timber connectors between the timbers and 25 mm washers to the nut ends.

Cut a 'birdsmouth's' out of the ends of the rafters no deeper than one third of their depth so that they sit on the supporting timber, and nail them in place.

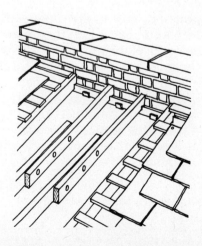

3

The roof covering may be laid on boarding, battens, or battens and felt. Piece-in a support for the roofing to match the surrounding construction. For a slate roof this will normally be battens of 50×19 mm or similar size.

Measure the slates or tiles and buy replacements of the same size. Continuing the pattern of the surrounding roof, nail slates in place using slater's nails, or fix other tiles in accordance with the manufacturer's instructions.

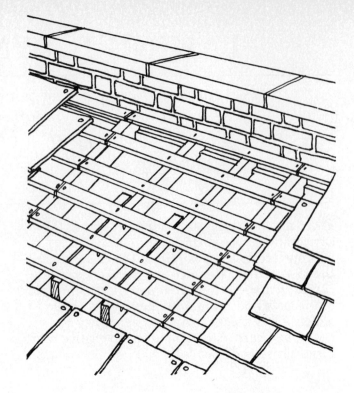

4

At the junction with a parapet wall, flashings or other weathering details should be made to match. Firstly repoint the wall where the chimney has been removed and replace any damaged bricks. If there is a lead or zinc flashing to the remainder of the roof, then preform a flashing of Code 4 lead or zinc, Gauge 14 as appropriate, but do not mix the metals or use either with another metal. Preform the flashing by bending it against a wooden batten, using a wooden mallet to get a straight joint. Rake out the mortar from a mortar course to the brickwork that is at least 150 mm above the top of the roof covering, and fit the flashing in place so that it penetrates at least 25 mm into the mortar course. Point the flashing in place with a 1:1:6 cement: lime: sand mortar, using small wedges to hold it in place while the mortar sets. The flashing should overlap the top of the roof slope by at least 150 mm and the flashings to either side by 200 mm.

If the junction with the parapet wall is protected by a mortar 'fillet' then place a 150 mm wide piece of slate adjacent to the wall and on top of the roof covering. On top of this slate, in the angle with the wall, form a mortar fillet about 150 mm up the wall and slightly concave. Using a 1:3 cement: sand mortar, smooth the surface of the fillet with a wet trowel and sprinkle it with neat cement. Work with the trowel until a smooth surface is obtained.

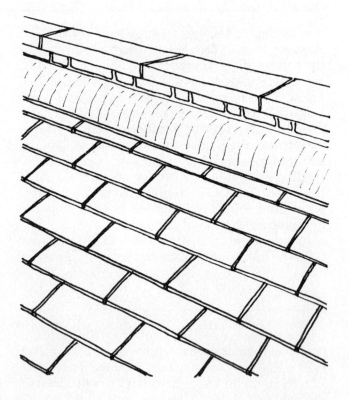

5

10.02
REBUILD CHIMNEY STACK

Chimney stacks are subject to movement resulting from temperature changes and frequently lean into the wind owing to the wind cooling one side more than the other. This movement weakens chimneys, forcing out the pointing and unless they have been adequately maintained, they will deteriorate to a point where they will require rebuilding.

Erect a scaffolding platform and protect the surrounding roof surface in a manner appropriate to the position of the chimney and the type of roof. Remove the chimney pots and carefully dismantle the chimney. Once the load of the pots and flaunching have been removed, old chimney stacks are often very easy to pull apart, and care should be taken to ensure that large sections do not fall. The chimney should be taken down until the brickwork is sound, or below the roof covering, taking great care that no bricks or mortar fall down the flues. The flues can be protected by stuffing a sack down each flue. The sack should have a cord tied around it so that it may be withdrawn.

1

In accordance with Sheet 2.16 mix up a 1:1:6 cement: lime: sand mortar and build up the brickwork so that it projects 150 mm above the roof covering on all sides, i.e. the brickwork steps down the roof. Lay a thin layer of mortar onto the brickwork and bed into it a bituminous damp-proof course.

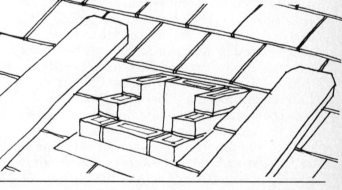

2

Continue building the chimney, ensuring that it is vertical, since any slight deviation from the vertical, combined with the effects of wind and thermal movement, could result in its collapse. The finished chimney should be 600 mm above the ridge or 900 mm above its own junction with any other part of the roof surface. To help protect the chimney from the rain, project the top two courses of brickwork by 38 mm so that water is thrown off the top of the chimney clear of the brickwork.

   As the brickwork is built up, render the inside to give each flue a 19 mm thick, 1:3, cement: sand lining. (2.05, 2.17.)

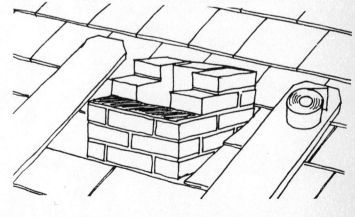

3

Bed a second bituminous D.P.C. in mortar on the top of the brickwork. Place the chimney pots in position over the flues. Build up a shaped topping so that water will be thrown clear, out of 1:3 cement: sand mortar incorporating pieces of broken brick. Polish the slope to the mortar with a wet trowel, sprinkling neat cement on the mortar and polish until smooth.

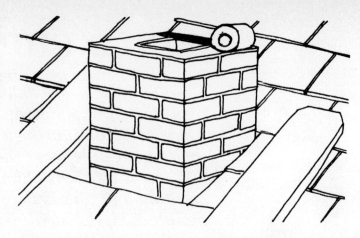

4

Before replacing the slates, incorporate 'L' shaped lead or zinc 'soakers' which are lapped into the slates, standing 50–75 mm up the face of the chimney and 100–150 mm along the roof. In the angle between the back of the chimney and the slope of the roof construct a back gutter of a length of ex 150×25 board supported on battens. This gutter must be covered with a single piece flashing which stands 100 to 150 mm up the chimney and 225 mm up the slope of the roof. This back gutter will normally be constructed out of lead or zinc formed and welded to give one continuous flashing. However, in a short-life house the back gutter can be made up out of Nuralite, or more simply by building up first a layer of Aquaseal 5 with a nylon reinforcing mesh bedded into it, then a thick coat of Aquaseal 40 followed by a second layer of mesh covering any open seams in the first layer, finish with a second layer of Aquaseal 40, topped with a coat of Aquaseal 5. The upstand to the soakers and the junction of the chimney with the lower roof slope can be covered with a lead or zinc flashing, or more cheaply with a fillet of 1:3 sand: cement mortar. The metal flashings should penetrate 25 mm into the mortar course of the brickwork, stepping down the sides of the chimney a minimum of 75 mm above the line of the roof slope. A cement mortar fillet should stand 75 mm up the side of the chimney and 75 mm along the roof slope and be concave.

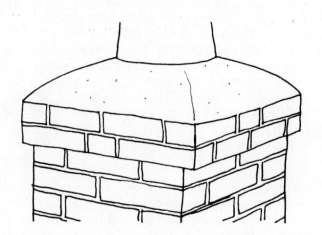

5

REPAIRING A CHIMNEY STACK

As routine maintenance, chimney stacks should be repointed where mortar has been loosened by thermal movement of the chimney and damaged flaunching, (the shaped mortar topping,) repaired or replaced.

Clean out the facing mortar from the joints to a depth of 10 mm with a plugging chisel and a club hammer.

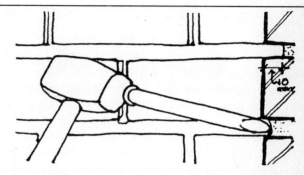

1

Brush the joints and the brickwork down to remove dust and old mortar. Brush water over the wall and the joints, soaking the brickwork so that it will not absorb moisture from the new pointing mortar.

2

Mix enough mortar to repoint about 1 square metre, using 1 part of Portland cement to 6 parts of sand by volume. Use enough mortar so that mortar is smooth, but firm, so that when a piece is cut off and pushed across the spotboard with a sawing action of the trowel it will roll into a 'sausage'.

3

Load some of the mortar onto a 'hawk' and, using a small pointing trowel, pick up a strip of mortar on the bottom edge of the face with an upward sweep of the back of the trowel. Rotate the wrist so that the bottom edge becomes the top edge and force the mortar into the joints, first a vertical joint and then the horizontal joint above and below it. Leave mortar flush with bricks.

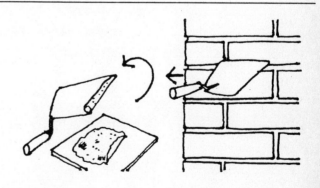

4

Pointing can be completed in a number of different ways such as 'flush', 'rubbed', 'recessed' and 'weather struck'. Of these the simplest is a flush joint. A flush joint is made by waiting until the mortar has started to go 'off' and then rubbing the joint, in one direction only, with a piece of dry sacking. Damp sacking will cause cement stains on the brickwork. Brush off any excess mortar when dry with a stiff brush.

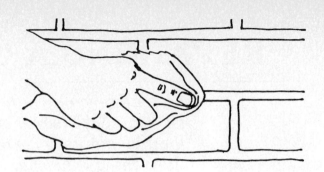

5

If the flaunching is badly damaged, hack it off with a 100 mm cold chisel or bolster, taking care that no rubble falls down the flues. If the flaunching is generally sound but cracked, use a plugging chisel to cut the cracks to about 25 mm wide. If the flaunching has been removed, bed a bituminous damp-proof course on the top of the brickwork before replacing the chimney pots on top of the flues. Rebuild the flaunching with 1:3 cement: sand mortar and pieces of cut brick. When filling cracks add some PVA adhesive to the mortar and paint the sides of the crack with PVA before filling with mortar. Polish the filling to the cracks, or the new flaunching, with a wet trowel, sprinkling with a little neat cement, until smooth.

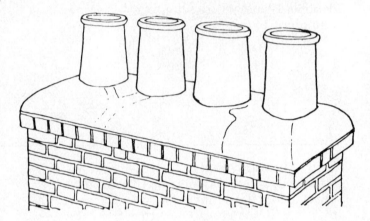

6

10.04
CAPPING-OFF CHIMNEY STACKS

When a chimney is no longer to be used for a solid fire it should be capped to prevent rain penetration. If the chimney is also in poor condition and is not going to be used for a gas fire, it should be taken down below the roof surface and ventilated into the roof space, since this will give fewer maintenance problems. Chimneys can be capped in a number of ways, but ventilation must be provided to prevent dampness resulting from condensation in the blocked off flues.

If the chimney is sound and the chimney pot is firmly bedded then a 'loose hood and spigot' or a plug can be placed in the top of the pot.

1

If the pots are not sound, take them off and hack off the old 'flaunching' which is the sloped concrete topping. Take care that nothing falls down the flues once the pot has been lifted off, tie a piece of cord around an old sack, and then block the flue with the sack. After the old flaunching has been hacked off, clean off the rubble. Use the cord to withdraw the sack before capping the flue. The flue can be capped in a variety of ways.

A If the brickwork is not sound or the stack is leaning, take off the bricks until the stack is reduced to about 600 mm in height. From the side away from the wind (chimney stacks lean into the wind) remove a brick from the side of each flue.

   Mix up a mortar of 1:1:6 cement: lime: sand and lay a 215×65 mm air brick in each opening so formed. Lay a bed of mortar on top of the bricks surrounding the flues and bed down a polythene or bituminous damp-proof course, lapping all the joints. Lay a second bed of mortar on top of the D.P.C. so that it slopes slightly in the same direction as the roof. Bed 50 mm thick precast concrete paving stones into the mortar so that it overhangs the chimney by more than 25 mm on all sides. Where more than one slab is necessary, butt them over the dividing wall between two flues and point the joint.

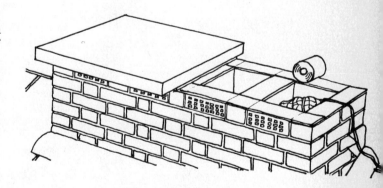

OR

B Either to the complete stack or one that has been reduced in height, lay a thin bed of 1:3 cement: sand mortar on top of the cleaned-off brickwork and bed into it a polythene or bituminous damp-proof course, lapping it at every junction.

Lay a second mortar bed on top of the D.P.C. and into it bed pieces of roofing slates so that they overhang the stack by 50 mm and the flues by 25 mm. Bed a half-round clay ridge-tile in mortar across the stack over each flue. Build up the mortar, filling it out with pieces of broken brick if necessary so that it slopes towards each side of the stack. Trowel the surface of the mortar smooth and then polish it with a wet trowel, sprinkling a fine layer of neat cement over it from time to time until it has a smooth finish.

C The stack can also be capped with a 'loose hood and spigot' or a clayware plug in the same was as for 'B' above, except the slate should oversail the flue sufficiently to support the capping device while the mortar flaunching is laid.

2

10.05
RENEW CHIMNEY POT

A cracked or damaged chimney pot should be replaced if the flue is to be used.

Stuff an old sack tied round with cord down the flue, below the bottom of the damaged pot. With a cold chisel and a club hammer, chip away the flaunching surrounding the damaged pot. If the flaunching is also in poor condition, it should be hacked off and replaced at the same time. Once the pot is free lift it off.

1

If the flaunching (shaped mortar topping) has been removed, bed a bituminous damp-proof course onto the top of the brickwork before replacing the chimney pot on top of the flue.

Make good the flaunching with 1:3 cement: sand mortar; polish it with a wet trowel sprinkling the mortar with neat cement until smooth and matching the remainder of the flaunching.

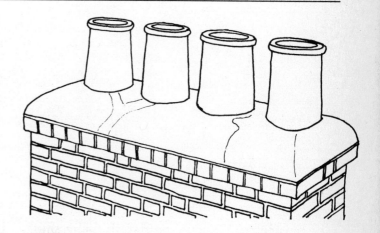

2

TAKE DOWN AND REBUILD PARAPET WALL

Parapet walls above roof level are exposed to the weather and may have become unstable if the pointing has not been maintained.

Erect a scaffolding platform and protect the roof surface to either side of the parapet wall in a manner appropriate to the position of the parapet wall and the shape of the roof. Carefully take down the parapet wall to the level of the first mortar course above the roof covering. To do this it will be necessary to chip off any sand: cement fillets with a cold chisel and to remove any metal flashings which should be retained for re-use. Clean off the old mortar to the top of the bricks.

1

The parapet wall should be rebuilt using the techniques for rebuilding a section of brickwork described in Sheet 2.16.

When rebuilding the parapet a damp-proof course should be included 150 mm above the roof surface to tie in with the flashings or fillets of mortar, if the wall has roofing to both sides. A damp-proof course should also be included beneath the coping stone. A wall which has no coping stone should have the second highest course of brickwork laid so that it projects by 50 mm to either side, and a cement: sand fillet added to help throw water off the wall. In exposed locations it is advisable to render a parapet wall. See Sheet 2.17.

2

10.07
RE-LAYING COPING STONES

Where coping stones top a parapet wall they are frequently loose due to failure of the pointing and mortar bed.

Erect a scaffolding platform and protect the roof surface to either side of the parapet wall in a manner appropriate to the position of the parapet wall and the shape of the roof. Carefully remove the coping stones and clean off old mortar to the underside of the stones, and to the top of the brickwork.

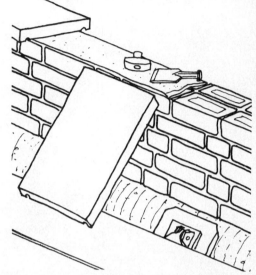

1

If any of the coping stones have broken or disintegrated, for example, due to frost action, a replacement may be made to match the length, depth and width of the existing stones. To the bottom of the formwork pin a length of waxed sash cord 15–25 mm in from each side to form a 'drip' in the new casting. Fill the formwork with a mix of 1:2:4 cement: sand: aggregate less than 15 mm, and poke with a stick to ensure that there are no air pockets in the casting. Tamp the top level with the formwork to compact the concrete and finally trowel the top with a metal float to give a smooth finish. After three days remove the formwork and the new coping can be laid.

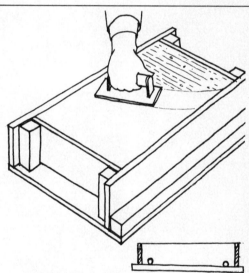

2

Mix up a mortar of 1:1:6, cement: lime: sand, until it is smooth enough to roll across a spot board with a bricklayer's trowel and lay a 5 mm mortar bed on top of the brick. Into this mortar, bed a bituminous damp-proof course, lapping all joints by a minimum of 150 mm. On top of the damp-proof course lay 10 mm of mortar spread with the point of the trowel and bed the coping stone. Cut off any mortar which is squeezed out. Point the junctions between coping stones with mortar and the joint below the stones.

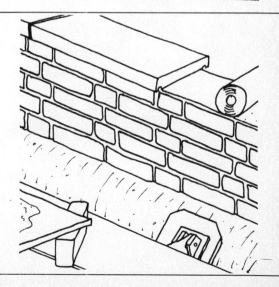

3

11
ROOFS

11.01
RE-CLIPPING SLATES

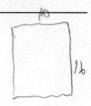

Slates work loose either because the fixing nails have corroded or because the slate has broken or laminated around the nail holes. Slates are brittle and can crack if walked upon.

Measure the size of the slates and obtain replacements of similar size. Slates are available in a number of standard sizes ranged from 12″×6″ to 26″×16″ with names such as 'Smalls', 'Duchesses', and 'Empresses' and there are also non-standard sizes used. New slates are expensive and second-hand slates can be purchased from some demolition merchants. It is worth looking around to find slates of the correct size, since it is normally difficult to patch a roof adequately with slates of the wrong size and cutting slates is time consuming.

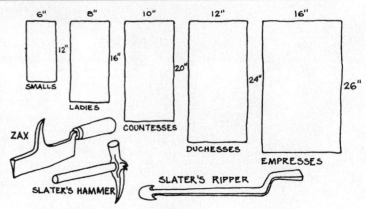

1

Slip a slate ripper up behind the damaged or slipped slate and hook the barb of the ripper round the head of one of the nails holding the slate in place. With a sharp downwards tug cut off the head of the nail. Repeat for the second nail and remove the slate.

2

A piece of lead, copper or zinc strip approximately 25×225 mm in size or a 300 mm length of 'slater's' copper wire is used to secure the new slate. Using a galvanised roofing nail, carefully nail the securing strip to the batten which is visible between the butt joint of the exposed slates. Take care not to hit the slates with hammer.

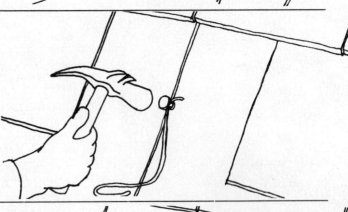

3

Gently raise the slates above the gap and slip under a replacement slate, so that its bottom edge is in line with the others in the row. Bend up the end of the securing strip so that the slate is held in place.

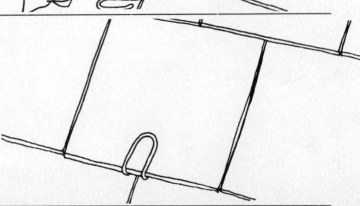

4

An area of slates which has been damaged can be reslated.

Measure the size of the slates and obtain replacements of similar size. Slates are available in a number of standard sizes, ranged from 12″×6″ to 26″×16″ with names such as 'Smalls', 'Duchesses' and 'Empresses' and there are also non-standard sizes used. New slates are expensive and second-hand slates can be purchased from some demolition merchants. It is worth looking around to find slates of the correct size, since it is normally difficult to patch a roof adequately with slates of the wrong size and cutting slates is time-consuming.

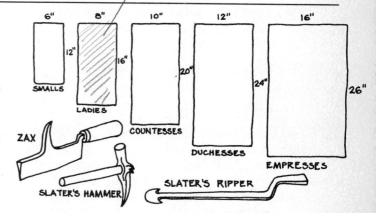

1

Slip a slate ripper up behind the damaged or slipped slate and hook the barb of the ripper round the head of one of the nails holding the slate in place. With a sharp downwards tug cut off the head of the nail. Repeat for the second nail and remove the slate. In this way remove the slates from the top of the section to be replaced until the fixing nails of the lower slates are exposed. Cut off the exposed nail heads with a pair of pincers and remove the slates. Do not attempt to pull the nails out with a claw hammer, since the lever action is likely to break the slate.

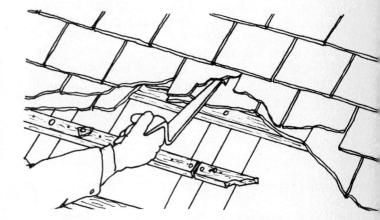

2

Cut off any broken battens above the middle of a rafter since ends which are unsupported will move when the slates are nailed in place and could result in cracked slates.

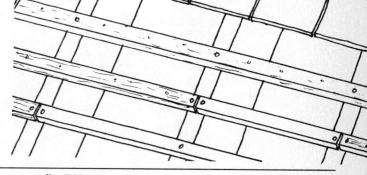

3

Starting at the bottom nail the first row of slates in position, using galvanised or aluminium roofing nails. Slates can either be 'head' or 'centred' nailed and normally overlap the next but one slate by 50–75 mm. Nail each successive row of slates until the second to last row, if the slates are head nailed, or the last row, if they are centre nailed, below the existing slates.

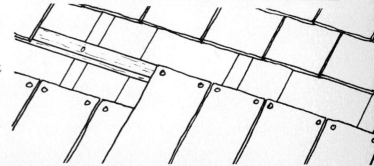

4

The last slates are held in position by strips of lead, zinc or copper approximately 225×25 mm in size, or by 300 mm lengths of 'slater's' copper wire.

Using galvanised roofing nails carefully nail the securing strips to the batten between the exposed slates, taking care not to damage the slates with a hammer. Gently raise the slates in the row above and slide the new slates into position and bend the securing strips so that they are held in place.

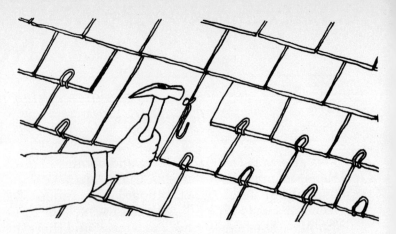

5

If a slate has to be cut, for example, adjacent to a hip timber or parapet wall, it may either be cut with a masonry saw, or a masonry disc attached to an electric saw, or cut in the traditional slater's fashion. First mark the cutting line on the slate and then place the slate with its cutting line overhanging the edge on a firm flat surface. Using the back edge of a bricklayer's trowel or a slater's Zax, chop along the cutting line, turning the slate over when the cut has reached half the length of the slate.

Nail holes can be made either with a masonry bit and drill, or by punching a hole with the spike of a slater's hammer, or with a blunt nail. The slate should be firmly supported before punching the hole, or else it will shatter.

from the under site, to get a countersunk hole

6

RESURFACING A VALLEY GUTTER

Many Victorian houses, particularly in London, were built with an 'M' or 'butterfly' roof which incorporates a central valley gutter running from the front to the back of the house. If not adequately maintained these can fail. A failed valley gutter which has a fall towards the rainwater downpipe and no large depressions can be recovered.

Clean off any dirt or silt deposit from the surface of the valley and carefully inspect it for any holes, bubbles or open seams which could be the cause of the leak. If none can be found, then check inside the roof space to see if the leak attributed to the valley is the result of water penetrating at a higher level and running down inside the roof. If a hole is found then proceed to resurface the valley.

1

To either side of the valley gutter remove the first two rows of slates using a slate ripper (see 11.01). This should be enough to expose the edges of the covering to the valley.

2

If the old covering, usually zinc, is sound and laying flat to the gutter the new covering may be placed on top of it, if not strip off the old covering and pull out or recess any nail heads.

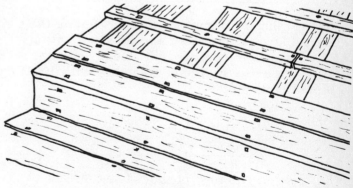

3

If the valley has a box section then into the bottom corners of the box nail a 45 degree 'tilting' fillet cut out of a piece of 50×50 mm (2″×2″) softwood. This is necessary so that the new felt covering will not have to bend through a right angle which will cause it to split. At the shallow end of the gutter it may be necessary to shape the fillet with a rasp or plane so that it matches in with the slope of the roof.

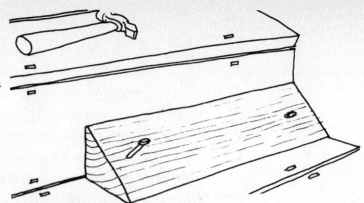

4

Starting at the outlet end of the roof, lay a strip of felt across the gutter. Bed the side nearest the outlet in mastic so that it sits over any shaped metal flashing to the outlet and nail the other side to the valley with galvanised felt nails. Lay the next piece in place, so that it overlaps the first by 75 mm (3″). Stick down the overlap with mastic and nail down the other side with felt nails. Continue in this fashion until the gutter is covered, making sure that the felt is in contact with the bottom of the valley and the tilting batten so that it is not unsupported anywhere since this could lead to the felt tearing.

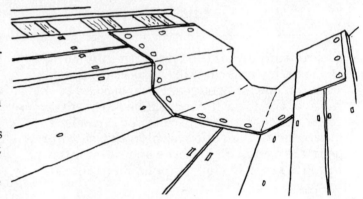

5

Cut strips of mineralized roofing felt about 1800 mm (6′–0″) in length to run up the slope of the valley. Starting at the outlet end cover the first layer of felt in mastic and bed into it a strip of felt so that it fits into the shape of the valley and its end does not coincide with a joint in the lower layer. Moving back up the gutter, mastic and bed down the next strip, overlapping the first by 100 mm (4″).

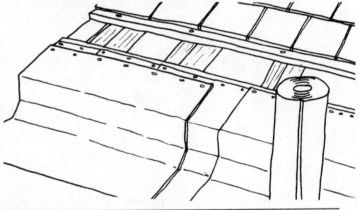

6

For a stronger covering use ordinary felt for the second layer as described and finish off with a third layer of mineralized felt, laid in mastic at right angles to the run of the gutter with 100 mm (4″) overlaps.

7

Replace the two rows of slates to either side of the valley, clipping the upper row as in 11.07. N.B. A more permanent covering is to have the zinc removed.

8

REBUILDING A VALLEY GUTTER

As noted in 11.03 many Victorian houses were built with a central valley gutter running from the front to back and these often fail. One common failure is that the central section of the gutter settles so that there is no longer a continuous fall from front to back and water collects in ponds in the gutter. Restoring a positive fall to such a gutter reduces the likelihood of future failure.

To either side of the valley gutter remove the first two rows of slates using a slate ripper (see 11.01). This should be enough to expose the edges of the covering to the valley which should then be removed.

1

Run a piece of string from the top end of the valley to the bottom and pull it taught. Using a spirit level check that there is a fall towards the outlet. If there is no fall, raise the end furthest from the outlet until a fall of 50 mm (2″) is achieved down the length of the gutter.

Cut and shape pieces of batten or plywood and nail them to the bottom of the valley gutter above the positions where the boards forming the base of the valley are nailed to supports (look for the old nailheads as a guide). These blocking pieces should stretch right across the valley and be high enough to touch the underside of the string.

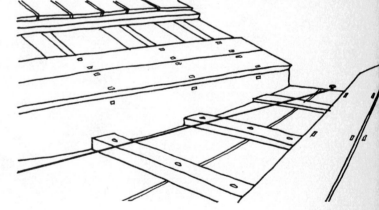

2

Cut a new bottom for the valley gutter out of 9 mm shuttering plywood. If the valley is a box gutter the bottom will have parallel sides, but if not it will taper towards the outlet end. Nail the plywood to the blocking pieces and sections of plywood above blocks.

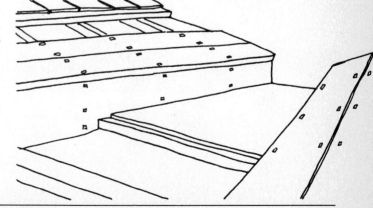

3

If the valley is a box gutter then cut a 45 degree tilting fillet from a piece of 50×50 mm (2″×2″) softwood and nail into the bottom corners of the box. At the shallow end of the gutter it may be necessary to shape the fillet with a rasp or plane so that it matches in with the shape of the roof.

If the boards at the side of the roof do not extend 450 mm up the slope from the new gutter, then extend them either with an old floor board or with plywood brought up to the same level. Recess all nail heads and smooth off any protruding corners.

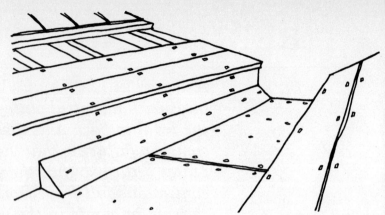

4

Re-cover valley as described in 11.03.

5

REPAIRING A ROOF TIMBER

A roof timber may require repair either because of damage or because it was badly constructed, for example, a rafter or purlin cut too short. This Sheet deals specifically with the repair of rafters whose ends have been damaged or have rotted. The principles can be applied to other repairs.

Support the affected rafters with 'Acrow' props, spreading the load on scaffold boards laid across the floor. If more than four rafters have to be repaired continue the propping down to the ground. Remove the roof covering over the affected area and 900 mm further down the rafters.

Cut off the damaged ends of the rafters at a point where the timber is firm. If the support to the rafters at the junction of the wall has also been damaged, attach a 75×50 mm timber to the wall using 'L' shaped brackets of 50×6 mm mild steel, set 100 mm into the brick courses at 600 mm centres and screwed to the timber. (See Sheet 11.06.)

1

Using the same section timber as the rafters, treated with preservative, bolt on extension pieces, which overlap the rafter end by 750 mm and are held in place with 3 No. 12 mm diameter coach bolts, with toothed timber connectors between them and 25 mm washers to the nut ends. Cut 'birdsmouth's' out of the ends of the rafters no deeper than one-third of their depth so that they sit on the supporting timber and nail them in place.

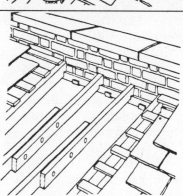

2

Replace the roof covering, renewing any battens and slates that are damaged or missing.

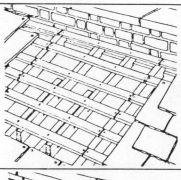

3

Fix a flashing or sand cement fillet to match the existing detail. (See Sheet 11.17.)

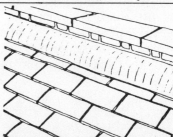

4

REPLACING A CORBEL SUPPORT TO A ROOF TIMBER

Rafters, wall plates and purlins are frequently supported on brick 'corbels'. In many houses this consists of a single brick projecting from the wall which has been too weak and has broken under the load. Provided the roof has not collapsed or settled, new supports can be added without removing the roof covering.

Where a wall plate has previously been supported by brick corbels it can be supported on 'L' shaped mild steel brackets set into the mortar course of the brickwork. First, out of 50×6 mm mild steel, make up, or have made up, some brackets which are the width of the wall plate, plus 100 mm long with a leg equal to the distance from the mortar course to the underside of the wall plate, plus half the depth of the wall plate long. Drill a 5 mm diameter hole in the leg, 12 mm from the end. With a sharp cold-chisel hack out the mortar at 600 mm centres along the mortar course. Tap the brackets into place so that they penetrate 100 mm into the brickwork and the vertical leg is hard up against the face of the wall plate. Point the brackets into the mortar course with 1:1:6, cement: lime: sand mortar. Where the bracket is not hard up against the underside of the wall plate, cut two wooden wedges and tap them, in opposition to each other, between the bracket and the wall plate. Do not force the wall plate upwards, drive the wedges only until they are firm. Screw the bracket to the wall plate.

Rafters which have lost their corbel support may be temporarily supported with props, while the corbels are cut off flush with the wall with a bolster. Then introduce a 75×50 mm wall plate supported on metal brackets as above, to pick up the ends of the rafters.

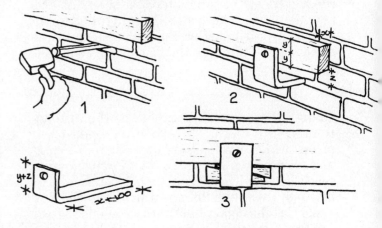

1

An individual roof timber may be supported on a galvanised mild steel joist hanger set into the brickwork. But it will not normally be possible to support the end in this way. Therefore a secondary strut must be nailed perpendicular to the rafter with its end cut to fit into a joist hanger set into the brickwork.

Alternatively, place a shaped blocking piece in the shoe of the joist hanger and nail the rafter to this block, also screwing or nailing the block to the hanger.

2

A NEW BOARD AND FELT ROOF

When a large area of roof covering has to be replaced it is often easier, quicker and cheaper to use a board and felt roof. In permanent work, 25 mm thick softwood boarding or exterior-quality plywood, or a particle board should be used, covered by three layers of felt. In short-life housing two layers of felt supported on thinner boarding is usually adequate.

Strip off the old roof covering, tiles, battens, etc., check that the roof timbers are sound and repair as necessary. Where roof timbers are not more than 450 mm apart provide a flat surface for the felt with second-hand floorboarding or 9 mm exterior-quality plywood. If the timbers are further apart or the roof is likely to be walked upon, then thicker boarding will be required. The plywood should be cut so that all sheets butt-joint over a rafter and a piece of 50×50 mm softwood should be nailed between the rafters to support joins at right angles to them.

When the roof is covered nail an ex 50×50 mm timber fillet to the boarding at the junction with any side walls.

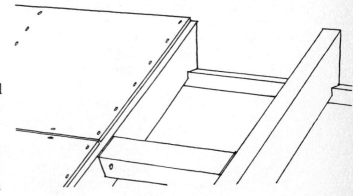

1

The first layer of roofing felt should be an asbestos or glass-fibre based felt with a roll weight of 55 lbs (25 kg) with a top layer of 80 lbs (36.6 kg) asbestos based, mineralised roofing felt. In three layer work the second layer is 55 lbs (25 kg) felt. The felt should be cut in advance of laying and laid flat so that it loses some of the curl of the roll. The first layer of felt is nailed in place, subsequent layers being bonded with hot bitumen or a cold bituminous mastic, such as 'Ruberoid' lap cement.

Starting at the bottom edge of the roof roll out the felt parallel to the bottom edge and nail it at 100 mm centres, with galvanised felt nails. At the junction with the wall, nail the felt to the tilting fillet and leave a free end standing 150 mm up the wall. Overlap any joins in the run of the felt by 150 mm. The next roll of felt overlaps the first by 50–75 mm and is similarly nailed in place, as are the successive layers, until the roof is covered. The top layer being nailed to the fillet and standing 150 mm up the wall, or else ending flush with the edge of the roof.

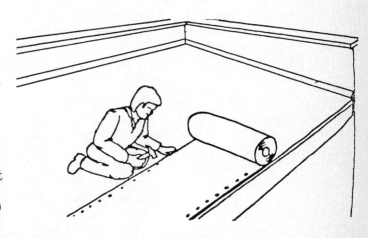

2

Form an 'L' shaped piece of mineralised roofing felt so that it will sit 100 mm on the roof and stand down the edge of the roof into the gutter. To form the 'L' gently warm the felt with a blow lamp and bend it over a batten, taking care not to crack it. Alternatively this section can be formed in zinc or Nuralite. Bed the 'L' section in hot bitumen or in lap cement, or a cold bituminous mastic.

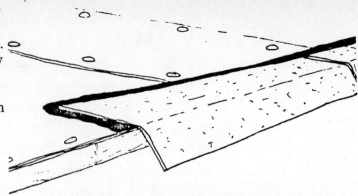

3

Apply a coat of hot bitumen or cold mastic the width of the roll and move across the roof rolling out the felt over the freshly laid adhesive. The first roll should be the one that the 'L' shaped section was cut from so that the joints will not coincide with the first layer. The first roll completely overlaps the leg of the 'L' shaped section, with subsequent rolls overlapping by 50–75 mm down the slope and 150 mm across the slope.

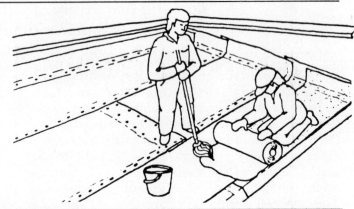

4

At junctions with walls the lower layer and the top layer, bonded together should stand against the wall, but not attached to it. A flashing piece of zinc, zincon or Nuralite is then formed and cut 25 mm into a mortar course in the brick or a saw cut in render so that it covers the upstand of the felt by 100–150 mm. The flashing is held in place by small metal wedges and pointed into the mortar course or render with 1:1:6, cement: lime: sand mortar. At internal corners the felt should be cut and folded so that it overlaps and an additional piece of felt added which extends 150 mm in each direction from the corner.

5

At any hip or junction lay the bottom layer of felt to the ridge lapping the top layers over the ridge and covering the ridge with an additional length of felt.

If a ridge or hip board projects more than 50 mm above the boarding, lay the layers of felt so that they stand up against and are nailed to the ridge/hip boards. Cover the hip/ridge with a metal, asbestos or clay ridge piece. The clay piece being bedded in 1:6 cement: sand mortar, the metal and asbestos sections being secured to the top of the ridge/hip boards with twist nails seated in compressible plastic lap washers.

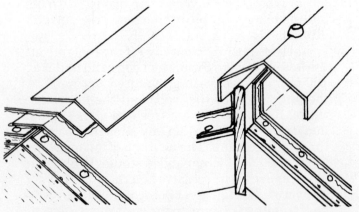

6

11.08
RENEWING THE COVERING TO A FLAT ROOF

A flat roof is normally considered to be any roof with a pitch less than 10°. The most common covering materials are zinc and roofing felt. Two layer roofing felt is adequate for most short-life housing, but three layer felt is normal in long-life work.

Strip off the old roof covering. Remove any battens used to support joins in zinc roofing and pull out or recess any nails. Piece in boarding where damaged to provide a flat even surface. Nail an ex 50×50 timber fillet to the boarding at the junction with any walls.

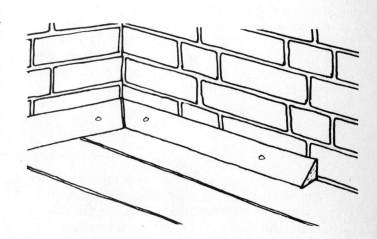

1

The first layer of roofing felt should be an asbestos or glass-fibre based felt with a roll weight of 55 lbs (25 kg) with a top layer of 80 lbs (36.6 kg) asbestos based, mineralised roofing felt. In three layer work the second layer is 55 lbs (25 kg) felt. The felt should be cut in advance of laying and laid flat so that it loses some of the curl of the roll. The first layer of felt is nailed in place, subsequent layers being bonded with hot bitumen or a cold bituminous mastic, such as 'Ruberoid' lap cement.

Starting at the bottom edge of the roof roll out the felt parallel to the bottom edge and nail it at 100 mm centres, with galvanised felt nails. At the junction with the wall, nail the felt to the tilting fillet and leave a free end standing 150 mm up the wall. Overlap any joins in the run of the felt by 150 mm. The next roll of felt overlaps the first by 50–75 mm and is similarly nailed in place, as are the successive layers, until the roof is covered. The top layer being nailed to the fillet and standing 150 mm up the wall, or else ending flush with the edge of the roof.

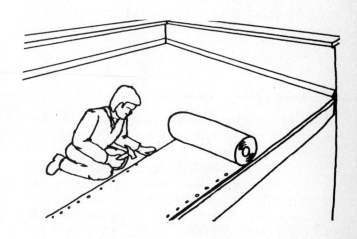

2

Form an 'L' shaped piece of mineralised roofing
felt so that it will sit 100 mm on the roof and
stand down the edge of the roof into the gutter.
To form the 'L' gently warm the felt with a blow
lamp and bend it over a batten, taking care not
to crack it. Alternatively this section can be
formed in zinc or Nuralite. Bed the 'L' section in
hot bitumen or in lap cement, or a cold
bituminous mastic.

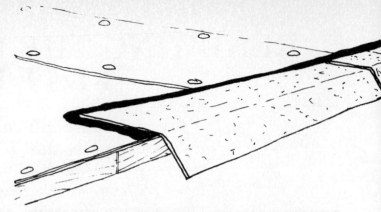

3
___

Apply a coat of hot bitumen or cold mastic the
width of the roll and move across the roof rolling
out the felt over the freshly laid adhesive. The
first roll should be the one that the 'L' shaped
section was cut from so that the joints will not
coincide with the first layer. The first roll
completely overlaps the leg of 'L' shaped section,
with subsequent rolls overlapping by 50–75 mm
down the slope and 150 mm across the slope.

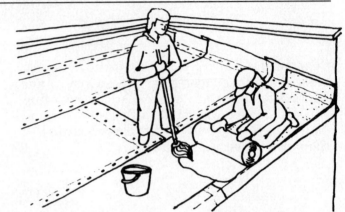

4
___

At junctions with walls the lower layer and the
top layer, bonded together should stand against
the wall, but not attached to it. A flashing piece
of zinc, zincon or Nuralite is then formed and cut
25 mm into a mortar course in the brick, or a saw
cut in render so that it covers the upstand of the
felt by 100–150 mm. The flashing is held in place
by small metal wedges and pointed into the
mortar course or render with 1:1:6, cement:
lime: sand mortar. At internal corners the felt
should be cut and folded so that it overlaps and
an additional piece of felt added which extends
150 mm in each direction from the corner.

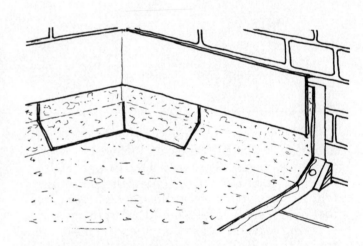

5
___

At an exposed top edge a similar 'L' shape to that
formed at the bottom edge may be lapped over
the felt. Alternatively an upstand may be made
by nailing a board to the edge of the roof so that
it projects 150 mm above. A tilting fillet is nailed
in the angle between the board and the roof and
felt lead up the board as a wall junction. A metal
coping is then nailed or screwed to the top edge
of the board so that it overlaps the felt by 100
mm.

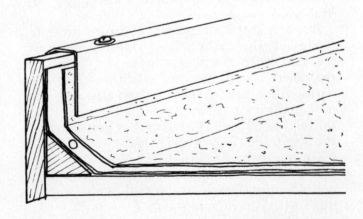

6
___

11.09
REPAIRING THE COVERING TO A FLAT ROOF

In some cases a flat roof covering may be essentially sound but require localised repair.

An Asphalt roof is a difficult covering to permanently repair since hot asphalt must be applied at set temperatures and permanent repairs are therefore best left to an expert. However, temporary repairs can be made by cleaning the area around a crack, applying a coat of Aquaseal 5 or Synthaprufe and bedding a nylon or pre-shrunk hessian reinforcing mesh into it while wet. When the surface is tacky apply a coat of Aquaseal 40, making sure that all the holes in the mesh are covered. Leave for twenty-four hours and finally recoat with Aquaseal 5. This method is adequate for cracks, the most common failure, but larger areas may need to be felted using a cold mastic adhesive, or covered with a thin layer of asphalt laid on a sheathing felt.

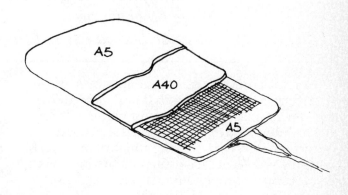

1

Metal roof coverings, particularly zinc tend to corrode with failure often being evident first on the upstands of the junctions between the sheets. The life of a zinc roof may be extended if the sheeting is basically sound, by cleaning off oxidation to the upstanding joints and then covering with 'Sylglass' or Aquaseal tape.

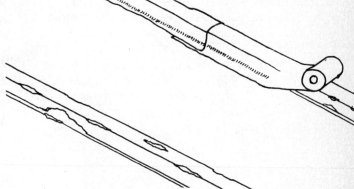

2

If a felt roof has been punctured the hole can be covered with felt bedded in mastic or hot bitumen, but it should be remembered that no joint should be open to the direction of the rain flow and the patch will have to be extended to the top of the roof. Attempting to lift other pieces of felt to provide a lap is not advisable since this is likely to cause more damage.

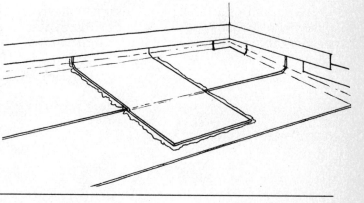

3

11.10
CLEANING AND REPAIRING A GUTTER

Guttering comes in a number of materials, most commonly zinc, cast iron and plastic, and a variety of shapes, including half-round, rectangular and ogee. A gutter may leak because it is blocked, because it does not have a correct fall or because it is broken or corroded.

Clean out a gutter using a scraper or a trowel and a brush, making sure that no debris go down the down pipe. Once the accumulated silt and debris have been removed wash the gutter clean with water, hosing being the simplest method. If the gutter does not leak, then no further repair is necessary, although a metal gutter will benefit from a coat of bituminous paint.

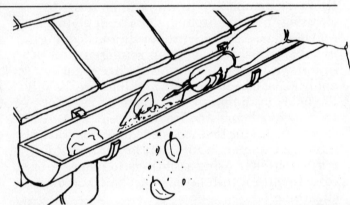

1

When a gutter appears to overflow at a point on its length removed from the downpipe, check that the gutter slopes towards the downpipe, with a spirit level. Where a low point is discovered stretch a string along the length of the gutter to check that it is localised. A localised low point can be eliminated by raising the gutter by screwing an additional bracket underneath it. However, when a number of lengths are sloping in the wrong direction the gutter should be taken down and re-erected to a fall. (See Sheet 11.11.)

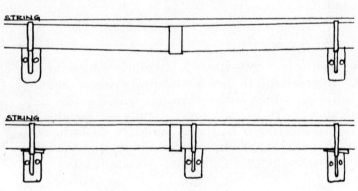

2

If the joints in guttering are leaking, smooth putty into the joint so that it is flush with the inside of the gutter and paint it with bituminous paint.

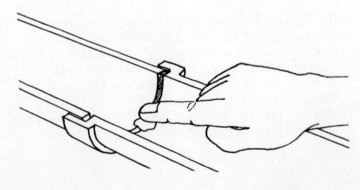

3

If a section of gutter is broken or holed it will normally have to be replaced. Different types of guttering are jointed in different ways, and an individual length in a run of guttering can only be replaced if the joints can be undone without damaging the gutter, and if a replacement piece of the same section and joint can be obtained. It is often simplest to replace a run of guttering with new plastic saving the good pieces for piecing-in elsewhere.

4

A small split or corrosion hole in a cast iron gutter can be temporarily patched. First open out a tin can and trim off the rims and the seam to provide a flat sheet. Form this sheet to the outside shape of the gutter and clean the gutter around the hole both inside and out, with a wire brush. Cover the tin with an epoxy adhesive and wire it to the outside of the gutter until the adhesive has set. Fill the hole flush with the inside of the gutter with the adhesive or an inert metal filler. When the adhesive is dry coat both the inside of the gutter and the tin patch with bituminous paint.

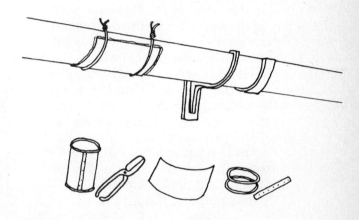

5

11.11
INSTALLING GUTTERING

Modern plastic guttering has push-together joints with some form of built-in seal. The joints are normally special fittings so that lengths may be sawn as required. Fittings and gutter lengths will not normally be interchangeable between manufacturers.

Tap a nail in the fascia board above the position of the downpipe and tie a string to this nail. Stretch the string out to the end of the gutter run. Level it with a spirit level and tap another nail into the fascia board at the end of the string and level with the first. Measure the distance between the two nails and divide this dimension by 200 to give the height of the end above the downpipe. Nail a second nail into the fascia this height above the first at the end of the run. Tie a string between the top nail and the downpipe nail so that it is taut, and it should now fall towards the downpipe at the rate of 1 in 200.

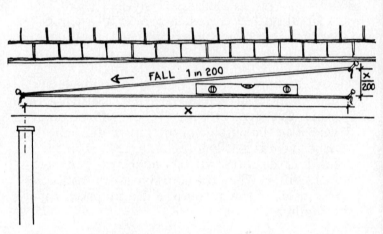

1

Making allowance for special fittings such as the stop ends and the downpipe outlet, screw gutter brackets to the fascia so that they are in line with the string at approximately 1 metre centres.

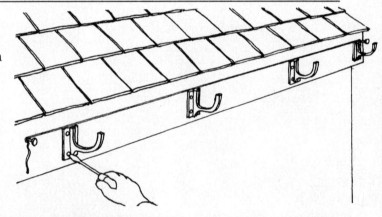

2

Cut lengths of gutter with a hacksaw and smooth-off burrs of plastic with a file or sharp knife. Push the fittings and sections of gutters together and snap the guttering into the gutter brackets. If the joints resist fitting do not lubricate the seals with an oil or detergent-based lubricant since this will cause a deterioration in the gaskets. Instead use water or water with a little soap applied to the gaskets.

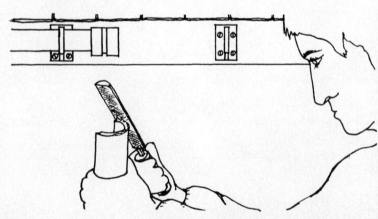

3

RENEWING A GUTTER BOARD

Gutter boards are frequently badly maintained because of their relatively inaccessible position. As a result they are frequently decayed.

Take down the guttering. It is not advisable to attempt to take down heavy guttering from a ladder, and a scaffold tower properly tied back to the building may be required. Once the guttering has been removed take down the defective gutter board.

If the board is fixed on the ends of the roof timbers check that they are sound and if necessary repair them. (See Sheet 11.05.) Paint the ends of the timbers with wood preservative. If the board is fixed against brickwork, usually by nails into wooden wedges, take out the wooden wedges and repoint the brickwork.

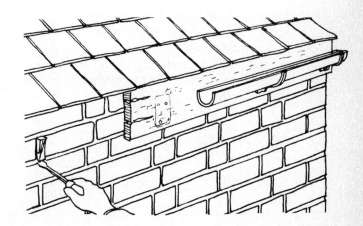

1

Using a similar size of timber cut the new gutter board, treat it with a clear preservative and paint it before fixing. If the board is fixed to the roof timbers nail it in place, recess, fill and paint the nail heads. If the board is fixed to the brickwork drill clearance holes for a 62.5 mm long No. 10 screws at 1.000 m centres and countersink the holes. Hold the board in position and mark the holes on the brickwork. Using a masonry bit, drill holes in the brickwork and plug them with plastic plugs. Screw the board into position, fill and paint the screw heads. Replace the gutters as Sheet 11.11.

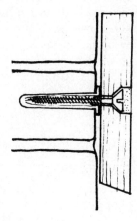

2

11.13
REPLACING A MISSING TILE

Tiles are usually clay or concrete and come in a number of sizes. Some are held in place by a locating nib which hooks over the tile batten, others are nailed in position.

Gently prise up the tiles above the broken one and attempt to unhook the nib from the batten. If the tile is nailed in place then use a slate ripper to snap off the nails. Take the tile to a builders merchant or demolition yard to use as guide when buying a replacement.

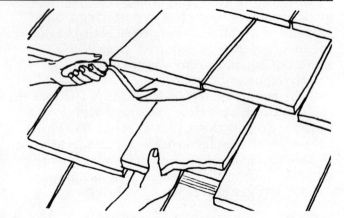

1

When replacing a nibbed tile, even one which was previously nailed, prise up the tiles above the missing tile, slide the new tile in position until the nibs have hooked over a batten. Ease the top slates back down onto the new slate which should now stay in position.

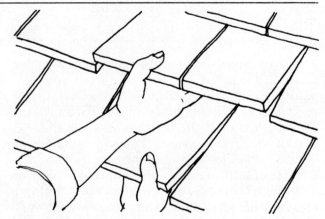

2

If the tile has no nib then it must be held in place by a clip made of copper wire, zinc or lead strip. Between the two tiles exposed by the removed tile locate the tile batten, if necessary by probing with a knife blade. Nail the wire or strip to this batten, ease up the tiles above and slip the replacement slate into place. Bend up the end of the wire/strip to hold the tile into place.

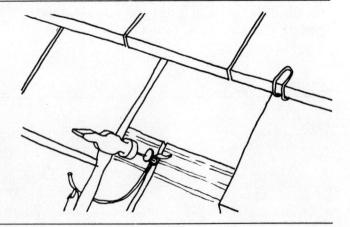

3

11.14
REPLACING A SLATE ROOF WITH CONCRETE TILE

When a slate roof is badly damaged it is common to strip off the old covering and replace it with concrete interlocking tiles. These are heavier than slates and the Building Inspector or District Surveyor will require some additional strengthening to the roof to be added.

Strip the old slates (and valley gutter if there is one). Recover the valley gutter as in 11.03 or 11.04. Take off all the old slate battens.

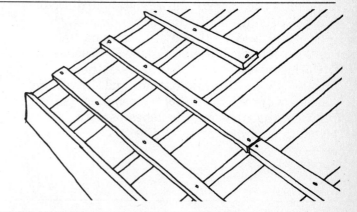

1

At the bottom of the roof slope nail a batten which will cause the bottom tile to tilt up slightly. Starting by overlapping this batten by 75 mm (3″) lay strips of lightweight tiling or sarking felt. Tack or staple the felt to the rafters, keep the felt taut and overlap each time by 75 mm (3″).

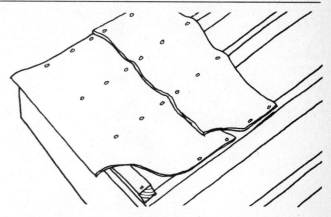

2

Interlocking roof tiles are held in place with nibs and have a minimum head and side lap which incorporates anti-capillary grooves. The head lap can be increased. Measure down the slope of the roof and determine how many equally-spaced whole tiles are needed increasing the head lap if necessary. Equally space ex 38 × 19 mm (1½″ × ¾″) preservative treated softwood battens down the slope, nailing them through the felt into the rafter. Take care not to rip the felt and butt or splay join battens over a rafter.

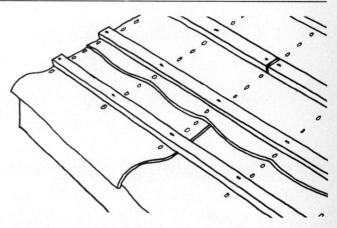

3

Starting at the bottom of the slope, hook the first tile over the first tile batten so that its end is supported by the tilting batten. Complete the first row and then hook on the next row of tiles and work up the roof.

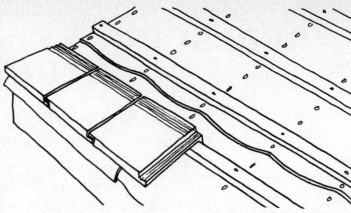

4
_____

The eaves tiles are cut out of a standard tile or can be specially made tiles depending on the type of tile used. At the eaves, before nailing in place the felt and battens, nail pieces of asbestos to the last rafter so that they oversail the wall by 50 mm (2"). Lay the felt, battens and tiles in the normal way. When the roof is complete point between the tiles and the asbestos with 1:3 cement: sand mortar.

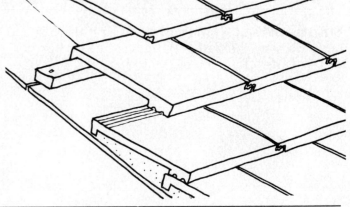

5
_____

11.15
REPLACING A DOWNPIPE

A damaged downpipe, when beyond repair, should be replaced before the discharge of rainwater down the wall causes failure of the pointing and damp penetration.

Remove the old downpipe. Many cast iron downpipes are held in place with metal spikes driven into the brickwork and these can be levered from the wall using a crowbar.

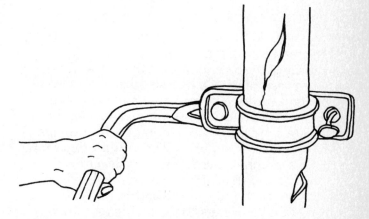

1

Measure the external diameter of the outlet from the gutter. Purchase a UPVC rainwater pipe which is either of larger internal diameter or has a collar of larger internal diameter than the external diameter of the outlet.

Slip the new downpipe around the end of the outlet so that it overlaps by at least 25 mm (1″) and fix it to the wall with saddle brackets screwed to rawlplugs in the brickwork.

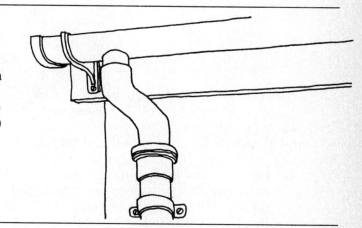

2

If the bottom of the downpipe discharges over a gulley, take the pipe down below the level of the gulley and cut the grating to fit tightly around the pipe so that no hole is left larger than the mesh of the grating. If the bottom of the downpipe fits into a sealed rainwater gulley, use a cold chisel to clean out the old mortar carefully from the collar. Fit the end of the pipe into the gulley and pack it around with hemp and putty or wet newspaper. Point around the bottom of the pipe with 'prompt cement'.

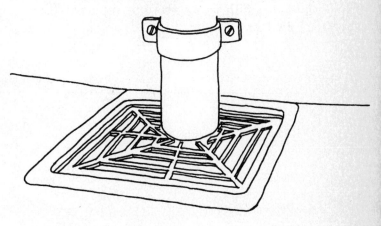

3

11.16
REPAIRING A DOWNPIPE

*Downpipes which leak can cause damp
problems both by spraying water onto brickwork
and by washing out the pointing to the
brickwork. Often leaks may be the result of
blockages.*

Place a bucket or a flat tin under the end of the
downpipe to catch any debris. If possible
disconnect the downpipe from the gutter. This is
often possible with cast-iron gutters and
downpipes which frequently have loose swan
neck connections. Using drain rods or a length of
flexible cane clear any blockages. If drainage
rods are used then brush out any silt deposits
using a brush attached to the rods. Otherwise
weight a length of string with a nut and feed it
down the downpipe; at the bottom end attach a
small bundle of rags to the string and draw it
through the pipe.

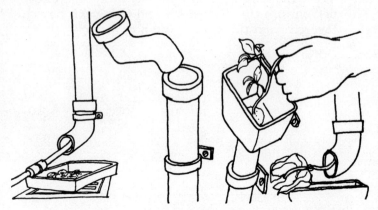

1

Small cracks in the downpipe can be patched by
binding the pipe spirally with 'Aquaseal' or
'Sylglass' tape. Alternatively a piece of
'Flashband' can be gently warmed and tapped
round the downpipe. A third method of repair is
to cut up a tin can and bind it around the
downpipe with 'Aquaseal' or 'Sylglass' tape, or
bond to the pipe using an epoxy adhesive.

   If the pipe is badly cracked or holed the
complete section will need to be replaced. (See
Sheet 11.15.)

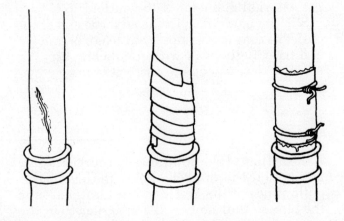

2

FLASHINGS

Flashings are used to protect the junction of one material or part of a building with another, from water penetration.

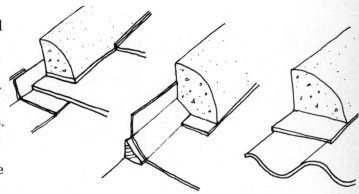

Cement : sand fillets are an inexpensive traditional form of water-proofing. They can fail due to cracking resulting from different movement of, say a roof and a wall, or because they are too permeable for their position.

Fillets are most effective when used to cover metal soakers in the case of slates, felt upstands in the case of felt roofs and other upstand details.

To reduce the possibility of the fillet cracking, place a 150 mm wide slate on the roof at the junction with the wall, lapping slates down the slope and build up a slightly rounded fillet of 1:3 cement: sand mortar, covering the slate and standing 150 mm up the wall. Smooth and polish the top of the fillet with a trowel. A water-proofing agent can be added to the mortar to increase its impermeability.

1

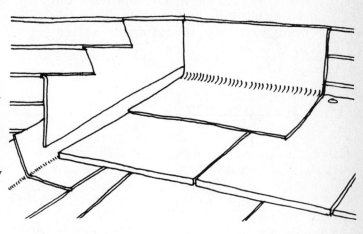

Metal flashings are usually made of zinc or lead. Lead is prohibitively expensive for short-life housing. A metal flashing stands down the wall, is located in a mortar course to brickwork or a cut line in render and covers the upstand of a roof covering or of metal soakers. At the top of a roof slope a flashing stands 150 mm up the wall and lays 150 mm down the roof slope. At the side of a roof the flashing stops 10 mm above the roof, or the angled fillets and overlaps the vertical stand of soakers or flashings. Its top edge may have to be stepped to fit into the brickwork. Flashings should be cut to step so that they are no less than 150 mm wide measured perpendicular to the roof slope.

The top of the flashing is bent so that it penetrates 25 mm into the brickwork. The flashing is held in position with wedges and pointed into the brickwork with mortar.

2

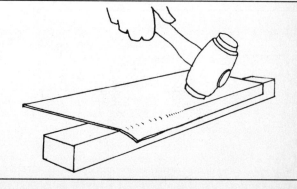

To form a zinc flashing bend it over a wooden straight edge using a rubber panel beater's hammer, or a wooden mallet. Do not overwork the zinc by too much bending as this will result in work-hardening and deterioration of the metal.

3

11.18
NEW CORRUGATED ASBESTOS ROOFING

An effective, relatively inexpensive and simple way to install roof covering is corrugated asbestos sheeting. The sheets come in a variety of sizes with purpose-made accessories for eaves, hips, ridges, etc. Asbestos roofing sheets should only be sawn, cut or drilled in well ventilated areas, while wearing a mask or respirator. All nail holes should be predrilled in the top of a corrugation. Due to the brittle nature of asbestos, it is advisable to use crawl boards to spread the load on the roof.

Strip off the old roof covering, including the battens, check that the roof timbers are sound and repair them as necessary. Asbestos sheets should be fixed in six places, twice in the centre, and twice in each of the top and bottom overlaps. The top and bottom overlap should be 150 mm and the size of the sheet will determine the positioning of the support battens. Nail 50×50 mm fixing battens to the rafters at centres necessary to fix the sheets.

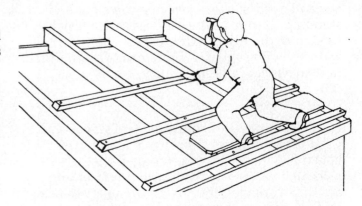

1

At the bottom of the roof fix the first sheet so that it overlaps the inside edge of the gutter, using galvanised twist roofing nails, seated in plastic compressible cup washers. Nail only the bottom and centre on the side away from the next sheet. Overlap the next sheet by one corrugation, drill through both sheets and nail the bottom and centre fixing to one side only. Proceed in this manner until the first row of sheets is in place.

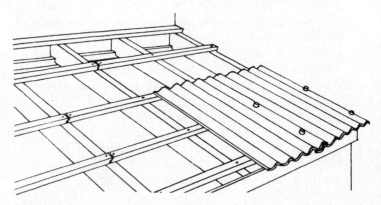

2

The next row of sheets overlaps the first by 150 mm and fixing is the same as for the first. Successive rows are laid in this way.

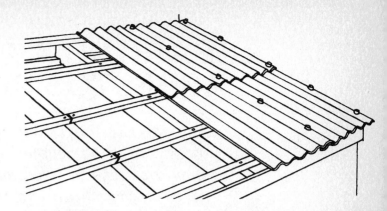

3

The last row of sheets is built up against the ridge or a wall and is fixed at top, bottom and centre, as each sheet is laid.

4

REPAIRING A CORRUGATED ASBESTOS SHEET ROOF

Asbestos sheeting is brittle and can be damaged by impact or by people walking on it. Boards should always be used when working on asbestos roofs to spread the load. Asbestos should be cut or drilled only in the open air, or in a very well ventilated space, while wearing a face mask, or respirator and goggles.

To remove a damaged sheet of asbestos, place a plank across the sheet below each set of nails and pull out the nails using a claw hammer, levering against the plank. The nails fixing the bottom of the sheet directly above the one to be removed will also have to be removed.

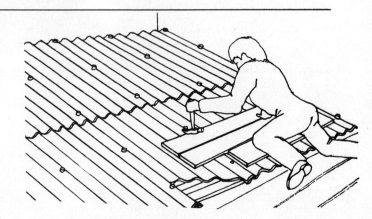

1

Once the nails have been removed, carefully take out the broken sheet and slide a replacement into position, so that it overlaps its neighbour on one side, and is overlapped by its neighbour on the other by 70 mm and laps above the sheet below and under the sheet above by 150 mm.

Drill fixing holes at the top, centre and bottom of each sheet to each side, on top of a corrugation. Nail the sheet in place with galvanised twist roofing nails, with their heads seated in purpose-made compressible polythene washers.

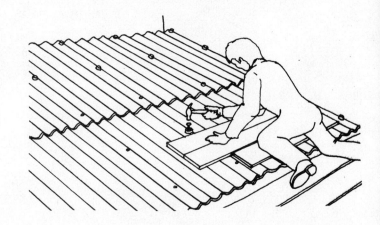

2

To repair a hair-line crack to an asbestos sheet, clean the sheet 50 mm to either side of the crack, using a wire brush and wearing a protective mask. Cover the crack with 'Sylglass' or 'Aquaseal' tape. This type of repair will not be successful if the crack is in the bottom of the trough of the corrugation.

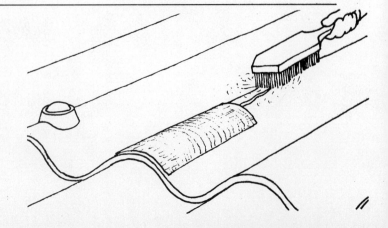

3

When covering the junction of asbestos sheeting and a wall with a cement : sand fillet, place a loose section of corrugated sheeting over the top of the sheets, 150 mm long or 150 mm wide pieces of slate down the sides of the sheet. Build the fillet up on these loose sections, not the corrugated sheeting. In this way movement of the roof will not break the cement : sand fillet.

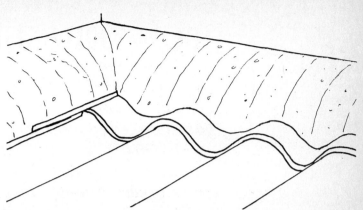

4

11.20
TURNERISING A ROOF

Turnerising is a technique by which a slate roof is covered with a continuous covering. It has the advantage of holding together slates or tiles which are in bad condition but has the disadvantage that it needs an additional layer of mastic every three years to remain effective and if it starts to leak it is very difficult to trace.

Clean off any moss or bird droppings from the slates and brush off any loose dirt. Push loose slates back into place and replace missing slates with another slate, or a piece of asbestos, lino or thick roofing felt.

1

Turn up any flashings around the sides of the roof so that the turnerising can be taken up under them.

2

Starting with a strip running down the slope, paint the slates with a coat of Aquaseal 5 or Synthaprufe, working upwards to force mastic into the joints between the slates. While the mastic is still wet, lay a strip of nylon reinforcing net or treated hessian on top. Bed the reinforcement into the mastic taking care to mould it into the ridges formed by the slates. Lay the next strip in the same way overlapping the first by 75 mm (3″).

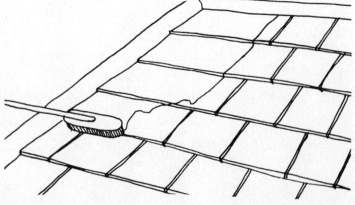

3

Apply a coat of Aquaseal 40 or Synthaprufe over the mesh, working upwards and allow to dry. Finally paint on another layer of Aquaseal 5 or Synthaprufe. When the final layer has dried it should not be possible to see any of the holes in the reinforcing net and the net should just be perceptible.

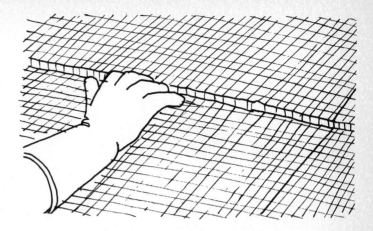

4 _____

Fold down the flashing to cover the edge of the turnerising. If there are no flashings then take the turnerising up the face of the parapet wall to the underside of the coping stone or the projecting brick course. If there is no projection then take the turnerising 150 mm (6″) up the face of the wall and then add a flashing (11.17). Ridge and hip tiles should be turnerised along with the remainder of the roof but with a layer of mesh which overlaps the top layers to either side by at least 100 mm (4″).
N.B. Synthaprufe is water soluble when it is wet so choose a dry day otherwise it will be washed off of the roof by rain.

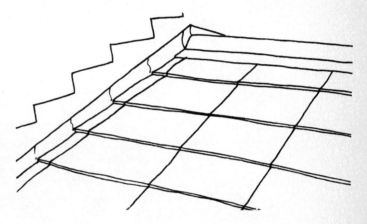

5 _____

12
DRAINS

The purpose of drainage is to dispose of waste water and sewage so that it does not cause a health hazard. In order to do this effectively drainage systems must be gas and water-tight and provide seals or traps to prevent noxious gases escaping.

Drains have to cope with three products, known as waste, soil and surface water, which are simply defined as:

Waste is the water from wash hand basins, baths, sinks, showers and bidets.

Soil is the effluent from W.C.s and urinals.

Surface water is rainwater from roofs and hard-paved areas.

In many districts, particularly older ones, the drainage system is combined, i.e. waste soil and surface water all go into the one sewer. However, increasingly dual systems are being used which have one sewer for waste and soil, another for surface water or storm water. Also where soil conditions permit, surface water is sometimes disposed of via 'soakaways' which are pits filled with rubble or pebbles, sited in back gardens. In rural or remote locations the house may be connected to a septic tank.

According to modern theory drains should be laid so that they can be easily rodded through, so that there are manholes at strategic junctions, and drains below buildings are avoided if possible. On older houses none of these principles may have been observed, or all of them, plus an extra lavish provision of manholes. Houses may be connected directly to the public sewer, normally sited in the street, or may first connect to a 'private' sewer running along the front or back of a number of houses before joining the public sewer. In Victorian terraced housing the drain will often run from a manhole in the backyard, under the house to the street – alternatively there may be no manhole. Where no manhole can be found, look for a piece of slate or stone flag which might conceal a shallow inspection chamber or a piece of clay or cast-iron pipe sticking out of the ground with an access cover on the head.

Drainage records are kept by the Local Authority and are available for public reference. However, these records may be inadequate for older property. The Local Authority are responsible for the construction and maintenance of public sewers and are empowered by the Public Health Acts to control the construction of drains discharging into them. Therefore if any alterations to the existing underground drainage is necessary, or new drainage has to be installed, then the Local Authority Building Inspectorate or Environmental Health Department should be informed.

Drainage Below Ground

Below ground drainage has traditionally been laid in glazed earthenware pipework, although many Local Authorities will now accept UPVC (Unplasticised Poly Vinyl Chloride) pipework which is much simpler to use.

Whatever the material used, drains must be constructed so that they are evenly supported, protected where they pass under walls or areas, such as driveways where vehicles may pass, jointed so that they will not leak, have the correct fall, are provided with water seals to prevent gases and rats escaping into a building or its surroundings, and be adequately ventilated.

Taking the above items in more detail the following practical points emerge:

(a) **Support** – Pipes should be laid on an even gravel bed and should not have to bridge over any holes.

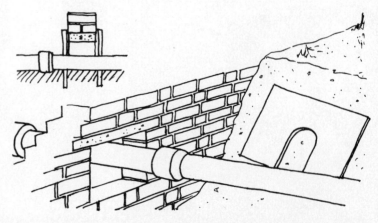

(b) **Protection** – Where a pipe passes through a wall, the wall should be carried on a lintel and space left around the pipe to allow for movement. Under roadways, driveways and parking places the pipe should be protected with concrete and some reinforcement introduced into the construction of the vehicle path. Pipes should be at sufficient depth to be protected from 'seasonal' soil movement which can be up to a metre deep in clay soil. New drains should have at least 750 mm from the top of the drain to the surface.

(c) **Jointing** – Earthenware pipes can be jointed with a ring of tarred hemp followed by 1:1 sand: cement mortar pointing, or by some form of butyl or polypropylene couplings. UPVC drainage systems incorporate patent push-fit jointing systems which if correctly used will not leak.

(d) **Fall** – It is very important to lay drains to the correct fall. Too steep a fall will cause the solids to be left behind. Too shallow a fall will mean inadequate sewage run-off, and either can result in blockage. New drains should be laid to a fall of 1 in 40 for a single house.

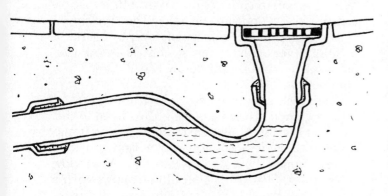

(e) **Seals** – With the exception of the soil stack, any connection to a drain should incorporate a 'U' bend containing water. The individual fittings connecting to a soil stack should also all be fitted with a trap containing a water seal. These seals stop sewer gases escaping into the building or its surroundings.

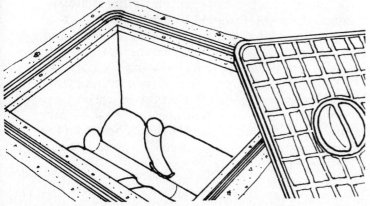

(f) **Access** – Manholes and rodding points must be provided so that all parts of the drain can be reached to clear blockages. This may be achieved by incorporating rodding access points at strategic positions.

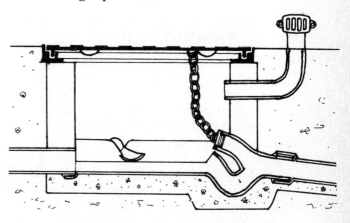

(g) **Ventilation** – Drainage runs must be ventilated to prevent the build-up of gases, and this is simply achieved by carrying the soil stack up past the last connection and the roof level and leaving an open end at least 900 mm (3'–0") above any window opening which is within 3 metres (10'–0").

Some local authorities require an interceptor or disconnecting chamber to be constructed before the connection with the public sewer. This prevents sewer gas entering the private drain but the interceptor manhole must be provided with a fresh air inlet which does not always have an effective seal.

External Drainage above Ground

External above ground drainage is concerned with the disposal of rainwater, either from roofs or from paved areas. Traditionally both are taken to the drain by means of a gulley. Gullies are normally square in plan with a cast iron or plastic grating. Below ground they sit on a 'U' shaped trap. When draining a paved area the gulley is placed at a low point and the surface sloped towards it, when taking rainwater from the roof the bottom of the rainwater pipe usually stops above the grating and a 'shoe' directs the water into the gulley.

Additionally, waste fittings may also discharge into a gulley, either directly or via a hopper in the rainwater downpipe.

The problem with gulleys is that the grating can become blocked with paper or fallen leaves and the waste or surface water cannot then run away causing flooding. These problems can be overcome by using a back inlet gulley which has a connection point which is separate from the gulley top, or by taking the pipe through a tight fitting cut out in the grating. Some local authorities do not allow waste fittings to be connected into the rainwater downpipe, or to discharge over gullies. In modern installations rainwater pipes are often connected directly to a pipe with a trap.

Internal Drainage above Ground

The drainage for most internal fittings is normally run down the outside of the building in old houses. Until a recent amendment to the Building Regulations which omits houses up to three storey, all new buildings have been required to fit internal drainage. The waste and soil are connected into a soil stack which in older houses is usually of cast iron and 100 mm (4″) diameter. Modern soil stacks are often made of UPVC. In older houses the soil stack is frequently used in conjunction with a separate vent pipe and the two pipes connected to the

The following table gives connection lengths and gradients, assuming that fittings have a 75 mm deep water-seal, a 'P', or Bottle Trap. 'S' Traps are susceptible to self-syphonage, and should not be used.

Fitting	Waste Size mm	Fall	Maximum Distance from trap to Stack
Bath	38	1:50 to	2.300 m
	50	1:10	4.000 m
Bidet	32	1:50 to	1.700 m
	38	1:10	3.000 m
Shower	38	1:50 to	2.300 m
	50	1:10	4.000 m
Sink	38	1:50 to	2.300 m
	50	1:10	4.000 m
Washbasin	32	1:50 to	1.700 m
	36	1:10	3.000 m
W.C.	100	104°	1.500 m *

* This table is based on recommendations included in the D.o.E. Design Bulletin 30. However, the GLC give a dimension of 2.400 m.

fittings, which are somewhat confusingly referred to as 'one pipe systems'. Three variations known as 'one pipe', 'modified one pipe' and 'modified one-pipe vented stack' systems are found to be quite common. Modern installations are usually a 'single stack' which just consists of a single soil pipe.

Connections to a soil stack which does not have a separate vent to each fitting must be made so that there is no loss of the water seal. The water seal is normally lost by self-syphonage, or by syphonage or back pressure from the stack. Both result from a discharge completely filling the diameter of the pipe and running at such velocity that it sucks out the water seal. Provided fittings are correctly positioned, waste pipes are of the right size and slope, connections are made into the soil stack in a proper relationship and adequate traps are provided, there are unlikely to be any problems from the loss of the water seal.

Waste connections to the stack should be vertically separate or directly opposite each other. Connections which are only marginally different in height can lead to problems with the waste from one flowing up the lower waste pipe. Where a waste connection would otherwise enter a stack opposite or below the W.C. connection it must be dropped lower by means of a 50 mm vertical section so that it enters the stack at least 200 mm below the W.C. connection.

The stack should be straight from the foot where it should have a large radius bend to the topmost fitting. Above the topmost fitting it may be bent since it is then purely a vent pipe and where it ends, 900 m (3′–0″) above any window within 3 m (10′–0″) it should be capped with a wire balloon or plastic grille to prevent birds falling into, or building their nests on top of the pipe.

Connecting waste pipes together can also result in syphonage of the trap and this is most simply avoided by running wastes separately to the stack or by using a combined waste of a larger diameter. Loss of the water seal is more a problem with washbasins than other fittings since they are designed to empty quickly, to carry away any soap scum. Sinks, showers and baths have relatively flat bottoms, so that even if the seal is sucked out by the main emptying the last of the water trickles slowly into the trap and reforms the seal. A number of anti-syphonage traps are available but these require more maintenance and should only be used if the pipework cannot be arranged to make them unnecessary.

Blockages

Working with existing drains and manholes can be extremely unpleasant, particularly when blockages have to be removed. It is advisable to wear protective clothing, rubber gloves and wellington boots and have some disinfectant to hand. Take care not to get raw sewage onto any cuts, grazes or open wounds, and if this happens then go to a doctor for an anti-tetanous injection.

Firms such as 'Dyno-Rod' specialise in work to existing drains, but they are not cheap and it is sensible to get an estimate. There are a lot of 'cowboy' plumbing firms who advertise their services for this sort of work but they will often be expensive and not actually do a good job. Unless someone has been well recommended by a friend it is better to rely on the national reputation of a firm who would find adverse publicity a deterrent to bad workmanship. If a blockage is between the last manhole on the house drain and the public sewer, the Local Authority may unblock it for little or no charge.

MAINTENANCE OF EXISTING MANHOLES

The manhole can be sited in the front or back garden, a basement well or even in a basement or cellar.

Clean off dirt from the manhole cover and rake out the channel around the rim. The cover is made of cast iron and is heavy, so care should be taken not to trap fingers, or to lift the cover in an awkward stance which could hurt the back. To lift a small, light-weight cover crouch astride it, knees bent, back straight, grasp one of the handles and lift one end by straightening the knees. If the cover will not move then loosen it by inserting the end of a crow bar under the edge, working around the rim rather than attempting to lever against any one point. If the handles are corroded, loosen the lid with a crowbar, lift the lid and slip a piece of wood below one corner and grip the edge to lift.

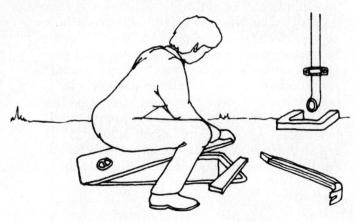

1

A heavy-duty cover or one with a concrete filled top can be rolled off using one, preferably two pieces of old gas barrel. As before, loosen the cover and with the crowbar in the centre of one end raise the lid and slip a length of gas barrel which is longer than the width of the cover under one corner, as far in as possible. Release the crowbar and move across so that it is outside of the pipe and again raise the cover. Push the pipe in so that it is at right angles to the cover and release the crowbar. Pulling the cover with the crooked end of the crowbar, roll it on the pipe placing the other piece of pipe in the path of the cover to provide a second roller.

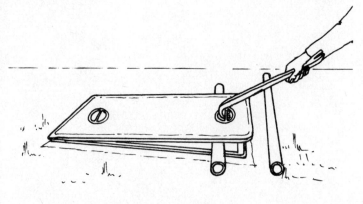

2

If the manhole is full of sewage or there are signs that it blocks, such as a 'tide mark' around the inside of the manhole, or pieces of paper stuck to the brickwork or to any step rungs, then rod the drains in accordance with Sheet 12.07. Before working in a manhole hose it down, and if it is one which is deep enough to climb into spraying the inside with a mixture of water and disinfectant will produce a healthier working environment.

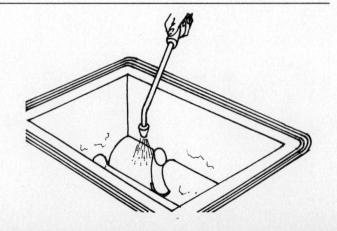

3

The bottom of the manhole has a glazed earthenware channel into which other pipes discharge. The base is formed out of concrete shaped to ensure that the sewage does not stick in the manhole. This shaping is known as 'benching'. If the benching is cracked repair it by chipping out the crack with a cold chisel and hammer until it is about 25 mm wide. Then mix up a mortar of equal parts by volume of cement and sand. Paint the inside of the crack with PVA adhesive, such as 'Unibond' and trowel the mortar into the crack. Smooth off the repair with a wet metal trowel until it matches the surrounding benching. A little neat cement sprinkled on the top of the repair will help the polishing of the surface.

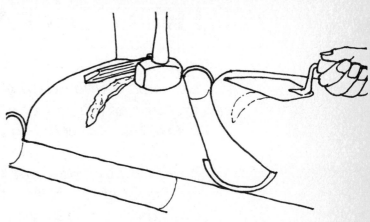

4

If the inside of the manhole is rendered, any cracks should be repaired in the same way as for the benching, but using a 1:3 cement: sand mortar. If the pointing to the brickwork has failed, repoint, using 1:3 cement: sand mortar and a flush joint (See Sheet 2.20). A cracked or chipped channel is more difficult to repair and a badly damaged channel will need to be replaced in the same way as for a new manhole (See 12.03). A small chip or hairline crack can be filled with 'prompt' cement, a rapid hardening fine cement mortar used for W.C. connections. Take care that the repair is flush with the pipe or it may trap solids and cause a blockage.

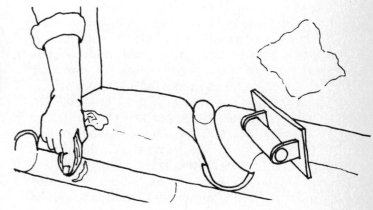

5

When the repairs are complete clean out the manhole cover frame with a wire brush, if corroded, and also clean off the rim of the cover. If the channel in the frame is filled with grease before the lid is replaced then a gas-tight seal will be formed.

   Replace the lid using techniques similar to those for removing it and take care not to trap any fingers!

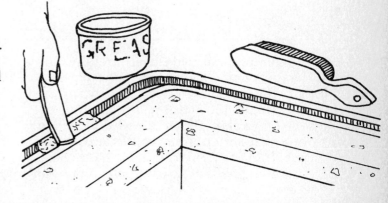

6

CONSTRUCTING A NEW MANHOLE

A new manhole will need to be built when connecting into existing drainage where none exists or at the end of a new drainage layout before the connection into the main sewer. Manufacturers of UPVC drainage systems also produce manholes and rodding points which save a lot of work. The manhole construction described is necessary when working with traditional clayware pipes.

Dig down to the existing drain and then another 225 mm below taking care not to damage the pipe. The hole must be large enough to take the manhole required and allow some working space. A manhole on a 100 mm or 150 mm diameter drain should be 450 mm wide if there are branches from one side, 750 mm wide if there are branches to both sides of the channel. The length is determined by allowing 300 mm for a 100 mm drain and 375 mm for a 150 mm drain, per branch on the side with most branches. If there is only one branch per side the minimum length should be 450 mm. These dimensions are internal to the manhole and the walls will be 225 mm thick brickwork. The existing drain will be in 600 or 900 mm (2′–0″ or 3′–0″) lengths and in order to fit in a new channel section it will be necessary to expose three lengths of pipe, if possible positioning the manhole central to the middle length.

1

With a hammer and cold chisel carefully chip out the centre pipe leaving the other pipes intact. In the bottom of the hole construct a form of timber that is 150 mm deep, the external size of the manhole plus 300 mm in each direction in plan and with the top 50 mm below the bottom of the pipe. Into the form pour a 1:2:4 cement: sand: small aggregate, concrete mix and tamp down level with a board. Cover with a piece of sack or polythene for two days and protect the hole.

2

If the hole is more than 1200 mm deep it may be necessary to hold up the sides with planks and struts. Do not work in deep holes with unsupported sides. Holes should be left open for as short a time as possible since the weather can weaken the soil, causing collapse and there is always a danger that someone will fall into an open hole.

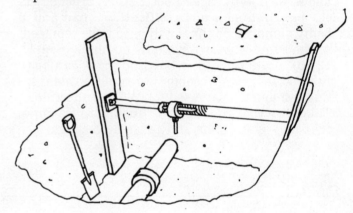

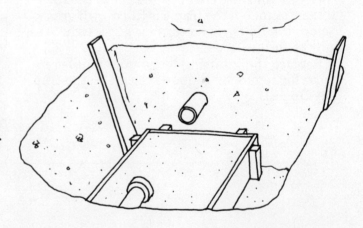

From the concrete base so formed build up a 225 mm (9″) thick brick wall to ground level. Leave holes in the wall through which the drain and branches can pass, supporting the brickwork on concrete lintels. (See Sheet 2.20C.)

3

In the bottom of the manhole insert a channel section in place of the pipe removed, bedding the channel in 1:6, cement: sand mortar on the concrete base of the manhole. Using brick pieces and mortar build up the bottom of the manhole to the height of the sides of the channel.

4

Each branch will discharge into the channel via a 'slipper'. Slippers are clay channels which are curved and are available in a number of different shapes to suit various connection angles. Position the slippers so that the cut-off end is directly above and in the line of the channel and bed them in place with a 1:5 cement: sand mortar. Between the slippers, using pieces of brick and 1:3 cement: sand mortar build-up curved shaped haunching. Polish the haunching with a metal trowel, sprinkling a little neat coment onto it whilst doing so.

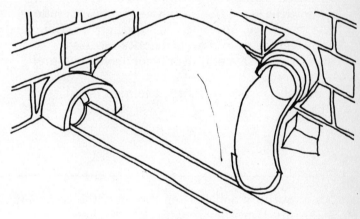

5

Connect the branch pipes into the collars of the slippers. To the top of the brickwork, bed a manhole. Cover frame in 1:3 cement: sand mortar. Once the connections to the manhole have been made, backfill around the outside and made good the surface, bringing it level with the frame. Grease the frame and fit the cover.

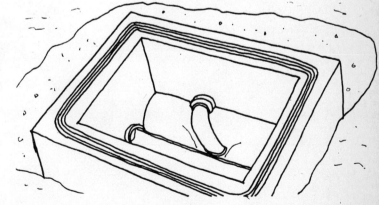

6

A missing, cracked or holed manhole cover is dangerous, since there is no longer protection from the hole beneath, or from the smells.

If the damaged cover is still in position remove it, whole or in pieces. First clean off the cover and the channel around the rim. Then loosen the cover with the end of a crowbar. Crouch astride the cover, knees bent, back straight and grasp a handle or the already raised edge and lift by straightening the knees. A heavy-duty cover may need to be rolled off. (See 12.02.2.)

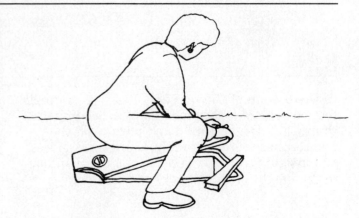

1

If the frame is damaged, or broken, chip out the mortar holding it in place with a club hammer and cold chisel.

Measure the size of the existing frame and purchase either a new frame and cover or just a cover to the same size. Manhole covers are made in a number of strengths to suit their location. Lightweight covers are adequate for use in garden areas, a medium duty for driveways, and heavy duty for roadways.

Bed the new frame in 1:3 cement: sand mortar.

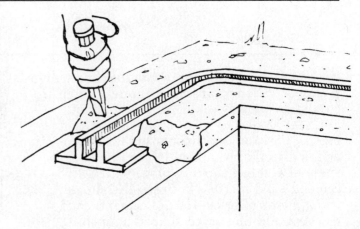

2

Clean out any debris from the manhole and make any necessary repairs (12.02). Place cover in frame having first cleaned out and greased the channel to the frame.

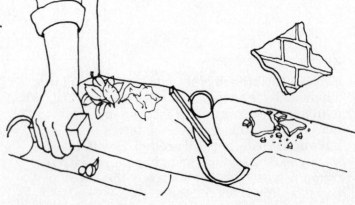

3

FITTING A NEW GULLEY

Gulleys are available in a number of different types and some come with an integral water trap or others will need to be fitted onto a separate trap. Gulleys should not be used without a trap. Common forms of gulley are open, back inlet and intercept. This description assumes the use of a clayware trap and gulley although UPVC are also available.

Bring the new drainage pipe to the gulley position (see 12.07) or if fitting onto an old drain carefully chip out a length of old pipe, cleaning out the collar. If the old pipe collar cannot be cleaned out, chop the end of the pipe level and fit a double collar. An unorthodox method of making a connection to an old pipe which whilst probably unacceptable to the authorities is apparently very effective when used for short-life houses consists of cutting the end of the old pipe roughly square, introducing a straight 'Multikwik' connector into the pipe and then connecting to the 'Multikwik' with UPVC pipework. The junction between the 'Multikwik' and the clay pipe is reinforced with prompt cement.

1

Fit a clay water trap to the end of the pipe and support the trap in weak mix concrete on top of shingle or gravel.

Position the gulley top on the trap and ram some hemp and putty or wet newspaper down around the gulley into the collar. Point the connection with prompt cement.

2

If the gulley is being used to drain a hard area, make good the surrounding paving so that it falls towards and is flush with the gulley. Pipes connected into a back inlet gulley can be pointed with prompt cement.

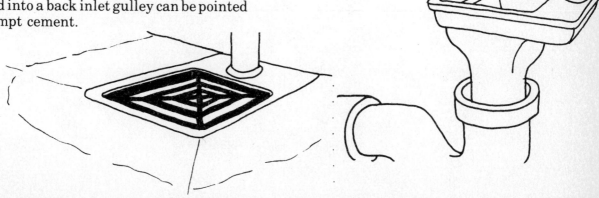

3

CLEANING EXISTING GULLEYS

Remove debris and rubbish from on top of the gulley grating. Pour a bucket of water into the gulley. If it drains away quickly then the blockage is cleared and the grating can be replaced.

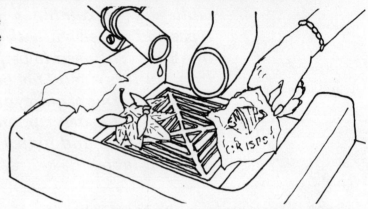

1

If the water drains away slowly, or not at all, then either the trap or the connection to the manhole or drain is blocked. Bail out water from the gulley with an old cup, or an old can with two holes punched at opposite sides of the rim and a wire handle joining the holes which can be submerged and then pulled out. Once the water is clear, remove any debris from the trap. Often the bottom of the trap will be full of silt and this can be scraped out by hand, wearing rubber gloves or with the scraper attachment from a set of drain rods. When silt and debris are removed, pour another bucket of water down the gulley.

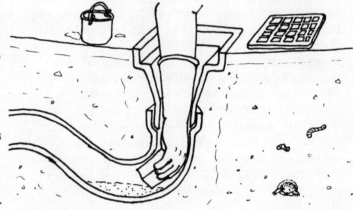

2

If the water runs away quickly except for the water seal which is only 125 mm deep for a 100 mm pipe, then the blockage is clear. Any remaining silt in the bottom of the trap can be flushed out with a water hose and the grating replaced. If the bucketful of water drains away slowly or not at all then the connection to the manhole or drain is blocked and needs rodding. (See Sheet 12.07.)

3

As previously noted this is not a pleasant task and professional help may well be sought. (See 12.01.)

Indicators that a drain might be blocked are — water not draining from gulleys, water coming up around the edge of a manhole cover, W.C. pan filling or slow draining when flushed, or unpleasant smells near the manhole.

Clean off the manhole cover and channel around the rim. Loosen the cover with the end of a crowbar, crouch astride the cover, knees bent, back straight and grasp a handle, or an already raised edge, and lift by straightening knees. A heavy-duty cover may need to be rolled off. (See 12.02.2.)

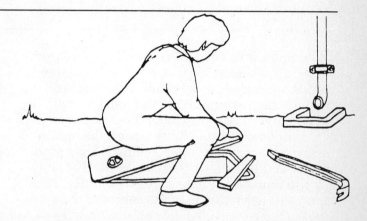

1

If the manhole is dry then get someone to send water down each of the connections by flushing the W.C. or putting buckets of water down the gulleys, filling a sink and pulling out the plug is another way. If the water comes through in a rush then the connection is clear, if nothing comes through, or there is only a trickle, then the connection is blocked.

If all the connections run free but water stays in the manhole or is slow to empty, or if the manhole was full when the cover was lifted, then the connection to the next manhole or the sewer is blocked. Lift the next manhole cover to see if the blockage is between the two, i.e. the second is dry, or further down the line, i.e. the second is also full.

2

Drain rods are available in three common varieties, canes, springs or plastic. All come in sections approximately 900 mm in length, which are screwed together. When using drain rods, the first section is inserted into the drain and the second screwed to it and so on. It is important always to turn the rods in a clockwise direction; if they are turned anti-clockwise they will unscrew and come apart in the drain.

From the dry manhole, rod up the drain with the 'corkscrew' attachment on the end, rotating the rods clockwise to break up the blockage.

When the rods are felt to have broken through, and to be rotating freely, continue to turn and withdraw the rods. A break through will usually result in a flow of sewage down the pipe. Next fit the semi-circular scraper attachment, push the rods back up the drain past the blockage, and pull back down, repeating until the blockage is apparently clear. If it is possible to get above the blockage, i.e. when rodding from a dry manhole back to a wet one, or rodding back from a manhole to the foot of a soil stack, which has a rodding eye, then finish by rodding through the remains of the blockage with the circular plunger, and then wash the pipe through with water.

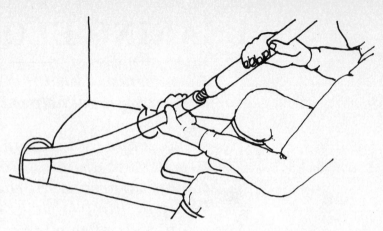

3

If a manhole is full and there is no dry point from which to rod then it must be cleared. If another operative manhole is available, the blocked manhole can be emptied with a bucket, but remember that sewage cannot be dumped on a garden or down a street drain since it is a health hazard. If there is no other manhole, then prod around in the drain with a piece of wood or pipe to try to remove any debris from the outlet. The outlet will normally be in the centre of the side nearest the road or the side at right angles to and furtherest down the direction of the flow. If the manhole is the last one before the public sewer, it may have an interceptor trap on the outlet with a rodding eye above. If so, the rodding eye cover will have to be removed before the blockage can be cleared. Fit the corkscrew attachment on to the rods and push them into the outlet or the rodding eye. Remove the blockage as before.

4

If the blockage cannot be removed, the drain may have collapsed. If a collapse is suspected between the last of the house manholes and the public sewer then contact the Local Authority Drainage Engineers. If the suspected collapse is in the 'private drainage system' it will have to be dug up and replaced and it is worth having a professional firm attempt to remove the block before considering relaying the drain.

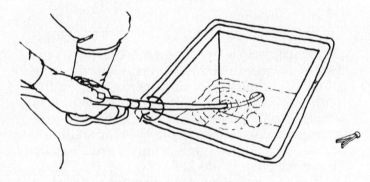

Drain rods can also be used to clear blockages in the stack. Rod up the stack from the manhole or from the access plate at the bottom of the stack. If neither of these positions are possible, then rod down the stack from the roof, but be sure to work from a sound platform before attempting to do so.

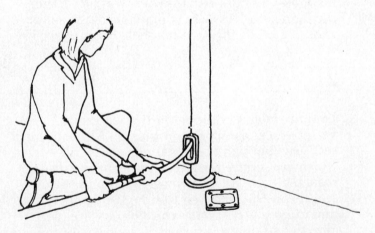

5

LAYING NEW DRAINS

Modern UPVC drainage pipes and fittings have made drain laying much simpler and easier than traditional clay pipes. However UPVC pipework is not accepted by all local authorities. Pipes and fittings for above ground drainage should not be used below ground.

Dig a straight trench between the two points to be served by the new drain. To check the required depth of the trench set up a 'shooting board' made up of a piece of floor board nailed horizontally between two stakes of 50×50 mm (2″×2″) softwood, at the connection end of the trench.

At the other end set up a second shooting board using a water level to mark the level of the other board and then measuring up from this mark one-fortieth of the distance between the two shooting boards before fixing the horizontal board at the higher mark.

Construct a 'T' from a piece of board as a cross-piece and a length of 50×50 mm (2″×2″) equal to the required depth of the top of the new pipe below the lower shooting board.

The bottom of the trench should be the diameter of the pipe plus 150 mm (6″) below the bottom of the 'T' when it is sited through, so that the cross-piece is in line with the tops of the shooting boards.

1

Line the bottom of the trench with pea shingle and rake it out to form an even bed. Fit a clayware to plastic connector-piece into the clay collar of the connection to the sewer. Pipes are always laid so that the collar end is highest so that the direction of flow is into the collar.

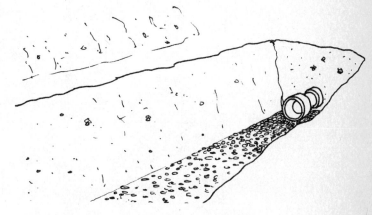

2

Push the first pipe into the connector, wetting the gaskets with soapy water if necessary. Using the 'T' rod check that the pipe is laid to the correct depth and fall and adjust the gravel bed as necessary. Make sure that the gravel bed is evenly compacted and that there are no depressions or holes below the pipe.

3

Connect the next pipe in the same manner. Branches, bends, gulleys and other fittings can all be push-fitted together in a similar fashion. Connections to the bottom of soil stacks should be made using large radiused bends or two 135° long bends. Once the pipes and fittings have been placed and the levels checked, cover the pipes with another layer of pea shingle to a depth of 150 mm (6″) above the pipe before back filling the trench.

N.B. A similar technique is used for clayware pipes, some of which are available with butyl gasket connections.

4

12.09
A NEW SOIL STACK

Most old houses will have cast iron soil stacks, some may even have lead, but modern stacks are usually installed in plastic. In order to blend in with older houses manufacturers now make black soil and waste systems. The design of the soil stack and its connections should be in accordance with the principles noted in 12.00.

At the base of the soil stack the below-ground connection to be used should have a slow, large radius bend to the drain. If a clay pipe is used below ground, then a special clay-to-plastic connector is first fitted into the clay pipe collar and a caulked joint made by ramming hemp and putty into the collar around the connector, followed by prompt cement.

1

The soil stack is then assembled by push-fitting the first length into the connector, taking care not to damage the sealing gaskets and clipping the stack to the wall with saddle clips. If the pipe gaskets are stiff they can be lubricated with soapy water. Pipes are fitted so that the collars are uppermost.

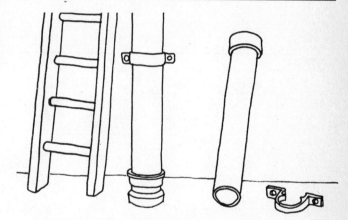

2

Connections into the stack are made by incorporating branch fittings for the W.C. or a fitting which has built in connection 'bosses' for waste fittings.

3

Alternatively a hole may be cut into the side of a straight length of pipe with a hole cutting attachment or by drilling a circle of holes inside the diameter of the required hole and finishing off with a half-round file. Into this hole a connection boss is either solvent-welded to the pipe or else held in position by a strap which is tightened around the pipe compressing a sealing ring. All bosses should be connected to the pipe before it is in position unless unavoidable.

Depending on the system used, the waste branches will either solvent-weld or push-fit into the bosses.

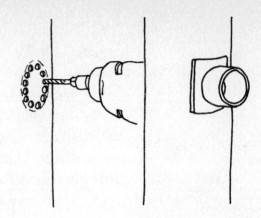

4

Above the topmost fitting the pipe acts as a vent pipe for the sewer and should be taken at least 900 mm (3′–0″) above any window within 3 metres (10′–0″). On the top of the pipe fix a wire balloon or plastic cage to stop birds nesting in or falling down the pipe.

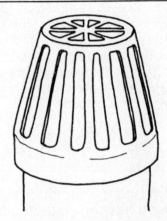

5

13
PLUMBING

PLUMBING – COLD AND HOT WATER SUPPLY

General Principles and Techniques

Before attempting to install particular fittings it is important to have an adequate knowledge of the principles involved in, and the techniques necessary for a plumbing installation.

13.01 Principles

A Water Supply

In towns and most villages the local Water Board supplies sterilised water, under pressure, via a mains pipe, usually located in the roadway. Each house is then fed by a communicating pipe which leads from the mains to a stop tap which is normally located under a small cast iron cover situated in the pavement or adjacent to the boundary of the property. This tap enables the Water Board to isolate a house from the supply.

The communication pipe is continued on into the house and a second stop tap is usually located just inside the wall at the beginning of the internal plumbing system. Typical locations are below the front steps in houses having a semi-basement floor, below the floor boards adjacent to the front door in houses with no basement and in a W.C. or below the kitchen sink in more modern houses. Sometimes a stop tap is located in the garden or even in an external W.C.

If a house has been standing empty it is likely that the plumbing system will have been vandalised in order to steal the pipework for scrap. In these cases it is not uncommon to find that the communicating pipe has been cut off flush with the external wall and simply hammered flat to restrict the water flow. If this has happened and water has been flowing within the house, apart from causing damage, it may also have resulted in the supply to the house being terminated. The Water Board may also have been requested to cut off the supply by an owner intending to keep property empty.

Termination of the supply is achieved either by digging up the road or pavement and capping-off the communicating pipe, or more simply by switching off the supply at the boards stop tap in the street. The stop tap which is operated by a simple rectangular section 'key' is the property of the Water Board, and strictly the Board should be asked to send someone, often referred to as a 'Turnkey' to turn on the stop tap. However, if simply testing whether or not the supply has been cut off in the street or temporarily isolating the supply to replace a defective stop tap, it is common for plumbers themselves using a key to turn the supply off or on. If the supply has been cut off before the Board's stop tap, it will be necessary to request a reconnection. Contact the local Water Board's area office, who will require an 'application for supply' form to be completed. Once in receipt of this form an engineer will provide an estimate for the cost of (re)connection. It is frequently necessary to pay for the connection in advance of the work being carried out and the whole process can take several months between application and provision of the supply. The Water Board's estimate will normally only cover the cost of reconnecting the supply up to their stop tap in the street, and, depending on the situation of the main, its age and the complexity of the connection the cost can be anything up to several hundred pounds.

B Water Storage

It is not uncommon to find houses where all the fittings run directly off the main's supply. This form of installation is not in line with modern practice and may be rejected by the Water Board. The reason for providing water storage within a dwelling and between the fittings and the main is to prevent a reduced or negative pressure sucking back contaminated water into the mains. A second advantage is that in the event of an interruption in the main supply the household has a reserve.

In some short-life houses the saving in pipework will be significant if no tank is used and in these cases the Water Board is unlikely to raise objections provided that:–
– There was previously no tank in the house.
– A non return stop tap with a drain cock is fitted at the beginning of the system.
– W.C. cisterns are fitted with anti-syphonage valves.
– Taps are positioned in relation to sinks, wash basins and baths so that their ends cannot be immersed in standing water.
– There is no hot water cylinder.
The Water Board will normally only check an

installation if a new connection or reconnection has been made.

Even where a storage tank is provided, it is normal for the cold tap in the kitchen to be connected directly to the mains for drinking water and it may also be necessary to supply an instantaneous gas-fired water heater from the mains in order to obtain the necessary water pressure.

C   Positioning of Appliances and Plumbing

In order to keep costs low it is advisable to plan your house layout so that kitchens, toilets and bathrooms are closely related, either being side by side or directly above each other. In the interests of ease and economy they should also be related to existing drainage positions, particularly toilets, since providing new soil stacks or connections for soil stacks can be expensive. Kitchen and bathroom wastes can, if necessary, be more easily diverted over greater distances and deposited into existing gulleys. (N.B. Only in areas where a single or combined drainage system is in operation.) (See 12.00 Drainage.)

Tanks are most usually positioned in the roof space, or on a platform over the stairwell, if the former is not possible. The relationship of the tank to the various appliances and rising main should be determined so that unnecessary bends and long branch runs of pipework are eliminated. The stop tap at the beginning of the system, where the main enters the house, should be at the lowest point and be provided with a drain cock or tap so that the system can be drained down if repairs or additions are to be made. Any low points on the system should be capable of being drained.

Long runs to isolated appliances should be avoided in hot water systems since it will take a long time for the water to reach the appliance, heated water in the pipe is wasted when the tap is closed and the distance may be too remote for the type of heating appliance used.

A maximum distance should be 12 metres (40'–0") including all bends. If the run is particularly circuitous with a lot of bends then this distance should be reduced since the pressure will be much less due to friction.

D   Materials

Plumbing fittings, pipework and appliances can be purchased in a variety of materials. In selecting the materials most suited to a particular need, consideration should be given to:–

Cost of material and fittings
Availability
Ease of use
Durability of material
Expected life of installation.

i. Supply Pipework for Hot and Cold Water

Copper – Copper pipework is not cheap and its price and availability are to some extent dependant on speculation in copper on the world stock markets. However, it is easy to use, can be easily bent to save fittings, is extremely durable, and even in short-life housing (of two years' life or more) is probably the best material to use since it can be salvaged and re-used if necessary.

Stainless Steel – Although introduced to rival copper pipe it is normally of similar price. Jointing techniques are similar to copper, but it is not so easy to work and more difficult to bend. It is not worth considering as a serious option unless other materials are in short supply.

Plastic PVC – There are a number of plastic systems on the market which are suitable for cold water plumbing and some which also claim to be suitable for hot water. They tend to be relatively inexpensive and easy to work with. Although readily available plastic hot and cold water piping has not been generally accepted by the building trade. This is due to its being relatively untested, susceptible to damage if knocked and the evidence that the main's pressure can cause the pipework to become brittle, and difficult to repair.

Some systems now on the market claim to have overcome these problems and are widely used in America.

Polythene – Polythene piping to B.S. 1972 is unsuitable for Hot water installations, but adequate for Cold water. It is relatively inexpensive, but somewhat difficult to obtain. It is easy to use, although probably best used when a minimum number of tight bends or branches are required. It will last for several years and as such is suitable for short-life use. It can be used to provide communication pipes and rising mains.

Mild Steel – Most commonly known as barrel, gas barrel or iron barrel, it is readily available, not cheap, and requires special thread-cutting equipment to work. It is not normally used for hot and cold water in domestic installation. Its most common use is for gas piping.

Lead – Lead is expensive, no longer readily available, difficult to work and can contaminate water. Although durable, old pipework can develop splits under pressure.

Others – In short-life housing, hose pipe can be used, which while cheap and easy to install does not last very long under pressure; about six months maximum.

Another alternative is clear polythene piping

which is cheap and easy to use, more durable than hose pipe but because it is clear allows micro-organisms in the water access to light, and a green growth exhibits itself in the pipework. Neither of these materials is acceptable to the Water Boards, or recommended for other than temporary use.

ii. Supply Pipework for Gas

Copper – Copper pipe, preferably jointed with solder, rather than compression fittings, is suitable for gas pipework in protected locations.

Mild Steel – While more difficult to work than copper, mild steel pipework is favoured by the Gas Board and should be used in vulnerable locations and if burying pipework in solid floors, or plastered walls.

Stainless Steel – Stainless steel pipework can be used, but the disadvantages noted above, in (i), should be considered.

N.B. No other materials are suitable for internal gas installations.

iii. Waste Water

Copper – Copper, while easy to work, is extremely expensive for waste piping and is now rarely used for this purpose.

Lead – Although some old installations are lead, it is not now used due to the high cost and the availability of more suitable materials.

Stainless Steel or Chromed Steel – This is rarely used in domestic waste systems, except perhaps where a waste trap below a sink or basin is exposed to view. It is more commonly used in public places where vandalism may be a potential problem.

Plastic – Waste systems are available in PVC, Polythene and ABS from a wide variety of manufacturers and plastic is now the most common material used for waste in the building industry. It is relatively inexpensive, readily available, easy to work and durable in this application.

Cast Iron – Cast Iron is expensive, difficult to work and is rarely used internally, except where liable to damage, or where there is a fire risk between dwellings.

iv. Baths

Enamelled Cast Iron – While heavy and expensive, cast iron baths are usually of the highest quality. Although the casting may fracture if struck a heavy blow with a hammer, they are normally very durable.

Enamelled Pressed Steel – More lightweight and less expensive than cast iron, pressed steel baths come in a variety of qualities, but all are usually durable, unless subjected to blows, which dent the steelwork or chip the enamel.

Perspex and Fibreglass – Lightweight, as expensive as the cheaper pressed steel baths, but usually available in more colours, these are susceptible to damage from scouring powders, cigarettes and heavy blows.

v. Sink Units

Stainless Steel – Probably the most common material for sink units with a wide variety of models and prices available. Durable, although the durability is affected by quality to some .extent.

Enamelled Steel – Enamelled steel or cast iron sink units are becoming more widespread, since a wide range of colours can be offered. The less expensive, more traditional enamelled sink units frequently suffer chipping of the enamel from hard use, e.g. dropped saucepans.

Stoneware – Glazed stoneware sinks are still available, but are more normally used for other than domestic purposes. They are durable, but can crack or shatter if subjected to hard use. The lack of an intergral draining board is usually considered a disadvantage.

vi. Wash Hand Basins

China or Clayware – The most common basins are made of china or clayware, they come in a variety of colours and patterns, and are usually adequately durable. However, they can shatter or crack if heavy objects, for example, glass shampoo bottles are dropped into them.

Glass Fibre – There are relatively few glass fibre basins on the market and they are susceptible to damage from scouring powders and cigarettes, and are not as durable as traditional china or clayware.

Enamelled Steel or Cast Iron – Enamelled basins are normally of the type which are inset into work surfaces or vanity units. They are durable but tend to be more expensive than clay or china ware.

vii. W.C. Pans

China or Clayware – Durable and easy to clean, this is the only type of material that is used for domestic W.C. pans. Available in a variety of forms ('S' trap, 'P' trap, two pieces, wash-down or self-syphoning) and colours.

viii. Flushing Cisterns

China or Clayware – Although the traditional, more durable material, clayware cisterns are now relatively expensive. Available both for high and low level operation.

Plastic – Cheap and available in a number of models including slim-line for awkward locations, plastic cisterns are normally perfectly adequate. Available for high and low level operation.

A Copper Pipe

Cutting

Copper pipe can be cut with a hacksaw, but if a lot of work is to be done it is worth borrowing or buying a pipe cutter. Always measure pipework to fit into the sockets of fittings.

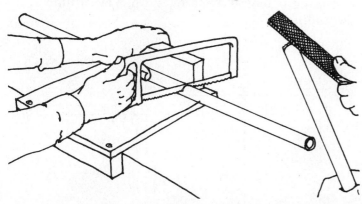

With a hacksaw, support the pipe and cut it across at right angles, taking care that the pipe does not drop and tear at the bottom of the cut, since this can distort the pipe. Clean off any metal burrs to the inside and outside of the pipe with a metal file. If the pipe is already connected, take care not to allow these burrs to remain inside the pipework otherwise they can find their way into tap washers, or gas jets, and cause problems, if not damage.

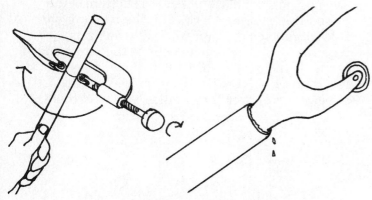

Using pipe cutters adjust the mouth of the cutters so that the pipe will slip between the two blades. Tighten the blades until they grip the pipe and then rotate the cutter around the pipe, holding and twisting the ball end to the blade adjuster, so that the pipe is cut through. Once the pipe is severed, inset the pointed end of the cutter into the cut end and rotate to clean out burrs, taking care not to leave any in the pipe.

Jointing

Before attempting any joint, the water must be turned off and the pipe free of water.

Capillary Fittings

Capillary fittings rely on a soldered connection to provide a gas or watertight joint. The most common and easy-to-use have inbuilt reservoirs of solder. Others are available without the solder and are cheaper. Once the technique of using capillary fittings has been learnt, they are cheaper and provide a joint that is less likely to leak than a compression fitting. However, they cannot easily be re-used. The key to good jointing in copper pipe is cleanliness. Grease, dust, and dirt can all cause a soldered connection to fail.

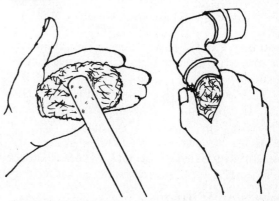

First polish the end of the pipe to the depth of the fitting socket plus 25 mm, with a pad of plumber's steel wool until it is burnished and shining bright. Place it somewhere clean, or support it so that the end is not in contact with anything. Next polish the inside of the socket, and also the outside at the end of the fitting with wire wool, until it too is shiny bright.

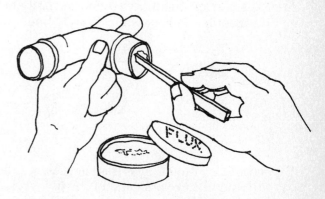

Open the tin of flux and with a clean sliver of wood, (a spill is ideal) kept in the tin for this purpose, apply a thin coat of flux to the inside of the fitting and the end of the pipe. Do not apply the flux with your finger which will probably be naturally greasy and may also introduce bits of dirt, steel wool, or copper burrs into the fitting, which could cause the joint to fail.

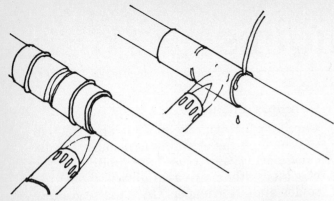

Fit the pipe into the fitting socket and heat the joint by playing a blowlamp around the pipe as much as possible. When using a pre-soldered fitting, heat the end of the fitting and the pipe so that the solder, once molten, will be drawn out of the fitting. The flux will bubble fiercely and spit just before the solder melts and a bright silver ring will then appear around the end of the fitting.

When using fittings without solder, heat the fitting until the flux begins to spit and then touch the top of the pipe against the end of the fitting with solder. If the pipe is hot enough the solder will melt and be drawn into the fitting and around the pipe by capillary action. Again a bright silver ring will be visible.

Clean off any excess flux with wire wool since flux left on the pipe will cause it to corrode.

Compression Fittings

There are two basic types of compression fitting, manipulative and non-manipulative. Manipulative joints should be avoided since they necessitate flaring out of the ends of the pipe. Fortunately non-manipulative compression fittings are most common and plumbers' merchants will usually supply these automatically when asked for a compression fitting. There are a number of manufacturers and pieces of their fittings will not normally be interchangeable. So if possible stick to one brand.

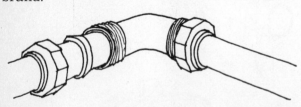

To achieve a joint simply unscrew one of the nuts, slip the nut over the end of the pipe, take the copper wedging ring, known as an 'olive', out of the fitting and slip it over the pipe so that the longer, shallower chamfer is towards the end. Push the pipe into the socket in the fitting so that it is fully home, slip the olive up to the socket, then engage the nut and tighten with the fingers. Finally give the nut three or four turns

with a spanner or wrench until it feels firm; do not overtighten. Stop the fitting turning by holding it with a wrench while tightening.

Bending Copper

Copper pipes can be bent to save fittings and to make a neater installation. However they should not be bent without proper support or else the pipe will flatten, and this will restrict the flow; the walls may crinkle, weakening the pipe and it may even split. There are three basic techniques for bending copper pipe, using a bending machine, bending springs or filling it with dry sand.

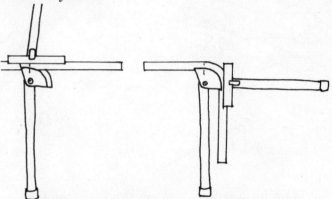

Bending machines are either portable or bench or tripod mounted. They are expensive to buy but can sometimes be hired; a portable bender is adequate for house plumbing where only 8, 15 and 22 mm copper pipe is being used. Bending machines are the most accurate method for bending pipes.

To use, mark the pipe where the bend is to start, slip it into the machine with the arms open and position the mark next to the bottom of the arc on the bending block. Slip the bending bar into place over the pipe and pull the arms together until the pipe is bent to the required angle. If the pipe is difficult to bend, more leverage can be exerted by slipping lengths of old gas barrel over the handles to extend them.

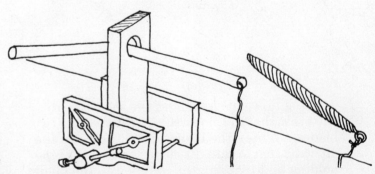

Bending springs are available to fit inside different diameter pipes. Before using the springs, firmly attach a strong cord to the end so that they can be withdrawn. Slip the springs inside the pipe so that they cover the area to be bent, pass the pipe through a hole drilled in a strong piece of wood and bend it by pulling on the ends of the pipe. When bending a pipe through right angles, move it two or three times so that the bend is not too abrupt. Withdraw the springs by pulling on the cord. A popular method of using springs is to bend the pipe over the knee, but this is not advisable since it can seriously injure the kneecap.

To bend a pipe using dry sand, first plug one end with a cork, then fill the pipe with sand, tapping the plugged end on the ground to ensure that it compacts. When full, plug the other end and bend in the same way as for springs, making sure that the plugs are adequate to withstand the pressure resulting from the bending and that all of the sand is cleaned out afterwards.

B Plastic Pipe

The Techniques apply for water systems, overflow piping and waste pipes.

Cutting

Plastic pipe can be cut using a hacksaw, taking care that the cut is square. Ragged plastic burrs can be removed using a fine metal file.

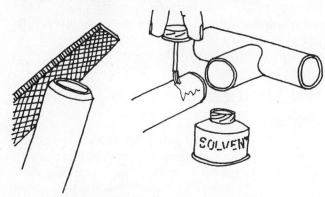

Solvent Weld Connections

Some waste-systems, overflow, and water systems, use a chemical solvent to effect a water-tight joint. The solvents are not always interchangeable between systems, since pipes can be made of a variety of plastics. The technique will vary with manufacturer and it is best to read the instructions carefully. However, the general principles are:

First cut the pipe square, clean off the end and put a 45° chamfer on the end.

Next slot the end into the fitting, make sure that it is located correctly in the socket and mark the pipe.

Clean the inside of the fitting and the end of the pipe with a cleaning solution applied with a clean cloth.

Coat the inside of the fitting and the end of the pipe down to the mark with a thin coat of solvent. Slot the pipe into the fitting and twist through 90° to ensure an even spread of adhesive and then leave the joint while the adhesive sets.

Push-Fit Connections

Most plastic waste systems have a push-fit system with the fittings containing a synthetic rubber ring (gasket) or rings to effect a water tight seal.

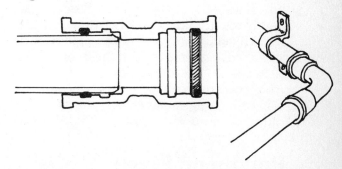

Cut the end of the pipe square and chamfer the end with a file. Lubricate the inside of the fitting with water, or soap and water, (do not use grease or detergent which causes some gaskets to deteriorate). Keeping the pipe square to the fitting, push it into place, twisting the pipe if it meets resistance. Take care not to dislodge the rubber gasket ring.

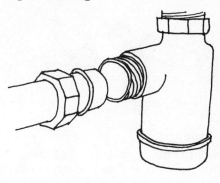

Compression Fittings

Some plastic fittings incorporate a form of compression fitting which relies on a nylon olive or a rubber ring to produce a seal.

Cut the end of the pipe square and clean it off, undo the nut and remove the sealing ring or olive. Slip the nut and the ring or olive over the end of the pipe and push the pipe into the socket of the fitting. Slip the ring or olive up against the mouth of the socket and then tighten the nut by hand. Do not over-tighten.

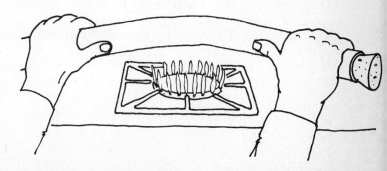

Bending Plastic Pipe

Plastic pipe is not easy to bend and fittings should normally be used for changes in direction. However if a slight bend or curve is necessary fill the pipe with dry sand and plug both ends. Rotate the pipe over a low flame; a gas cooker jet is ideal, taking care not to scorch the plastic, until soft. Gently bend the pipe to the required shape and remove from the flame. Hold the pipe in the required shape until cool; do not cool with water since this will cause the pipe to become brittle. A jig made of nails hammered into a piece of scrap wood will save tired arms while the pipe cools.

C Polythene Pipe

'Poly' pipe is available to BS 1972, Class 'C' or 'D', which is low density or to BS 3284 which is high density. Low density to Class 'C' (blue markings) is the most suitable for domestic use.

Cutting

Poly pipe can be cut with a hacksaw, the end of the pipe being cleaned up with a craft knife or a fine metal file.

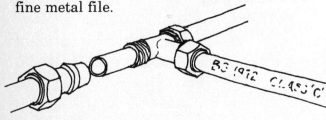

Connections

Poly pipe is normally joined using compression fittings. Kuterlite and Conex both manufacture special brass fittings but these can be expensive and are often not readily available. If using purpose-made fittings ensure that they are for the appropriate class of pipe, since poly pipe must be fitted with liners or else the pipe will deform. The diameter of the liners is different for each class.

For Class C poly pipe a length of 15 mm copper pipe can be used as a liner and ordinary $\frac{3}{4}''$ compression fittings or 22 mm fittings with 'Polyrings' (manufactured by Conex) substituted for the metal olives, may be used to make a cheaper connection.

To make a connection insert the liner into the pipe, slip the nut of the fitting and the olive or polyring over the end of the pipe and fit the pipe into the fitting. Tighten up the nut of the fitting, first by hand and then with a wrench or spanner. Do not over-tighten.

A cheaper method of jointing polypipe has been developed by short-life housing users which allows copper capillary fittings to be used.

Take a 100 mm length of 15 mm copper pipe, clean up with plumber's wire wool and apply flux to the pipe. Next clean and flux a 15 mm

olive and slip it over one end of the pipe, place it 25 mm from one end of the pipe with the flat slope of the olive facing away from the end of the pipe. Heat the pipe with a blowlamp and touch solder against the edge of the olive so that solder is drawn under the olive. Wipe off any molten solder with a piece of cloth and allow to cool.

This piece of copper should then be fitted into copper fittings and all joints requiring heating made.

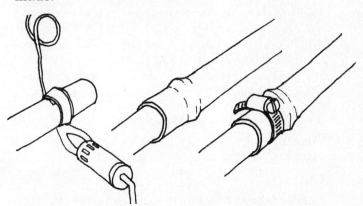

Place a jubilee clip over the end of the copper pipe, wet the end of the 'polypipe' and slip it over the end of the copper pipe and the olive. The polypipe should pass 50 mm past the olive, slip the jubilee clip back over the polypipe and tighten it adjacent to the olive.

D Mild Steel

Cutting

Barrel should be held in a pipe clamp or against a bench hook and sawn through with a hacksaw. Remove any metal burrs with a fine metal file.

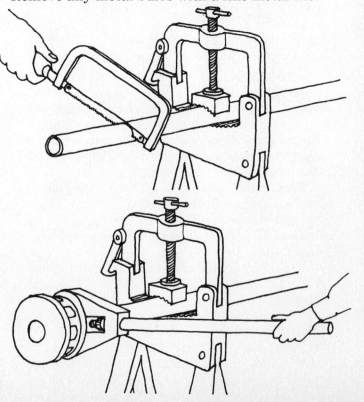

Connections

Barrel connections are made by screwing together pre-threaded pipes and fittings. Although some standard lengths of pipe can be bought pre-threaded they do not give significant flexibility and it will almost certainly be necessary to cut male threads on to the pipes. Fittings usually come with a British Standard Pipe (B.S.P.) female thread. To cut threads on to the pipe it is necessary to buy or hire a pipe clamp, a set of thread-cutting dies and a die rachet with handle. If hiring check that the dies are sharp and have not been damaged.

Fit the pipe into the clamp so that the end protrudes by 150 – 200 mm (6″ to 8″) and fit the correct sized dies into the rachet head. Slip the guide shaft over the end of the barrel and keeping the dies square to the pipe, bring down the handle to start the cut.

Cut the thread by using a pumping action, stopping at regular intervals to turn the die back about a quarter of a turn to release any metal cuttings and to add cutting oil to lubricate the dies. Continue until a thread the full depth of the die has been cut.

Clean any metal cuttings and oil off the new thread and try it in a fitting to check the thread. The metal to metal threads will not produce a gas or water-tight fit on their own and there are two common methods of producing a seal.

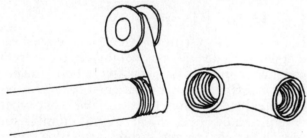

Either smear the thread on the end of the pipe with BOSS White or wrap the thread in PFTE (Poly Fluoro Tetro Ethylene) tape, about three times around the thread, working in the direction that the fitting will screw on. Screw the pipe into the fitting, tighten with a Stilson wrench. Do not attempt to overtighten, since this could damage the threads.

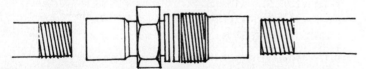

When joining in between two fittings it will be necessary to use a different form of connector on one end of the pipe since screwing in one end will screw out the other. This can be overcome by using a union coupling. This has two halves which are pulled together compressing a fibre washer, by a loose nut. Fit the halves of the connector to each of the pipes to be joined, insert the fibre washer, wrap the thread in PFTE tape and tighten the locking nut.

Bending

Barrel can be bent with a bending machine in the same way as copper pipe but due to its thickness and resistance to bending, a bench, rather than a portable bender is usually necessary.

E Lead

Cutting

Lead can be cut with a hacksaw and any metal burrs then cleaned off with a knife. However, it is particularly important to remove all lead shavings from the pipe since lead is poisonous.

Connections

Working with lead is difficult and lead is very expensive. The only connection that it is essential to know is joining lead to copper, since a great number of service pipes are still lead and any alterations or repairs to lead pipework are best done in copper.

This joint is known as a 'wiped' or Taft joint and is easiest to do when the open end of the lead pipe is vertically below the copper. If this is not possible or the pipe is in a difficult location, then practice on some pipe off-cuts, or else get a plumber to do the connection.

(a) If the pipe is long enough, gently bend it so that the end of the pipe is vertical. Cut the end off square with a hacksaw, plug the end of the pipe with some cloth, and scrape off any lead shavings from the cut end with a knife or a file. Carefully remove the plug so that no shavings fall down into the pipe.

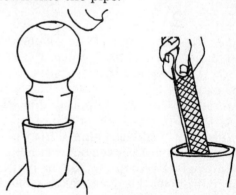

(b) Using a conical piece of wood, known as a tampin or any other conically-shaped piece of wood or hard plastic, such as a screwdriver or bradawl handle, form a bell mouth to the end of the lead pipe by supporting the pipe in one hand and tapping the forming implement with a hammer.

(b) Rotate the form to ensure that an even conical mouth is produced, deep enough for a piece of copper pipe of the same internal diameter as the lead, to fit 23 – 30 mm into it.

Plug the end with a piece of cloth and clean the inside of the bell with a knife or file until the metal is bright. Carefully remove the plug and the scrapings.

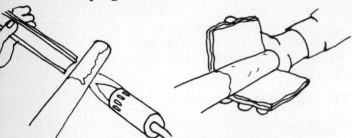

(c) Take a piece of copper pipe of the same internal bore as the lead and at least 200 mm long. Clean off the first 100 mm with wire wool until it shines and apply flux using a clean sliver of wood. Heat the copper until the flux sizzles and then rub a bar of plumber's metal (a form of solder) along the pipe until the fluxed area is completely covered. Remove from the flame and wipe with a fluff-free pad of cloth (wiping cloth). Remove any excess solder. There should now be a smooth even coating of solder over the end 50 mm of the pipe. This process is known as 'tinning'.

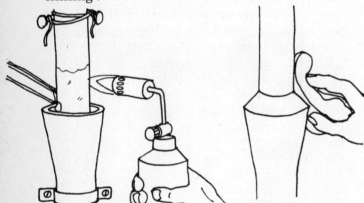

(d) Place the tinned end of the copper into the bell in the end of the lead pipe. Support both pipes, so that they are firmly positioned, using pipe clips or by tying or wiring them to nails hammered into the wall. Apply tallow (flux for lead) to the tinned section of the copper, the inside and end of the lead pipe. Gently play the blowlamp on the lead but do not over heat it or it will distort and begin to melt, before heating the copper just above the mouth of the lead pipe. Start melting plumber's metal into the mouth of the joint and push it down with the wiping cloth, so that a ring of solder is built up. Finally wipe of any excess solder so that a chamfered ring is formed between the end of the lead pipe and the tinned copper. Leave to cool until cold before removing the supports and carefully bending back into position or turning on the water to test the joint. A bad joint cannot be repaired; the lead pipe will have to be cut back and the process repeated.

F   Hose or Flexible Plastic Pipes

These can be cut with a sharp knife and joined either with patent hose pipe connectors or with copper pipe, olives and jubilee clips as described earlier for poly pipe.

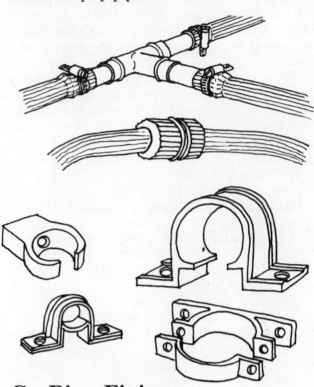

G   Pipe Fixings

In order to keep it in position, to stop it from distorting under its own weight, to stop it from oscillating under vibration and to help prevent leaks starting, all pipework must be supported or restrained by clips. There are two basic types of clip, saddle clips, which are put on after the pipe is in position and straddle the pipe, and plastic pipe clips which are positioned before the pipe. The pipe is then pressed into the clips which spring closed around it. Although the plastic pipe clips look neater, they have only one fixing, so are less reliable and must be accurately positioned before 'popping' the pipe into place. Also if a pipe has been inadequately clipped extra clips cannot be added without removing the pipe. Saddle clips have two fixings and can be added after the pipe is run. They are the more versatile.

Clip Spacing

Material	Vertical Spacing mm	Horizontal Spacing mm
Copper Pipe	1200	600
Polythene	600	300
Mild Steel	3000	2000
Plastic (supply)	1200	600
Plastic (waste)	1200	900
Plastic (soil)	1800	

EXTERNAL CONNECTION TO THE MAIN

Sometimes the main connection will have been cut off so that no end is available inside the house.

Check that the water has been switched off at the external stopcock. From the position that the old communication pipe came through the wall and the position of the Water Board's stopcock in the street, judge the line of the communication pipe. Carefully dig down to expose the pipe.

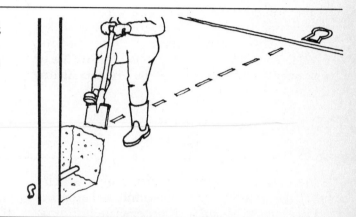

1

If the supply is only being connected for a short time then it is adequate to expose the communication pipe, adjacent to the house, cut back the pipe to give a clean, square end and connect a piece of copper pipe to it, using a Taft joint to lead (See 13.02 E) or a threaded end with an iron to copper connector (See 13.02 D) for galvanised steel. The copper pipe should be wrapped in 'Denzo' or Sylglas' tape to give it some protection against acids in the soil and pieces of slate, tile or brick placed over the pipe when the hole is filled in to protect it from gardening damage.

2

If the supply is a 'permanent' reconnection, it is probably worth replacing the whole of the communicating pipe from the Water Board's stopcock. Dig out the trench so that it is about a metre deep and if possible take it under the building so that the water main can rise on an internal wall. Where it passes through the wall, place a piece of larger diameter plastic waste pipe through the wall to form a sleeve.

3

Line the bottom of the trench with sand or a fine gravel. The communication pipe can be laid on 15 mm polythene pipe to B.S. 1972 Class D (green marking) and the Water Board can be asked to make the connection to their stopcock. Alternatively a stub of the old communication pipe can be left protruding from the Board's stopcock. A 200 to 300 mm stub of copper pipe is then attached to this pipe with a Taft joint if the old pipe is lead (See 13.02 E) or an iron to copper connector if the pipe is galvanised steel. Attach the poly pipe to the copper pipe with a compression fitting, with an insert. (See 13.02 C.) Cover the pipe with about 150 mm of fine gravel or sand and then lay pieces of slate, tile or brick over the line of the pipe before back filling the earth.

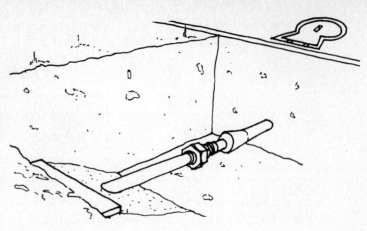

4

To the end of the communicating pipe which enters the building, attach a combined stopcock and draincock. If the pipe enters the building through the external wall, wrap insulation around it up to the stopcock.

5

INTERNAL CONNECTION TO THE MAIN

When the main has been cut off inside of the house a new internal connection can be made provided a sufficient length of pipe is left.

Check that the water has been switched off at the external stopcock. If not, either ask the Water Board to turn off their stopcock or use a key made by hammering flat the end of a piece of $\frac{1}{2}''$ gas barrel, but take care not to damage the shaft of the stopcock.

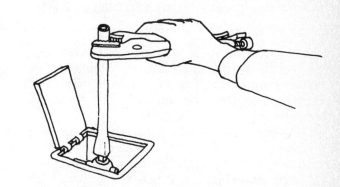

1

Cut off the damaged end of the communication pipe. The communication pipe will normally be in $\frac{1}{2}''$ diameter lead. Connect to the stub end, a 300 mm length of copper using a wiped or Taft joint (See 13.02 E). If the entry pipe is galvanised mild steel, then a B.S.P. thread will have to be cut into the end of the pipe. (See 13.02 D.) Once the thread has been cut, wrap it round three times with PFTE tape and screw on an iron to copper connector, having a BSP thread on one end and a capillary or compression fitting on the other. Fit a 300 mm length of copper into the connector.

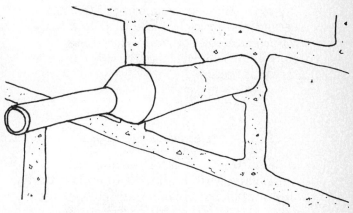

2

Connect a combined stop and draincock or a stopcock followed by a draincock to the stub of copper pipe. A stopcock with a non return valve is preferable. They have an arrow marked on the outer casing indicating the flow direction. Both stopcock and draincock are fitted with compression fittings. The connection is now ready to take the rising main.
N.B. All pipework against an external wall should be insulated or lagged to prevent frost damage.

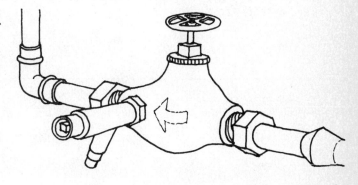

3

13.05
RISING MAIN

The Techniques described apply equally to the provision of a new rising main or the replacement of an old, and assume that the Water Board's connection has been brought into the house to a stopcock, which is fitted with a drain-off valve. (See Sheet 13.04.)

A position for the main should be selected which involves the minimum number of bends and an economic pipe run. The main can be run in polypipe or copper. The main should not be sited on an external wall if possible.

If a water tank is to be fitted the rising main need only serve the tank, the cold tap at the kitchen sink and a high pressure instantaneous gas-fired water heater, if fitted.

Where no tank is fitted, the main should be taken up to the highest room where fittings are to be served and branches taken off to other rooms. For example, the main rises to a bathroom with branches en route to the kitchen and a separate toilet.

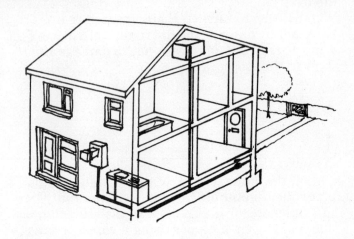

1

If no tank is fitted then after the stopcock, fit a non-return valve with built in draincock so that no contaminated water can be sucked back into the mains. Connect the pipe to the stopcock, either copper (See 13.02 A) or polypipe (See 13.02 C), adequately clipping in position en route, run to the points to be served. If the pipe is on an external wall wrap it in insulation to protect it from frost.

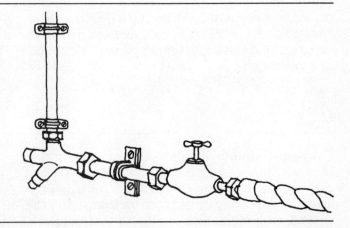

2

13.06
COLD WATER STORAGE TANK

*When water is being stored it is normal to
provide a fifty-gallon actual capacity water tank
for a dwelling with an independent hot water
system, an eighty-gallon tank when it serves
both the cold water and a hot water cylinder.*

The tank should be situated in the roof space, or
as high above the highest draw off position as
possible, for example, on a platform over the
stairwell. A full tank is very heavy, a
fifty-gallon tank weighing nearly a quarter of a
ton. The load must therefore be spread as much
as possible. If practical, locate the water tank
over a partition or load-bearing wall on the floor
beneath.

Construct a platform by laying four pieces of
75×50 mm s.w. across the ceiling joists at 300
mm centres, so that they span a minimum of
four ceiling joists. On top of these timbers nail a
piece of 22 mm blockboard or chipboard, large
enough to take the tank. If a galvanised metal
tank is to be used the platform can be
constructed of floorboards, but with modern
polythene or glass fibre tanks it is essential that
they sit on a flat even surface, or else splitting
can occur due to uneven stresses setting up in
the tank bottom. Avoid siting the tank platform
in the centre of the span of the ceiling joists and
if the joists look undersized, or in poor condition
seek advice about the way to support the tank,
rather than risk it coming through the ceiling
when full.

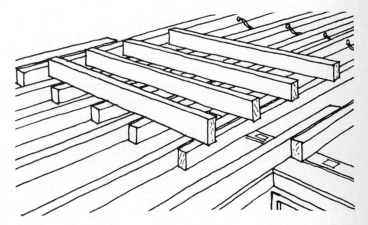

1

The tank may be galvanised steel (either new or
second hand), glass fibre or polythene. The size
of the tank will often be limited by the size of the
access hatch. A fifty gallon tank will have a
volume of approximately ten cubic feet (0.270
cubic metres), but this may be achieved in a
number of different proportions, so that a tank
should be available to fit through your hatch.
Flexible polythene tanks are also available
which can be folded up and pushed through, but
in my experience they have a tendency to split.
Two tanks can be linked together to give a
required capacity of this if necessary.

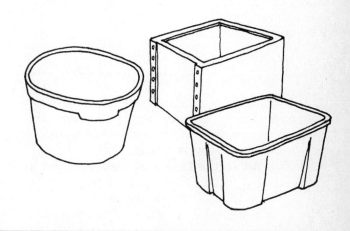

2

Before putting the tank up into the roof, but
after checking that it will fit through the hatch,
the holes for the inlet, outlet and overflow can be
cut.

The inlet hole is situated about 50 mm below the tank rim, and will normally be served by a 15 mm supply.

The overflow is situated about 10 mm below the tank rim and is one pipe size up from the supply, i.e. 22 mm for a 15 mm supply, 28 mm for a 22 mm supply. The outlet is sited 50 mm above the bottom of the tank and is usually 22 mm.

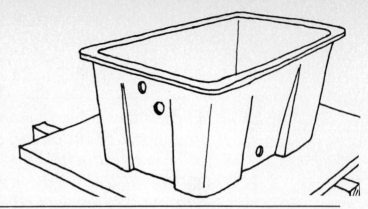

3

The outlet and overflow are connected to the tank by means of tank connectors. These are usually compression fittings attached to a piece of threaded pipe which has two back nuts and two compressible washers. A hole is made in the tank just large enough for the threaded pipe to pass through, one back nut and a compressible washer are placed on the pipe, which is put through the hole and the second washer and nut are then placed on the pipe. When both nuts are tightened so that the washers are compressed a watertight seal is achieved.

The inlet is fitted with a ball valve which will normally have its own tank connector built in.

To cut holes in the tank, or hole, cutters, which are available in sizes to match the threaded section of the connectors. If no tank or

hole cutters are available, mark the external diameter of the tank connector threads on the side of the tank and make a series of drill holes around the inside of the cut out. Finish off with a half-round file, checking with the tank connector until the hole is large enough.

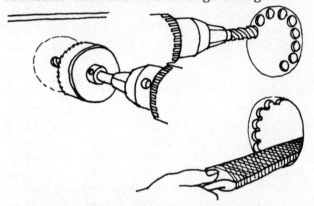

4

The tank connectors and ball valve are now fitted to the tank and the nuts tightened to compress the washers. Place the tank on the tank platform and hook up the water supply to the ball valve. A gate valve should be positioned on the inlet pipe to allow the tank to be isolated. The overflow should be taken out of the roof space and the end positioned so that it discharges outside the building, or if this is not possible, over the bath. Overflows can be run in plastic pipe, solvent-welded to a plastic tank connector.

The outlet should have a gate valve adjacent to the tank to enable the down feed to be shut off.

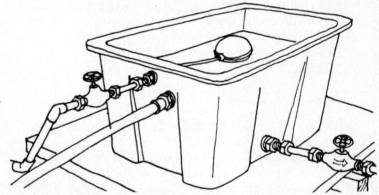

5

Once the tank is connected check that it does not leak and adjust the water level by bending the ballcock arm so that the water level is about 25 mm below the overflow outlet.

Place a lid on the tank and insulate the top and sides with glass fibre quilt or polystyrene slabs. Do not insulate under the tank. Wrap the inlet and outlet pipes in the roof space with insulation.

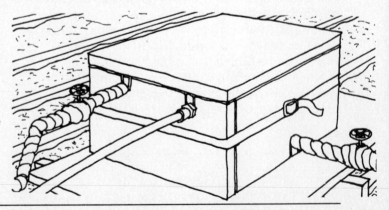

6

TAPS

Taps are available in brass, cast metal and nylon. The most common sizes are ½″ for wash basins and kitchen sinks, and ¾″ for baths. There are a variety of special purpose taps which take special washing machine or garden hose attachments, as well as a whole range of different designs both in single and mixer taps.

Metal Pillar and Mixer Taps

Clean around the tap hole in the fitting, removing any protective paper, if new, old putty if second-hand. The hole in the fitting will normally be square and the tap may have a corresponding square shank on top of the long tap thread. If the tap has a separate chromed rose plate, screw this over the thread. Apply putty to the bottom of the tap and the rose plate, if fitted, and place the tap in the hole. Slip on a washer; these are usually polythene, square, with a central, circular section which is raised, screw on the back nut and tighten until the tap is firm. This may be tightened using a 'basin spanner' which is capable of fitting up into restricted spaces. Clean off any putty squeezed out from around the base of the tap.

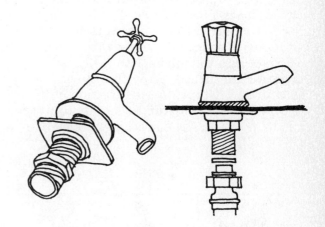

The water supply is connected to the tap with a tap connector which relies on a fibre washer to make a seal. Wrap some PFTE tape around the bottom of the thread in the direction that the nut turns. Slip the fibre washer into the tap connector and slip the tap connector onto the end of the tap thread. Tighten up the nut of the tap connector, with the basin spanner if necessary, until firm. Note all soldered joints to the supply pipe should be complete before attempting to connect the tap.

1

Nylon Taps

All nylon, or nylon with metal outer casing taps are becoming increasingly common. They are fitted to bath, basin or sink in exactly the same way as for ordinary taps. However, the connection to the water supply is more delicate, since the nylon tap thread is easily damaged by a normal tap connector. If a tap connector is used it is very easy to get the brass nut cross threaded in which case it cuts through the nylon thread, or to over-tighten the connector causing a compression of the nylon thread which later begins to leak.

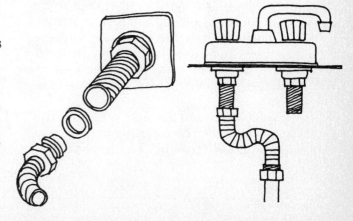

Therefore when using nylon taps a special flexible fitting must be used. This is fitted to the supply pipe by a compression fitting. The flexible section is then bent so that the tap connector fits below the tap thread. A washer is fitted into the connector and it is then carefully screwed on to the end of the tap thread until finger tight. A quarter turn with a basin spanner should be sufficient to make a water tight connection.

Bib Taps

Bib taps are wall mounted and may be used with a ceramic sink, to provide an outside tap, or where a wall mounted tap is required. The taps are available in cast brass or chrome finish with matching back plate elbows. The back plate elbow is connected to the pipework by a compression fitting and screwed to the wall. The tap screws into the elbow with a British Standard Pipe thread. Wrap the end of the thread in PFTE tape, in the direction of the thread, and screw into the back plate until the tap is firm and in the correct position.

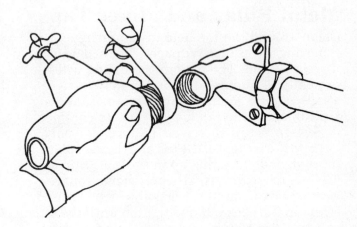

Tap Maintenance

Taps rely on a fibre or rubber washer to stop the flow of water which wears with time causing the tap to drip and sometimes producing a 'hammering' noise in the pipes when the water is turned off suddenly. To replace a washer first switch off the water to the tap. Unscrew the chrome shield, protecting it with a cloth if it is necessary to use an adjustable wrench or spanner. Raise the bottom of the shield and using a spanner on the brass nut this reveals, unscrew the tap mechanism. Undo the securing nut and remove the worn washer from the back plate. It is advisable to take the old washer along when buying a replacement since there are a variety of washers available. Fibre washers are best since they can be used for both hot and cold water, while rubber washers can only be used for cold. Replace the washer and re-assemble the tap.

If the tap leaks around the shank, turn off the water, undo the screw holding the head in position and gently tap it off. Unscrew and

remove the covering shield. If the knurled knob around the shaft is loose tighten it and turn the water back on. If it still leaks turn the water off again, remove the tap mechanism and unscrew the knurled knob using a pair of pliers. Screw out the shaft of the tap and remove the 'O' ring. Replace the 'O' ring and re-assemble the tap, do not over-tighten the knurled knob.

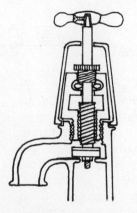

If a second-hand bath is going to be used, ensure that there are no chips in the enamel, no distortion in the surface and that the old taps and waste fittings can be removed. Scale build-up on the enamel can be removed by using spirits of salts. Care should be taken when using this acid to protect the skin and eyes. Demolition and scrap merchants' yards often provide a good source of high quality, big, old, cast iron baths, which are relatively inexpensive.

Position the bath so that there is room to work, if the end of the bath with the taps is to go against the wall, leave a gap for a shelf, or if that is not possible, choose a bath which has side taps.

Fit the legs or cradles on to the bottom of the bath. These usually slot into locating grooves for cast iron baths, or bolt into flanges welded to the bottom of pressed steel baths. In order to spread the load of the bath, which in use weighs several hundredweight, place two pieces of 75×50 mm timber across the span of the joists and stand the bath on these timbers. Measure the distance from the underside of the bath to the floor and check that it is sufficient to fit in a waste trap. If not pack the bath up further, do not cut a hole in the floorboards as this would make it difficult to unblock the trap without damaging the ceiling below.

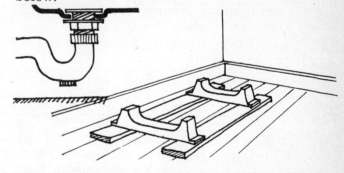

1

Turn the bath on its side to fit the waste which will normally be 1½″ but may be different on some old baths. If using a second-hand bath use a stilson wrench to undo the locking nut on the old waste. If the nut will not move or the thread is damaged, then turn the bath upside down and cut down through the waste outlet and the locking nut with a hacksaw taking care not to cut into the bottom of the bath. Remove the waste fitting and clean out any old putty.

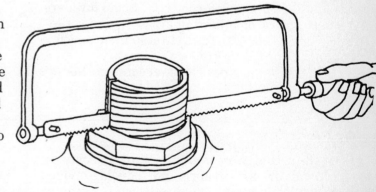

2

The new waste fitting can have a long threaded section which is slotted to accept an overflow attachment or be shorter with no slot if a combined trap and overflowing fitting is to be used. Do not use a slotted waste with a combined trap and overflow. Turn the bath on its side. Undo the locking nut from the waste. The waste must have a watertight seal to the bath which is provided either by a compressible rubber washer or by applying a continuous ring of putty to the back of the flange. Place the waste in position in the bath slip on a washer, the overflow ring and another washer, if a combined system, and then the locking nut. Tighten the nut until the rubber washer is compressed or some of the putty squeezes out from around the flange. Do not over-tighten.

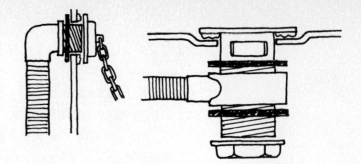

3

Locate the overflow in the hole provided in the bath and tighten the cover grating down, either onto a rubber washer or onto a ring of putty. If the overflow is combined with a trap then position the trap, ensure that the compressible washer is not twisted and then screw onto the end of the waste fitting until hand tight. A further quarter of a turn with a wrench should ensure a watertight seal.

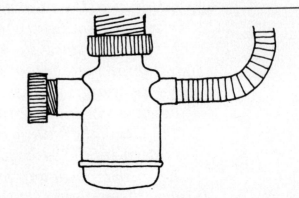

4

The taps are $\frac{3}{4}''$ and may be pillar or mixer taps, they are usually fitted with the cold to the right and hot to the left. Fit the taps as described in Sheet (13.07).

There should be a 22 mm supply from the cold tank and the hot water supply to the bath taps. If only a 15 mm supply is available then step up the size of the pipe with a 22 mm to 15 mm reducer.

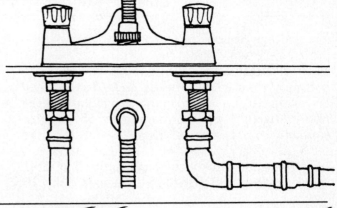

5

Position the bath on the spreader timbers and adjust the feet or pack the cradles so that the sides of the bath are level – this will ensure that the water runs away correctly. Some builders place a brick or a hard quarry tile under the adjustable feet of the bath to stop them sinking into the spreading timbers.

Fix the bath in position and connect the taps and waste. (13.07.)

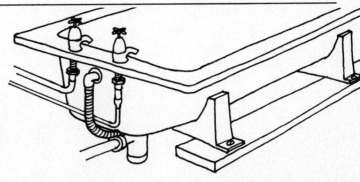

6

It is important, particularly if the bath is boxed-in, that there is a watertight seal between any wall or built-in surround. This is provided by a silicone mastic such as Down Corning or Evode Bath sealant which is squeezed out of a tube through a nozzle which is provided. Smooth the mastic with a wet finger, or a wet smooth piece of metal, for example a spoon handle. The seal will remain flexible and this is necessary since there will be some movement between the bath and the wall when the bath is filled or in use. Putty which dries out, or other fillers which are not flexible are therefore not suitable.

7

INSTALLING A WASH BASIN

The waste to a wash basin is normally $1\frac{1}{4}''$ diameter, and the overflow will normally be integral in the moulding of a clay basin, necessitating a slotted waste outlet. There must be a watertight seal to the basin which is provided either by a compressible rubber washer or by applying a continuous ring of putty to the back of the flange. Place the waste in position in the basin, to the underside slip on a washer and the locking nut. Tighten the nut until the rubber washer is compressed or some of the putty squeezes out from around the flange. Do not over-tighten since this could crack the basin.

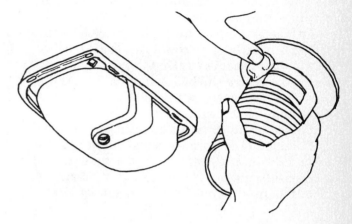

1

The taps are $\frac{1}{2}''$ and normally fitted with the hot on the left and the cold on the right. Fit the taps as Sheet 13.07 – they will require a 15 mm supply. Take care not to over-tighten the locking nuts as this might crack the basin. Bed the plug and chain fitting in putty and secure in the hole provided in the basin.

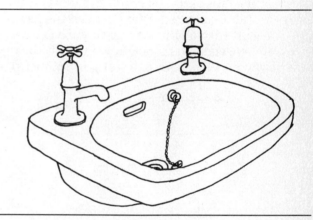

2

If the basin is to be supported on a pedestal then fit the pedestal and basin together; they are normally located by a second locking nut around the basin waste being tightened down against a rubber washer on the pedestal. Stand the pedestal against the wall and mark the position of the brackets which will hold the basin back to the wall. Check that the basin is level and then drill and plug the wall. Screw the brackets into position with brass screws.

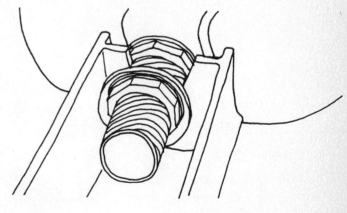

3

If the basin is to be supported on brackets then mark the wall approximately 750 mm above floor level, and using a spirit level draw a horizontal line. The brackets may be gallows or towel rail brackets, or for small basins they may simply fit in slots in the rear of the basin, or have a ring support which fits around the basin waste outlet. For gallows or towel rail brackets, position the brackets so that they are correctly spaced to receive the basin and make sure they touch the line on the wall. Mark the positions, drill and plug the walls and screw the brackets into place using brass screws. Place a bed of putty on top of the brackets and check that the basin is level. If the wall will not take an adequate fixing a pedestal or leg brackets should be used to ensure a firm support.

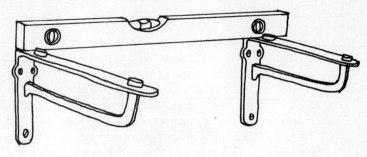

4

Connect the taps and waste, hiding them behind the pedestal is required. Seal between the basin and the wall with a silicone mastic such as Dow Corning or Evode Bath Sealant. Smooth the mastic with a wet finger or a wet piece of metal.

5

INSTALLING A SINK UNIT

Pressed metal sinks are normally designed to be supported on a sink base unit and are available with draining boards to the right or left. The unit will often have a drawer below the draining board and a fake drawer in front of the sink. Most units can be simply converted from left to right by unscrewing the blank front and changing it over with the drawer, although the drawer tracks may also need to be changed. The sink top is usually held in place by simple swivel toggles or 'L' shaped fasteners.

It is important that the top of the unit is level before the sink is positioned.

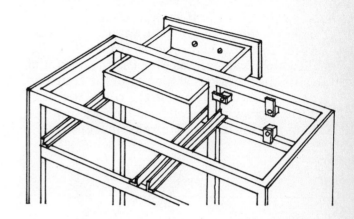

1

Some sinks are made to be inset into a work surface and are provided with a template to enable the surface to be cut accurately. Position the cutting template (if the template is missing, make one from newspaper) on the work surface so that there are no obstructions beneath it which will obstruct the sink bowl and the pipework. Transfer the cutting line from the template to the work surface using carbon paper, or by first blacking the back of the template with a soft pencil. Inside the area to be cut out drill a hole behind the line. Starting in the hole with a padsaw or a jigsaw cut out for the sink and smooth off any rough areas with a rasp or file.

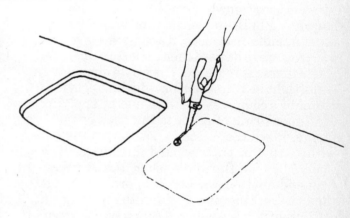

2

The inset sink will normally be held in position by a number of swivel fasteners on the underside, which sometimes must be screwed to the inside of the work surface.

In order to ensure a watertight fit around the sink, bed it in putty or a sealing gasket if provided. If using putty, place an even ring of putty around the opening, put the sink in place and push down to spread the putty. Swivel the fasteners under the work surface and tighten-up the screws. Trim off any excess putty so that there is a continuous line of putty around the edge of the sink.

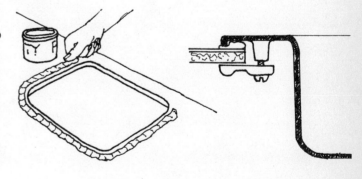

3

If no sink unit is available, or wanted, then the sink top can be supported on a purpose-made frame. This can be simple or as complex as required, but should be made so that the edges of the unit are supported, with a raised batten to support the upstand if incorporated.

Do not attempt to screw through any part of the sink unit to hold it in place. Instead hook 'L' shaped shrinkage plates over the inside rim of the sink unit and screw them into the frame or wedge lengths of batten into the rim of the sink and then screw pieces of wood to both these battens and the frame. The frame must be level.

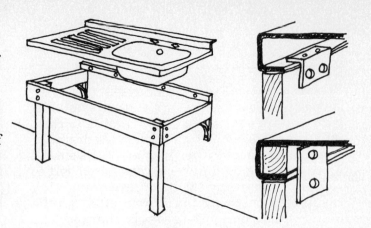

4

Whichever means of support is to be adopted for the sink, the waste, overflow, taps and plug attachments should all be fitted to the sink before it is positioned. Fit the taps as Sheet 13.07. The waste fitting can have a long threaded section which incorporates a slot if the sink has a built-in overflow, or an overflow attachment is to be used. If a combined overflow and trap are to be used then a shorter, unslotted waste fitting is required. The waste must have a watertight seal to the sink which is provided either by a compressible washer or by applying a continuous ring of putty to the back of the flange. Place the waste in position in the sink with washer or putty around the flange, to the underside on a flexible washer, the overflow ring and another washer (if appropriate), and then the locking nut. Tighten the locking nut until the rubber washer is compressed, or some of the putty squeezes out from around the flange. Fit the overflow and plug chain holder attachments, tightening them down onto a compressible washer, or a ring of putty.

The sink may now be connected to the water supplies and the waste.

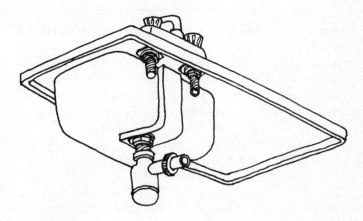

5

INSTALLING A W.C.

Where an old W.C. pan has been removed or is to be replaced, carefully tap round the pan behind the trap section about 150 mm from the connection, with a cold chisel and hammer. Take care not to smash it out causing pieces to fall down the connection. Having tapped all round the pipe, tap once with a hammer, which should cause it to break off, and remove the pan. Stuff some newspaper or some rag into the mouth of the connection, below the bottom of the pan connection and carefully chip out the remains of the pan and the cement connection with a cold chisel. Work into the pipe and take care not to damage the cast iron, or clayware (if ground or basement floor) collar. Unscrew or chip out the remains of the old pan pedestal.

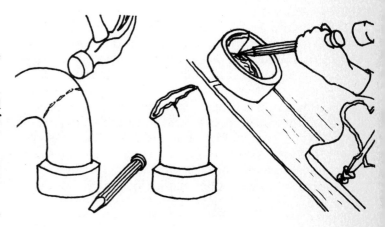

1

W.C. pans are available with an 'S' trap to suit a floor connection, with a 'P' trap to suit wall connections, or 'Two-piece' with a swivel bottom section to suit off set floor connections. However, some manufacturers are now only making 'P' trap pans since adaptors made by 'Multikwik' can be used to connect them to the outlet.

The choice of pan is governed by the type of cistern, high or low level, conventional or slim fit, and the position of the outlet.

Having selected the type of pan place it on the floor in the position and check the alignment for the connection.

2

If the pan has an 'S' trap which fits directly into the connection, place the pan in position with the pan outlet correctly aligned with the connection. Screw the pan to the floor with brass screws which do not rust. If the pan sits on a solid floor then bed it in 1:3 cement: sand mortar, or hack out 25 mm diameter pockets below the fixing positions with a cold chisel. Fill these with 'prompt' cement or 1:3 cement: sand mortar, immediately place the pan, screw into the cement with brass screws and leave for the cement to set.

To make a joint between the outlet and the pipe, first ram putty into the collar around the outlet, about 10 mm thick, then on top of the putty add a ring of hemp, followed by another ring of putty and tamp well down. If no hemp and putty are available, then damp newspaper or brown paper will also provide adequate caulking. Finish the connection by tamping 'prompt cement', or rapid hardening cement, into the connection and trowel a smooth chamfer from the collar to the pipe. (Prompt cement is also used to joint the two halves of a two-piece pan).

3

If a 'Multikwik' adaptor is to be used first determine whether one, two or three pieces are necessary. These connectors comprise a pipe with a rubber flanged spigot piece which fits into the connection collar, or to other connectors. The connection to the pan is made by fitting the pan outlet into a pre-greased socket which is also protected by rubber flanges. A number of straight and bent pieces are available. Make up the necessary connection by cutting and push fitting together the various pieces. Using the sachet of lubricant provided, grease the inside of the 'Multikwik' socket and push onto the pan outlet until it is fully home and pull out the bell-shaped skirt to sit around the pipe. Push the flanged spigot of the 'Multikwik' into the connection. Fix the pan to the floor as in 3 above.

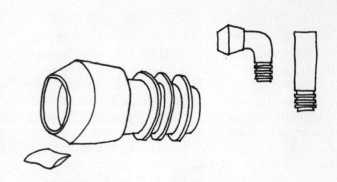

4
_____

If the pan is to connect to a plastic soil stack a 'Multikwik' adaptor may be used or if the connection is a simple straight connection, most manufacturers of plastic soil systems produce a simple rubber sealing sleeve which fits over the pan outlet and forms a seal when outlet and sleeve are pushed into the connection pipe.

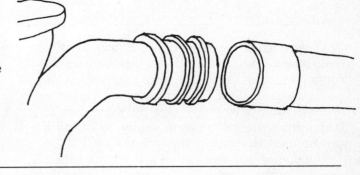

5
_____

13.12
CISTERN AND FLUSH PIPE

Cisterns can be high or low level. Low level cisterns are most common in modern installations and can be 'slimfit' or close coupled, or have two action flushing. With minor variations, they are all installed in a similar fashion, with the exception of close coupled cisterns and pans which have to be coupled together before fixing either pan or cistern. For the others:

Once the pan has been correctly positioned determine the siting of the cistern which should be behind, square to and symmetrical to the pan for low level cisterns, behind or to the side and slightly back for high level cisterns. Mark the position of the cistern and the position of the overflow. If the overflow is to be taken through the wall adjacent to the cistern position then cut a hole with a masonry drill or cold chisel before fixing the cistern.

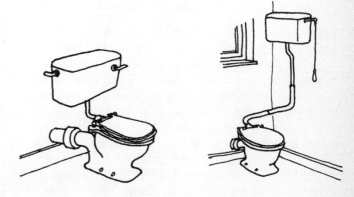

1

The cistern will be held in position by brackets or screws through the rear wall of the cistern, or both. Mark, drill and plug the wall and screw the brackets into place. Mount the cistern on the brackets and screw through the rear wall with brass screws. If the plaster and brickwork is too bad to provide a secure fixing, hack off the plaster and rawbolt a plywood or blockboard fixing board to the brickwork, flush with the plaster.

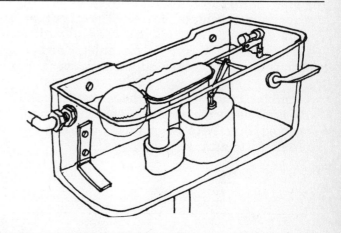

2

Connect a plastic overflow pipe to the overflow outlet and a 15 mm cold water supply to the inlet pipe, using a tap connector. Most modern cisterns have plastic inlet pipes so that all the soldered connections to the supply pipe must be carried out before it is joined to the cistern, and care must be taken not to cross thread the tap connector which will damage the inlet pipe causing it to leak.

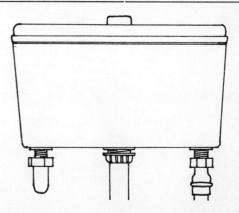

3

For a low level cistern a single flush pipe is cut to length and the top end connected to the bottom of the cistern by a compression fitting which should be hand-tightened, with an extra quarter of a turn with a wrench to ensure that it is watertight. For a high level cistern a two piece flush pipe, if it is behind the pan, or a three piece if it is to the side, will be necessary. The pieces are cut to length and slotted together to form the shape necessary to get from the cistern outlet to the pan inlet. Although the push fit should be watertight the pieces can be solvent welded to give extra certainty. Once again the top of the pipe is fitted to the cistern outlet via the compression fitting.

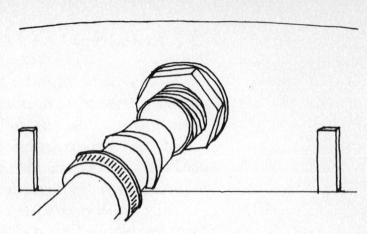

4

The bottom of the flush pipe has a radiused bend and a straight section which fits into the back of the pan. This junction is sealed with a 'cone' of which there are two varieties. The better kind has an inner conical section which fits around the pipe and into the pan inlet, with an outer sheath which fits around the outside of the pan inlet. The simpler type has a bell end which fits around the pan inlet and narrows to a sleeve which fits around the pipe. To fit the first, wet it with water and push it over the end of the pipe, bend back the outer sheath and locate the end of the pipe in the pan inlet. Roll the outer sheath back over the outside of the inlet. The other type is simply slipped over the end of the pipe which is then pushed well into the pan inlet. The bell mouth of the cone is then pulled back over the inlet.

N.B. For both types of cistern check that the inlet valve is of the correct type, high pressure when connected directly to the mains, low pressure when fitted to a tank.

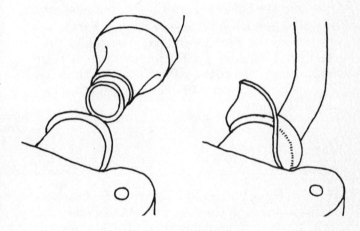

5

13.13
FITTING A HOT WATER CYLINDER

Hot water cylinders are normally made of copper, and are available as direct or indirect. They are heated by a heating coil from a heating boiler, or a back boiler to a fire, or by an electrical element known as an immersion heater. A direct cylinder is not to be recommended, except possibly in 'soft' water areas, since the heating of the water causes a scale build up like the 'furring' in an electric kettle. In an indirect cylinder water in a coil is heated in a closed system so that there is minimal scale build up. The water to be used circulates around the outside of the heated coil and becomes hot enough for use but is less prone to scale build up.

Purchase a cylinder for use with a boiler or an immersion heater, or both and position it if possible in an airing cupboard on the top floor. Adjacent to the main water storage tank in the roof fit a feed and expansion tank.

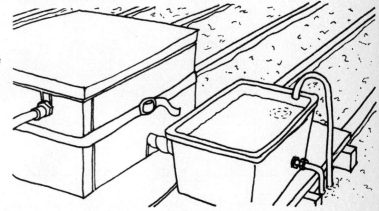

1

The connections to the cylinder are made so that the hot water tap connections are made off a circuit which returns to the cylinder. Off this circuit which is connected into the female connection to the top of the cylinder an expansion pipe is taken up to the main cold water tank and bent over so that it will discharge into the tank. A connection from the cold water storage tank is taken down and connected to the female connection at the bottom of the cylinder.

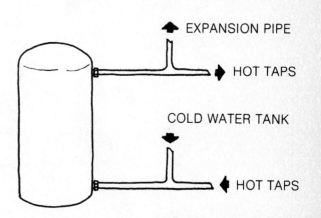

EXPANSION PIPE

HOT TAPS

COLD WATER TANK

HOT TAPS

2

Heating coil connections depend on the form of heating. If there is only an immersion heater then a supply is taken from the feed and expansion tank and connected to the bottom male connection with an expansion pipe connected to the top male connection, taken up to the feed and expansion tank where it is bent over to discharge into the tank. For the electrical connection (See 9.08).

When the heat is being provided by a boiler the feed pipe from the tank is connected to the boiler. From the boiler one pipe is connected to the top male connection of the cylinder and the expansion pipe to the tank is a branch off this connection. A pipe connects the bottom male connection on the cylinder with the boiler.

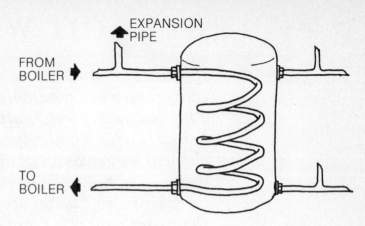

3
_____

Insulate a hot water cylinder with a jacket and lag or insulate hot water pipes to prevent heat loss, particularly when they pass through unused spaces. Some heating 'packs' are available which combine a hot water cylinder with a feed and expansion tank and are ready insulated. They should be connected in accordance with the manufacturer's instructions.

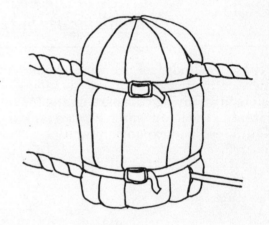

4
_____

13.14
REMOVING OLD PLUMBING

Before removing a redundant fitting or system it is important to make sure that the water supply is turned off and the system or the part serving the fitting drained down.

Turn the main stopcock off (clockwise).

Open the taps or flush the cistern to check if water is still flowing. If no water comes from the taps, or if the water flows, but then stops as the feed pipe empties, or if the cistern does nor refill once flushed then proceed to drain down.

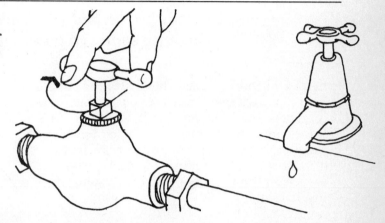

1

If water continues to flow from the taps or the cistern refills then check that the stopcock has been turned the right way, and if it has then look in the roof spaces, over the stairwell or sometimes on top of the roof, for a water tank. If there is a tank containing water, depress the ballcock to see if water is coming up to it from the rising main, if not then the main stopcock is probably working.

On the distribution pipe leading out of the tank there should be a stopcock. If there is not, then, unless a stopcock can be found between the tank and the fitting the tank will have to be drained.

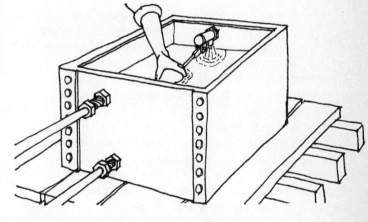

2

In order to drain down the system first open all the taps until the water stops to flow. Place a bucket below the drain cock and let the remainder of the water out of the system. Remove the fittings either by cutting through the pipework or by undoing the connections. If the fittings are not being replaced, before turning on the water cap off all dead pipes. Pipes can be capped with purpose-made caps, either capillary or compression for copper pipework. Alternatively a piece of pipe can be cleaned up, hammered flat and the end bent over. Clean the pipe again, flux and solder. This will usually be adequate for a temporary stop.

When fittings are to be re-used, take care when removing pipes, taps, waste fittings, etc.

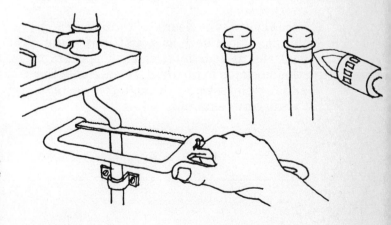

3

From time to time Blockages are inevitable, and are most common in kitchen sink wastes, where congested cooking fat or oil, can clog up with bits of vegetables, hairs and tea leaves to form an efficient plug. Regularly flushing the waste through with hot clean water, or a solution of washing soda is a good preventative precaution.

When a sink, bath, or basin blocks, take a rubber plunger, place it over the waste outlet and press up and down with the handle. If no plunger is to hand a pad of cloth, such as a folded tea towel will sometimes work. The plunger works by alternately increasing and decreasing the pressure on the blockage which will sometimes cause it to dislodge.

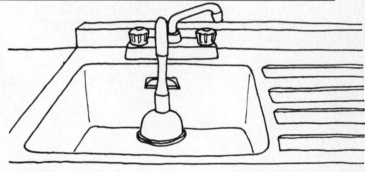

1

If the plunger fails then bail all of the water out of the blocked fitting. Place a bowl or bucket under the trap on the waste outlet. If there is very little room, for example, between the bottom of a bath waste trap and the floor, slide a shallow baking tray underneath. The trap is now opened:–
– for a bottle trap simply unscrew the bottom section by hand, holding the upper section so as not to put stress on the connections.
– for a plastic 'P' or 'S' trap, unscrew the bottom section again steadying the upper pieces to avoid straining the connections.
– for lead or copper traps there is normally a circular plate on the bottom of the 'U'. Place the shaft of a screw driver between the raised horns on this inspection plate and unscrew the plate (anti-clockwise).

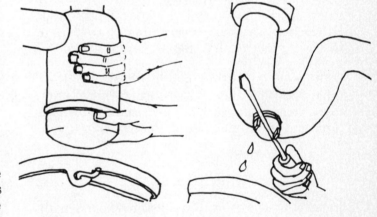

The trap can now be cleared of the blockage, a flexible implement such as a knitting needle may be useful to clear out a lead or copper trap. Once the blockage is removed, re-assemble the trap and run clean water through the waste to carry away any remaining solids.

2

If the blockage is not in the trap then use a flexible metal drain cleaner to rod out the waste. Alternatively remove the covers of any rodding points built into the waste and break up the obstruction with a drain rod. If the waste is a plastic push fit system, and there are no rodding points then the pipework can be carefully eased apart to give rodding access.

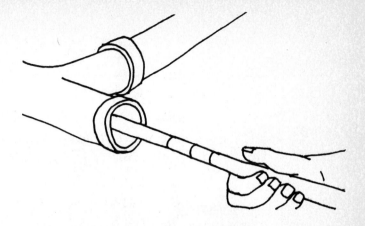

3
___

If a W.C. blocks, bail out some of the water and agitate the pan outlet with a large rubber plunger or with an old-fashioned mop. If this fails to clear the blockage then the soil stack will need to be rodded through. (See 12.07.)

4
___

13.16
STOPPING AN OVERFLOW

When an overflow is running it should not be ignored; overflows when left to run can cause damage to brickwork, damp penetration, plaster failure, and if drains are blocked, even minor flooding. At least the running overflow is a waste of clean water.

The overflows to W.C. cisterns and roof tanks are controlled in the same way so that these instructions apply equally to each:

Open the tank or cistern and examine the ball valve. Common problems with the ball float and arm are:
i. The ball has worked loose and fallen off.
ii The ball has developed a leak and is water logged.
iii. The arm is bent so that the water level necessary to close the valve is above the overflow outlet.

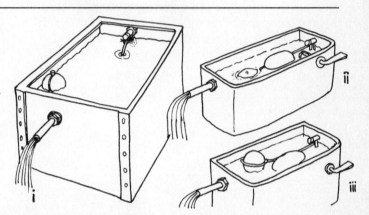

1

The remedies are simple:
i. Screw the ball back into the arm and check the setting.
ii. Buy a new ball and screw it onto the arm. It is worth switching off the water, disconnecting the arm and taking it along to ensure that the ball will fit. Some cisterns have specially shaped floats so make a note of the make.
iii. Bend the arm down so that the valve shuts off when the water level is about 25 mm below the overflow outlet.

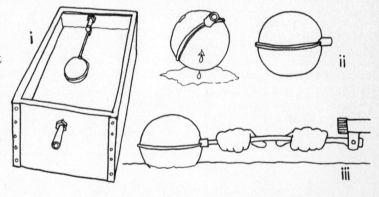

2

If none of these remedies work then the washer is probably worn. Switch off the water. There are a variety of ball valves in use but the basic principle for replacing the washer or diaphragm is the same, first remove the ball arm which is usually held in position by a split pin, second, undo the cap nut on the end of the valve, and third, remove the diaphragm or the piston holding the diaphragm. Take the old diaphragm along when buying a new one and before re-assembling the valve clean off any calcium deposits. Re-assemble in the reverse order. Switch on the water, allow the tank to fill and adjust the ball arm if necessary.

3

14
GAS

14.00
GAS PLUMBING

The principles and techniques of gas plumbing are very similar to those for water. However the dangers are far greater and in recognition of this fact the installation of gas appliances is covered by the Gas Safety Regulations (1972) which set out strict conditions under which such work may be executed. The readers are advised not to attempt gas installation work unless they have previously gained a sound practical knowledge of plumbing techniques and unless they are willing to have the installation tested by the Gas Board before connection.

The Gas Safety Regulations in particular require that installation pipes and appliances are installed or altered by 'competent' persons in accordance with the regulations. Pipework is required to be 'of good construction and sound materials' and an installation must be 'tested to verify that it is gastight and examined to verify that it has been installed in accordance with the regulations'. Pipework must be adequately supported, protected from damage, positioned so as to avoid accidental damage, cross electrical wiring at right angles, pass through walls by the shortest route and be protected against any likely movement in the wall. It should not run through wall cavities, and when passing through a solid floor the pipe must be protected by a sleeve which must not allow gas to be trapped between pipe and sleeve but will allow for movement in the pipe.

Gas appliances must be suitable for the type of gas supplied, i.e. natural gas at present but pre 1971 most areas were supplied by town gas and some older appliances still exist. There must be a correctly installed flue to remove the fumes caused by the burning gas, a supply of air to enable the gas to burn, the room must be adequately ventilated and the appliance must be in proper working order.

The gas main, stopcock and meter are all the property of the local Gas Board and the consumer is not allowed to tamper with them. The Gas Board have two common methods of disconnecting a supply of a house that has been left empty, they will either remove the meter and cap the supply pipe or they will dig up the supply pipe and cut it off in the street. Even if the Gas Board have only removed the meter they may decide to take the opportunity of a request for supply to renew the connection to the main. A connection that involves a new service pipe can be expensive, ranging from one to several hundred pounds. The expense may be reduced if the gas meter is situated in a meter box sited on the outside wall of the house or even on the back of a boundary wall. This has the advantage of reducing the length of the Gas Board service pipe and because the meter is installed in a box provided by the Gas Board, to which they have one key, it enables the meter to be read when no one is at home.

In many old houses the gas meter is situated in the hallway or under the stairs and this is no longer acceptable since no gas appliance should be sited in an escape route in case of fire unless enclosed in a fire proof box. In practice the Gas Board will usually request that the meter is resited.

When taking possession of an old house contact the local Gas Board and check that the gas supply is on. If the supply has been disconnected ask for an estimate for the cost of reconnection, agree a meter position with the board and instruct them to carry out the reconnection. The Gas Board may take some time to carry out a reconnection and will often require payment in advance. Meanwhile install the new gas piping or check and modify the existing installation. Adjacent to the agreed meter position leave a 22 mm pipe to which the board can connect the meter. The Gas Board will test the installation before connecting the meter and householders should ensure that this test is carried out.

Gas pipework can either be run in copper or mild steel pipe, no other material is acceptable. The techniques for jointing the pipework are the same as those for plumbing. (See 9.02).

The gas supply is normally 22 mm in diameter and 22 mm pipework should be run inside the house with 15 mm connections to appliances.

The flow of gas is controlled by a stopcock on the supply side of the meter. The stopcock is operated by a handle secured to a square shank. The shank is marked with a line which is at right angles to the pipe when closed and open when it is in the line of the pipe. The handle will normally be fixed so that it is in line with this marking but this is not always the case.

14.01
MAINTAINING EXISTING INSTALLATION

If the gas installation has not been used for some time and the pipework is old gas barrel, obviously installed before 1971, it is advisable to check it very carefully for gas leaks. In older installations threaded joints were sealed with hemp and 'Boss White' and there is evidence that these joints deteriorate when natural gas is supplied. It is much drier than town gas, causing the hemp to dry out and become brittle. However, if the pipework is apparently sound and is to be used, examine it and make alterations as necessary.

Trace all the pipework, lifting floorboards to make sure that an open end has not been left. In particular look for holes in the floorboards next to fire places which may indicate that a gas fire connection has been removed.

If an open end is discovered where the pipe has been cut through then unscrew the severed section of pipe from the next fitting using a pair of grips or a stilson wrench. The end of the pipe can be blocked off with a plug or a cap depending on the thread on the pipe. Purchase a plug or cap of the appropriate diameter. Clean off any rust or old jointing compound from the threads with a wire brush. Wrap the 'male' thread with three turns of PFTE tape wound in the direction of the thread. Tighten the plug or cap with a wrench.

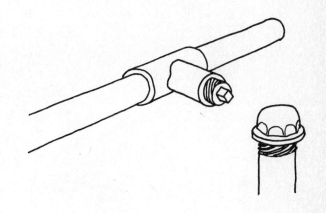

1

If an alteration or addition is to be made to the existing installation first ensure that the gas is turned off. Unscrew a plug or cap to the end of the pipe or cut through a section of pipe and unscrew each end from its fittings with a wrench. Clean off the threads at each end and insert a copper to iron connector, using PFTE tape to seal the threads. Between the two copper to iron connectors insert copper pipework with 'T' branches to the appropriate fittings.

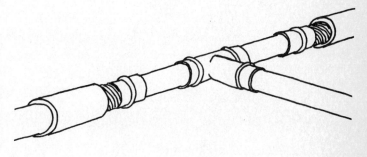

2

If the gas supply is already on then check each connection in old pipework for a possible leak. Switch off all appliances, turn off all pilot lights and make sure that no one is smoking and that there are no naked flames or faulty electrical fittings which may be sparking. Turn on the gas at the stopcock and watch the meter dial. If the needle or digits move, however slowly, then there is a leak or a pilot light has been left on. Check all appliances and if they are all off but the meter continues to register a gas flow then there is a leak. Smell each joint; natural gas has an additive which gives it a strong smell and if a leak is suspected drip an equal solution of water and washing up liquid onto the joint. If the liquid bubbles then there is a leak. Re-do the joint and re-test. Even when moving into a house which has a gas supply turned on and metered it is worth asking the Gas Board to run a pressure test if the installation is old or if minor alterations have been made.

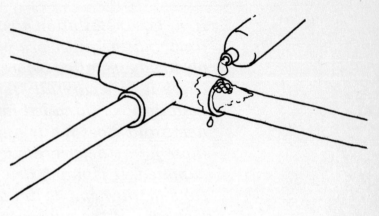

3

RUNNING NEW GAS PIPE

New gas piping should be run in a position where it is unlikely to be damaged and should be either mild steel barrel or copper pipe. Copper pipework is quicker and easier to install although the material is more expensive.

From the meter position take a 22 mm pipe so that it runs to any appliance that requires a 22 mm feed, such as some models of multipoint water heater, and also acts as a 'rising main' to any floor where more than one gas appliance is to be installed. Off this 22 mm pipe take 15 mm branches to serve the various gas appliances.

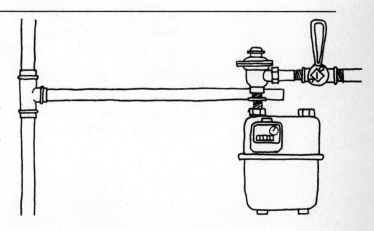

1

Take care not to allow dirt, copper shavings, plaster dust etc. to enter the pipes and plug open ends of pipe with pieces of rag when leaving work incomplete. Cap ends of pipes which have not been connected to appliances, leaving an extra-long piece of pipe to allow for the plugged ends to be cut off.

Fix appliances in accordance with Sheets 14.03, 14.05, 14.06 and 14.07.

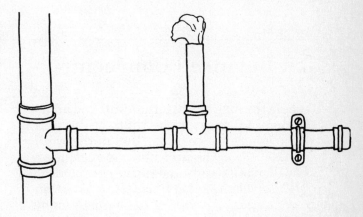

2

14.03
FITTING A GAS FIRE

A gas fire which is floor-mounted must stand on a hearth of incombustible material. This can be achieved by sitting a gas fire on an existing hearth or by forming a hearth of an incombustible board secured to the floor. Gas fires are served with 15 mm supplies which can be reduced to 8 mm within 1 metre of the gas cock.

Run a gas supply to a gas cock adjacent to the gas position. The gas cock should be positioned so that it is unlikely to be kicked or damaged by, for example, a vacuum cleaner.

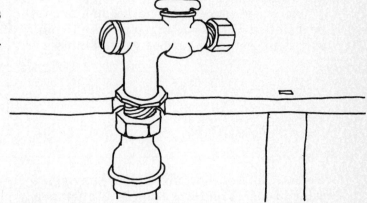

1

Back Balanced Convector Fire

Cut a hole through the external wall and adjust the two piece flue set to the width of the wall. Tape the joint and insert the flue in the wall. Mount the body of the fire, minus the casing on to the wall using screws and rawlplugs coupling it to the flue at the same time. The connection between the gas cock and fire can be made using 8 mm copper with or without a chrome finish. The connections are made by compression or threaded fittings and PFTE or 'Boss White' should be used on the threads of the fittings to ensure a gas tight connection. Replace the outer casing to the fire.

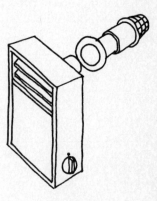

2

Conventional Gas Fire

Make sure that the chimney has been swept and that if the pot has been removed the flue has been capped in such a way as to allow the passage of the equivalent of 0.017 square metres (27 square inches) of free air. A specially made clayware plug, a loose hood and spigot or a 225×225 mm air brick should give an adequate airflow. (8.04, 10.04.)

Block off the fireplace with a non combustible board or brickwork and cut or leave a hole to accept the flue. (8.01, 8.03.)

Position the fire so that the flue outlet extends into the slot in the blocking up of the fire place. If the fire is to be wall mounted ensure a strong fixing to the blocking up which should preferably be brick or blockwork rawlplugged and screwed.

The connection between the gas cock and the fire is made in 8 mm copper, with or without a chrome finish. The connections are compression or threaded fittings and PFTE tape or 'Boss White' should be used on the threads to ensure a gas tight connection.

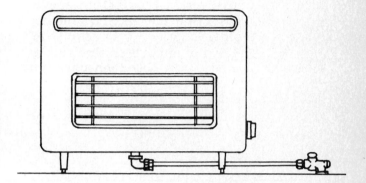

3

INSTALLING A GAS COOKER

Run a 15 mm gas pipe to behind the gas cooker position and take it vertically to 900 mm above the floor. Fit a gas cock to the pipe and a further short length of pipe. Securely clip the gas pipe to the wall. To the end of the pipe fit the female socket of a bayonet cooker-hose connection.

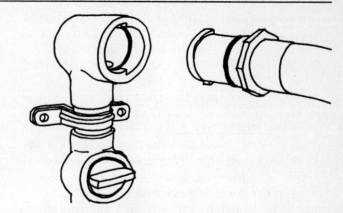

1

To the back of the cooker fit the end of the cooker hose. Cooker hoses are available with both male and female threaded ends; a check should be made of the fitting on the back of the cooker. If a wrong hose is available the fitting on the cooker can be converted using a converting fitting i.e. male to female thread. Seal the threads with PFTE tape or 'Boss White' and tighten the fitting with a wrench. The bayonet end of the hose is located into the bayonet socket of the pipe.

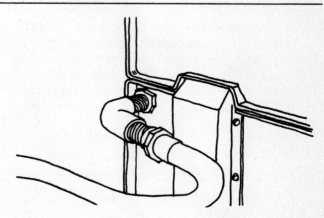

2

Some hoses are fitted with a wire which is shorter than the hose and is fitted to the wall or the supply pipe to stop the cooker being pulled too far.

3

14.05
INSTALLING A GAS MULTIPOINT WATER HEATER

When installing a multipoint water heater always invest in a new back balanced model or re-use one you have used in another house. Back balanced heaters are safer than the conventionally flued models. It is possible to buy second-hand water heaters which are sometimes offered with a 'guarantee'; however they frequently break down and often the time, energy and the cost of spare parts will reduce or negate the value of the 'bargain'.

All fittings served by a multipoint water heater should be within a 12 m (40'–0") pipe run and the heater should serve no more than three points.

On an external wall mark the size of the opening for the flue terminal and cut out a hole using a club hammer and bolster. Cutting a hole from the outside will do less damage to the external brickwork but it is not usually possible unless the heater is being fitted on the ground floor or scaffolding has been erected.

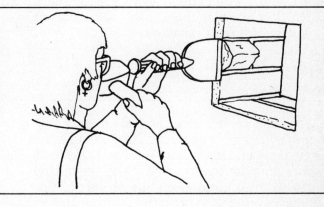

1

The balanced flue set is made up of two pieces which slide over each other to take up the thickness of the wall. Adjust the flue set to the appropriate thickness, tape the joint between the sections and position the flue in the wall. Screw the flue backplate to rawlplugs in the internal wall and make good the brickwork and point around the flue on the external wall with 1:3 cement: sand mortar. It is important that no part of the flue grating is obstructed and the flue should not be closer than 300 mm (1'–0") to any object.

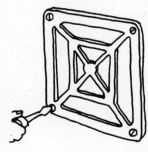
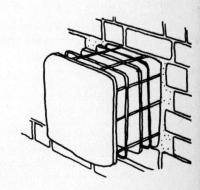

2

Remove the front casing of the heater and offer it up to the inside of the flue terminal. Mark the wall at the fixing positions and take down the heater. Using a masonry bit, drill and plug the wall to take 50 mm (2") No. 12 screws. Peel off the backing strips to the adhesive sealing gasket and stick it around the flue terminal. Hold up the body of the heater against the flue and screw it to the wall. Fit and tighten any bolts securing the flue to the body of the heater.

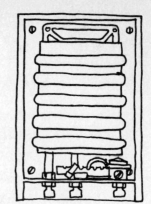

3

The inlet and outlet pipes will vary in position and size depending on the make of the heater. A common set of connections is a 22 mm gas supply with 15 mm water for both the inlet and the outlet. All of these connections are usually made by special tap connectors which come with the heater. These connectors are not always copper but can be soldered to copper. If the heater is being fed directly from the mains it will be necessary to fit on a governer valve to reduce the pressure into the water supply. Fitting a gate valve into the water supply and a gas cock onto the gas supply will make it easier to disconnect the heater if a fault develops.

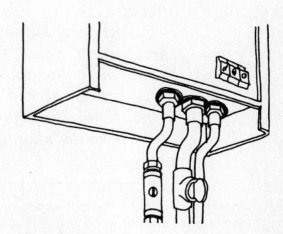

4

Fit the front casing onto the body once the connections have been made. Turn on the water and the gas and if the connections do not leak depress the pilot light button. Keep the button depressed for a minute to allow the air in the pipe to clear and then press the ignition button. Once the pilot light is lit continue to press the button until the pilot light has warmed up the valve sufficiently for the flame to stay lit when the button is released.

5

Water heaters should be regularly serviced, a small internal leak can often cause a great deal of damage if it remains undetected. The Gas Board offer service contracts which are relatively inexpensive and include inspections. As such they are a wise investment.

6

14.06
INSTALLING A GAS SINK POINT WATER HEATER

Sink point water heaters vent their fumes directly into the room and should only be allowed to run for 5 minutes. They are not suitable for filling a washing machine or a bath.

Take the outer casing off the water heater, hold it up to the wall, mark the positions of the fixing holes and place the heater to one side. Drill the wall with a masonry bit and plug the wall with rawlplugs. Screw the body of the heater to the wall using No. 12 screws.

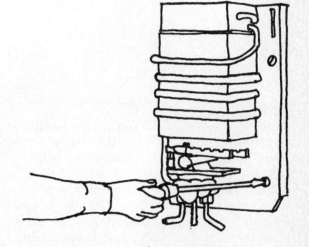

1

The connections on the bottom of the heater will normally be 15 mm to the water supply and outlet and either 15 mm or 9 mm ($^3/_8''$) to the gas. Insert a gate valve on the water supply and a gas cock on the gas supply to allow for disconnection of the heater. Make the connections between the tap connectors provided and 15 mm copper pipe, using a reducing fitting if the gas is 9 mm ($^3/_8''$). Fit compressible washers in the tap connectors, wrap PFTE tape around each thread, screw on the connectors and tighten them with a wrench or basin spanner. Do not over-tighten.

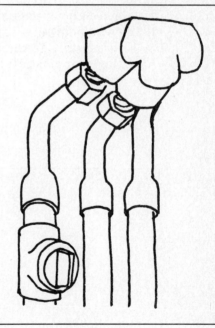

2

Replace the outer casing of the heater. Turn on the gas and the water. Check that the connections do not leak and if not then light the pilot light. Adjust the flame so that it burns blue and allow it to heat up the valve controlling the main gas supply before turning on the water.

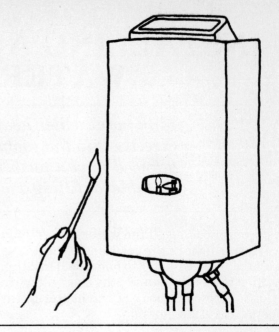

3
_____

Before using the heater the room must be fitted with permanent ventilation, either in the form of a fixed vent in the window or an airbrick through the wall. The simplest method is to replace a pane of glass with one in which a circular vent has been fitted. It is possible to ask a glass supplier to cut a circular hole in the glass and a number of proprietary vents are available.

Alternatively knock a 225×150 mm hole through the wall using a club hammer and cold chisel. To the outside wall point in an airbrick using 1:3 cement: sand mortar. To the inside cover the hole with a plaster or plastic fixed vent with a built-in insert screen.

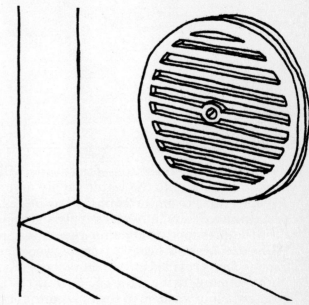

4
_____

15
DECORATING

15.01
PAINTWORK

A Brushes and Rollers

Always buy good quality brushes and rollers, since they will last longer and give a better finish if taken care of and used properly.

1

Brush care

When using a brush for an oil-based paint, such as gloss paint, it can be left suspended in water overnight if it is to be used again the following day. Make sure that the water covers the bristles completely and that the brush does not touch the sides or the bottom of the container.

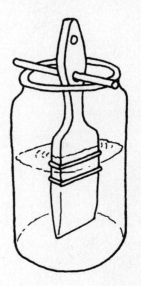

To clean a brush which has been used for oil paint, scrape off excess paint on the side of a tin or with an old table knife. Put some white spirit, turpentine or paint remover (not stripper) into a jar and work the brush bristles in the liquid. When the brush is apparently free of paint pour some detergent-based washing-up liquid onto the bristles and wash the brush under the tap. Repeat the process with clean white spirit or paint remover followed by washing in hot water and detergent. Wash through until clean and shake out any water.

When using emulsion paint, simply wash the brush through with hot water and detergent until clean. Shake out any water.

Store bristles flat and wrap them, when still damp, in newspaper to keep them in good condition.

Roller Care

If work is to be stopped for more than twenty minutes the roller should be cleaned. Scrape off excess paint or roll it out on old newspapers.

When using oil paint, soak the roller with white spirit, turpentine or paint remover and work paint out of the roller with the fingers. Coat the roller in detergent-based washing up liquid and wash under hot water until clean.

For emulsion paint, wash the roller in hot water and detergent until clean.

Wrap rollers in newspaper when still damp.

2

B Paint Stripping

Paint stripping is a long tedious process and should only be started if the surface to be painted is in too poor a condition to paint again, or if the wood is required stripped for decorative effect.

When stripping timber for decorative effect a lot of time will be saved by removing all doors, shutters, and any unfastened panelling and taking it to be stripped in a caustic soda bath.

The fixed timber is best stripped with a paint stripper rather than a blowlamp since this will result in scorch marks unless great care is taken. Finish off with plumber's steel wool soaked in paint stripper or caustic soda. When using paint strippers always wear old cothing and rubber gloves. Wash away paint stripper immediately, if it comes in contact with the skin.

Apply paint stripper with a brush, wait until the paint bubbles and then strip off with a shaving hook or stripping knife. A conventional paint stripper may require several applications to work through the layers of paint.

A thixotropic paint stripper such as 'Klingstrip' is spread over the paintwork to a depth of about 3 mm, and then covered in polythene. After several hours, depending on the number of layers of paint, remove the polythene, scrape the stripper back into the tub for re-use, and then scrub the remainder of the paint off with warm water and a stiff bristled scrubbing brush.

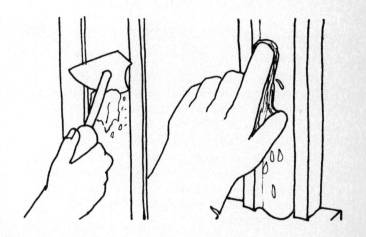

3

For repainting, old paintwork need only be stripped if it has old runs and drips, has become crazed or is starting to flake off. To strip paintwork, use a gas blowlamp, or a gas torch which tend to be easier to use and more reliable then the old fashioned paraffin blowlamps. In addition, a stripping knife, a triangular shaving hook and one or more combination of shaving hooks are necessary.

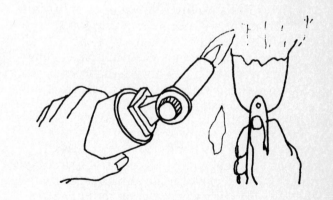

4

Start by stripping mouldings first, beginning at the top and working down, play the blowlamp over the moulding until the paint melts and then strip off, working downwards using the combination shaving hook, fitting its curved shapes into the moulding. Having stripped all of the mouldings, strip the panels or flat areas starting at the bottom of each panel, working from right to left if right handed. Play the

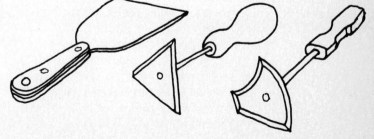

blowlamp over the paint to soften it and strip it off with the stripping knife.

Do not use a blowlamp near glass, since the heat will cause it to crack. Paint next to glass should be stripped using a paint stripper.

A blowlamp should not be used when stripping oil paint from metals, plastered walls, asbestos sheeting, or close to glass. In these cases paint strippers should be used.

C Surface Preparation
Walls and Ceilings

i Gloss Paint

Wash down the gloss paintwork with warm water and sugar soap. Wash away all traces of the soap with warm water and leave to dry. To provide a key for the new paintwork, rub down with a fine sandpaper, either by hand or using an orbital sander. Repair small cracks and bring up the level of areas where the paint has flaked off, using a filler such as Polyfilla. Sand any filled areas down to match the level of the existing paintwork.

ii Emulsion Paint and Washable Distemper

Wash down the paintwork with sugar soap and warm water; rinse off any soap. There is no need to rub down the wall but fill any cracks or damaged areas as for gloss painted walls.

iii Non-Washable Distemper

Non-washable distemper is usually found on ceilings, sometimes in conjunction with a lining paper. It is water soluble and must be removed to provide a sound base for new paintwork.

Soak the surface with water; a water spray used for plants is useful. Allow the water to soak in, spray again and use a stripping knife to remove the distemper. When all of the distemper or distemper and lining paper, has been removed, wash down with sugar soap and rinse with warm water to remove all traces of the glue base of the distemper.

iv Wallpaper

If the wallpaper is firmly stuck to the wall, brush off any dust and wipe it down with a damp cloth. The dyes used for some wallpapers may come through the paintwork and the only way to find this out is to paint a test strip.

If the wallpaper is not firmly stuck to the wall, or is obviously several layers thick, or the dye shows through, then the paper should be stripped. Soak the paper with water or a wallpaper stripper. When the glue has softened, use a stripping knife to remove the paper. If the wall has been covered with a vinyl paper, peel off the top vinyl layer. A washable paper should be scored with a wire brush to allow the water to penetrate through to the glue. Once all of the paper has been removed, wash down the wall with sugar soap and rinse with warm water, to remove all traces of wallpaper adhesive.

v Damp Stains

Brown stains caused by damp patches which have dried out should be sealed with a sealant such as 'Damp Coat'. This treatment will only work if the cause of the dampness has been eliminated.

A white fluffy salt deposit may appear through paintwork in areas of new plaster which has been damp and is not yet dried out. Take off the paint and brush off the salt deposit and allow the area to dry before coating it with sealant prior to repainting. If the deposit continues to appear fifteen to eighteen months after the plasterwork was completed, or the plaster does not dry out, then look for other causes, such as a failed damp-proof course, missing roof tile, broken rainwater pipe or leaking pipe.

Woodwork

i Stripped wood

Woodwork which has been stripped with a blowlamp should be rubbed down with a fine-grade sandpaper, working with the grain. Any scorch marks must be thoroughly sanded to remove charred wood.

When woodwork has been stripped with caustic soda or a chemical stripper it should be thoroughly washed down with warm water to remove any trace of the chemical. If a very strong caustic soda solution has been used it is advisable to wash the woodwork with a solution of vinegar and water to neutralise any caustic which is present before rinsing with clean warm water. Leave to dry before sanding down with fine sandpaper, working with the grain.

Before repainting stripped wood, rub down any knots and cover them with two coats of knot sealer or knot stopper.

ii Gloss Painted

Wash down gloss painted woodwork with sugar soap and rinse with warm water. To provide a key for the next layers of paint rub down with wet, wet and dry sandpaper, of 280 to 400 grade.

To repair a dent or localised flaking or blistering, clean off the damaged paint with a scraper, fill the area with a filler and rub down to match the existing paintwork. Give the filler a coat of undercoat and rub down with wet and dry paper.

D Painting

Never start painting an area which cannot be finished in one session; don't leave a wall or a door half-painted overnight, or even for a meal, as this will result in the paint forming an edge and a join mark will be visible when painting is resumed.

Never overload the brush, since this will only result in drips or runs, as well as paint flicking off the brush or running onto the handle. Dip the tip in the paint and remove any excess paint on the rim of the can.

i Gloss Paint

When painting woodwork with gloss paint start by painting any mouldings, then the panel surrounded by the moulding and finally the flat areas surrounding the moulding. Gloss paint should be applied to large flat areas in about 600 mm (2'0") squares, starting in the top right-hand corner, if right handed, working down in squares, before moving across to start the next strip. In each square apply the gloss paint in a number of vertical strips, then, without reloading the brush, the square with horizontal strokes, then vertical and horizontal strokes until the brush moves smoothly across the surface. Reduce pressure on the brush while brushing out so that the brush marks will be worked out. Finish with vertical strokes. When applying each subsequent section brush towards the join so there is no overlap at junctions between squares.

Always paint edges and corners adjoining the square before painting the square. Non-drip or jelly gloss paint should not be brushed out to the same extent. Do not stir non-drip gloss, but all other gloss paint should be stirred for three or four minutes to ensure that the pigment is thoroughly mixed.

ii Emulsion Paint

Start by painting the edge against the ceiling or at the top of the area to be painted and apply the paint in horizontal bands about 200 mm wide, working from the top down. Apply emulsion paint in the same way as for gloss paint, brushing out to achieve an even paint film. Emulsion paint does not show brush marks.

Applying emulsion paint with a roller, start by painting edges and corners with a brush. Fill the sloped paint tray to about one third of the way up the slope. Push the roller backwards and forwards in the paint and then pull it back up the slope to remove excess paint. Apply the paint with alternate diagonal strokes, finishing off with straight vertical strokes of the roller.

Stir emulsion paints for three or four minutes before using, to ensure that the pigment is well mixed.

iv Outside Painting

Choose a day when it has been dry for several days and is likely to stay dry for two more. The weather should be warm, but not so hot as to cause the paint to blister. Paintwork can be damaged by frost, so do not choose a day when frost is forecast. Windy days are also to be avoided, since windborne dust, leaves and debris will stick to and damage new paintwork.

Techniques of paint application are the same as those for internal work, but exterior quality paints should be used. External paintwork which is subject to sunlight, frost, wind, and rain, deteriorates more quickly than internal paintwork, and it is worth buying good quality paints (consult the *Which* report), rather than having to re-do external decorations more frequently.

iii Ceilings

When painting ceilings, use the same technique for applying the paint but work away from the window wall and, if possible, work off a platform, or a scaffold board, supported by two step ladders, rather than from a single step ladder.

15.02
WALL PAPERING

Walls should be prepared in the same way as for painting, except that porous walls should be sealed with a coat of size or wallpaper paste. Leave the size to dry and rub the wall down with sandpaper before hanging any wallpaper.

Wallpaper should be hung starting at the side of the main window and working towards an unbroken wall. Lengths of paper should butt rather than overlap, but where an overlap is unavoidable, for example at corners, overlap towards the window so that the edge does not cast a shadow. Adjacent to the window, mark the wall one paper's width from the frame or the edge of the opening. Drop a plumb line down the wall and mark a vertical line through the mark.

Set up a table for pasting and on it mark the length of the wallpaper required. Wallpaper lengths should be about 100 to 150 mm longer than the height of the wall. The mark on the table can be positioned so that one length of the table top, plus the distance from the left-hand end of the table to the mark, is the required length. With patterned wallpapers, after cutting the first length, match the pattern before cutting the next length and trim off any excess on the length. Cut all of the wallpaper before starting to hang, numbering each length so that there is no confusion.

Mix up the paste in a clean bucket and tie a string across the top of the bucket. Lay the first length of paper on the table with the top of the paper to the right of the table. Dip the brush into the paste and wipe off any excess on the string. Working from right to left, paste the centre strip of the paper lying on the table. Move the paper to overhang the back edge of the table by 3 mm and brush out the glue to that edge. Pull the paper back to overhang the front edge by 3 mm and brush glue back to the front edge. Fold over the pasted length with a loose roll and move the rest of the length onto the table, pasting in the same way. If any glue gets on the face of the paper remove it immediately with a damp cloth. Clean off any paste on the table top before pasting the next length.

Hang the pasted paper up against the mark on the wall and brush the paper out smooth with a paper hanger's brush, or a wad of dry cloth. Use the point of the scissors to score the junction with the ceiling, peel back the paper and cut off surplus paper along the scored line. Brush the paper back into position. Trim paper at the bottom of the length and around obstacles in a similar fashion.

When papering into a corner, cut a width of paper so that it will go 6 mm around the corner. Hang the paper in the normal manner and lap the extra round the corner. The next length of paper should overlap the 6 mm section and this is hung to the angle of the corner.

When papering a chimney breast or similar section of wall, drop a vertical line down the centre of the breast and work outwards to the edges.

To fit around light switches and other electrical fittings, push the point of the scissors into the paper at the centre of the fitting and cut diagonally to about 3 mm past the corners. Then trim the paper to sit around the fitting. Alternately, trim the paper to overlap the fitting by about 2 mm, switch off the mains, loosen the front of the fitting and smooth the paper down behind the cover, taking care not to get paste into the fitting. Ensure that only a slither of paper is behind the cover.